ULRICH ZWINGLI
EARLY WRITINGS

ULRICH ZWINGLI
EARLY WRITINGS

Edited by Samuel Macauley Jackson

Wipf and Stock Publishers
EUGENE, OREGON

Wipf and Stock Publishers
199 West 8th Avenue, Suite 3
Eugene, Oregon 97401

Ulrich Zwingli Early Writings
By Zwingli, Ulrich
ISBN: 1-57910-297-2
Publication date: October, 1999

PREFACE

THE first collector, editor and publisher of the works of Huldreich Zwingli was his scholarly and devoted son-in-law, Rudolf Gualther, who married his daughter Regula, became pastor of St. Peter's in Zurich in 1542 and succeeded Bullinger as antistes in 1575. He translated more than thirty of Zwingli's German treatises into Latin, which gave them a much wider constituency. These translations, along with the works originally in Latin, he brought out in 1545 and prefixed to the three volumes in folio an elaborate *Apologia pro Zuinglio*, which was also separately published. To Gualther's three volumes a fourth was added,[1] consisting of biblical annotations furnished by Leo Jud and Kaspar Megander, either directly from their notes of Zwingli's

---

[1] Opera | D. Hvldrychi Zvin | glii, uigilantissimi Tigurinæ eccle | siæ Antistitis, partim quidem ab ipso Latine conscripta, partim | ueró è uernaculo sermone in Latinum translata: omnia | nouissime recognita, & multis adiectis, | quæ hactenus uisa non sunt. | Salvo semper et incolvmi or- | thodoxae ecclesiae ivdicio. | [Device commonly used by Froschauer (often also spelled Froschouer) as a play upon his name, Frosch meaning a frog, a tree with frogs about it.] | Iesvs. | Venite ad me omnes, qui laboratis & onerati estis, & ego| requiem uobis præstabo. | Matthæi xi. | (There is nothing said on the title-page about this being the first volume, nor is there any date, or name of publisher. On the reverse of the page is the familiar woodcut of Zwingli.)

The other volumes have these title-pages, confining the transcript to the differing words: Opervm | D. Hvldrychi Zvin | 'glii tomus secvndvs, continens | τὰ πολεμικὰ, id est pugnas, quæ ipsi cum Pontificijs, | Anabaptistis, & alijs aduersarijs suis | intercesserunt. | [Device, also often used by Froschauer, a boy riding a frog, with other frogs around.] (The rest of the page as above.)

Opervm | D. Hvldrychi Zvin | glii tomvs tertivs, ea, qvae in Genesim, | Exodum, Esaiam & Ieremiam prophetas, partim ex ore illius |excepta, partim ab illo conscripta sunt, unà cum | Psalterio Latinitate donato, cõtinens. | [Device as above] (the rest of the title-page the same).

lectures or from what he had himself written out. This edition was reprinted in 1581.[1]

The third edition is the one familiar to all modern students of Zwingli, and which has well served them for many years. It was collected and edited by Melchior Schuler and Johannes Schulthess.[2] It separates the Latin from the

In Evangelicam | historiam de Domino nostro | Iesv Christo, per Matthaevm, Marcvm, | Lucam, & Ioannem conscriptam, Epistolasqê aliquot Pauli, | Annotationes D. Hvldrychi Zvinglii | per Leonem Iudæ exceptæ & æditæ. | Adiecta est Epistola Pauli ad Hebræos & Ioannis | Apostoli Epistola per Gasparem Megandrum. | [Device of tree with the frogs about it.] | Matth. xi | Venite ad me omnes qui laboratis & onerati | estis, & ego reficiam uos. | Tigvri excvdebat Christophorvs | Froschouerus Mense Augusto, Anno | M.D.XLV. |

[1] Opervm | D. Hvldrichi Zvin- | glii, vigilantissimi Tigvrinae | ecclesiæ antistitis, partim qvidem ab | ipso Latine conscriptorum, partim verò é uernaculo | sermone in Latinum translatorum | pars prima. | Accesservnt hvic æditioni svb | finem eiusdem authoris epistolæ selectiores de | varijs rebus scriptæ. | Catalogum & seriem eorum, quæ hoc libro conti- | nentur, post Apologiam inuenies. | [Device] Salvo semper et incolvmi or- |thodoxæ ecclesiæ ivdicio. | Iesvs. | Venite ad me omnes, qui laboratis & onerati estis, & | ego requiem vobis præstabo. | Matthæi xi. | Tigvri | Excudebat Christophorus Froschoverus, | Anno M.D. LXXXI. | (The device is geometric.)

Opervm | D. Huldrichi Zvin-| glii pars secunda, con- | tinens τὰ πολεμικὰ, id est pv- | gnas, quæ ipsi cum Pontificiis, Anabapti- | stis, & aliis aduersariis suis | intercesserunt. | Elenchvm omnivm, quae hoc | volumine continentur, versa pagi- | na exhibebit. | [Device, boy riding a frog] (then the same as above to the end).

D. Hvldrichi Zwin- | glij Annotationes in Genesim, E- | xodum, Esaiam & Ieremiam pro- | phetas, vnà cum Psalterio | per eundem Latini- | tate donato. | [Device, boy on a frog] | (and same as above to the end).

D. Hvldrichi Zvin- | glii in plerosque Novi | Testamenti libros, qvorum e- | lenchum post præfationem & indicem re- | peries, annotationes ex ipsius ore | exceptæ per Leonem | Ivdae. Adiecta est epistola Pauli | ad Hebræos, et Ioannis apostoli epistola | per Gasparem Megandrum. | [Device, boy on frog] | (and same as above to the end).

[2] Huldreich Zwingli's | Werke | Erste vollständige Ausgabe | durch | Melchior Schuler und Joh. Schulthess | Erster Band | Der deutschen Schriften | erster Theil | Lehr- und Schutzschriften | zum Behufe des Ueberschrittes | in die evangelische Wahrheit und Freyheit | von 1522 bis März 1524. | Zürich, bey Friedrich Schulthess. | (1828.)

(All the contents of this volume which were written in German along with the exposition of the Sixty Seven Theses for the First Disputation, also originally in German, are given in Latin translation, and this translation is sometimes called Vol. I. of Zwingli's works. It bears this title: Huldrici Zuinglii | opera | completa [editio prima |'curantibus | Melchiore Schulero et Io. Schulthessio | Volumen primum | Germanica origine scripta | quorum pars

German treatises and puts them in different volumes. In this edition the letters by and to Zwingli are included. The edition is in eleven parts and a supplement.

prima continet | didactica et apologetica | pro consequendo transitu | in evangelicam veritatem ac libertatem | ab anno 1522 usque ad Martium 1524 | Turici apud Fridericum Schulthessium. | 1829. |)

The other volumes have these title-pages, transcribing what is distinctive on each: Huldreich . . . | Zweyten Bandes erste Abtheilung. | Der deutschen Schriften | zweyter Theil | Lehr- und Schutzschriften | zum Behufe des Ueberschritts | aus dem Papstthum in die evangelische Wahrheit und Freyheit | vom April 1525 bis 1528 | betreffend die Täuferey sämmtliche | und | betreffend die streitige Abendmahlslehre | von 1526 bis Januar 1527. | Zürich, bey Friedrich Schulthess | 1830. |

. . . Zweyten Bandes zweyte Abtheilung | Der deutschen Schriften | dritter Theil | Lehr- und Schutzschriften | betreffend | die streitige Abendmahlslehre | von 1527 bis July 1528 | liturgische und poetische sämmtliche | und | vermischte kleinere meistens politische |von 1522 bis July 1526 | Zürich, in der Schulthess'schen Buchhandlung | 1832. |

. . . Zweyten Bandes dritte Abtheilung. | Der deutschen Schriften | vierter Theil, | apologetischen, kirchlichen, geschichtlichen, | grösstentheils | politischen Inhalts, | aus dem letzten Zeitraume, | von 1526 bis 1531. | Zürich, Druck und Verlag von Fr. Schulthess. | 1841. |

Huldrici Zuinglii | opera | completa editio prima | curantibus | Melchiore Schulero et Io. Schulthessio | Volumen tertium | Latinorum Scriptorum | pars prima | Didactica et apologetica | pro evincendo transitu | in evangelicam veritatem et libertatem | ab anno 1521 ad 1526 | Turici ex officina Schulthessiana | (F. Schulthess und S. Höhr.) | 1832.|

. . . Volumen quartum | Latinorum Scriptorum | pars secunda | Didactica et apologetica | ab anno 1526 usque ab obitum auctoris | ceteraque varia | poëtica paedagogica philologica historica | Accedunt | sermones vulgares in Psalmos | lingua plerumque vernacula. | Turici ex officina Schulhessiana | 1841. |

. . . Volumen quintum | Latinorum Scriptorum | pars quinta | Exegetica Veteris Testamenti | maximam partem | Turici ex officina Schulthessiana | (F. Schulthess und S. Höhr) | 1835.

. . . Voluminis sexti tomus primus | Latinorum Scriptorum | pars sexta | Exegetica Veteris Testamenti residua | ac de Novo Testamento Evangelia | Turici . . .| 1836. |

. . . Voluminis sexti tomus secundus | Latinorum Scriptorum | pars sexta | Exegetica Novi Testamenti | residua. | . . . | 1838. |

. . . Volumen septimum | Epistolarum | a Zuinglio ad Zuingliumque | scriptarum | pars prima | Turici apud Fridericum Schulthessium | 1830. |

. . . Volumen octavum | Epistolarum | . . . | pars secunda | . . . | 1842. |

Huldrici Zuinglii | opera | a M. Schulero et Jo. Schulthessio | edita. | Supplementorum fasciculus | continens | minora scripta hactenus reperta omnia tractatus et epistolas | curantibus | Georg. Schulthessio et Gasp. Marthalero | ecclesiae turicensis ministris. | Turici ex officina Schulthessiana | 1861. |

The fourth edition[1] is that now appearing. It was projected by two Swiss scholars who had paid particular attention to the Reformation in that country, Emil Egli, professor of history in the university of Zurich, and Georg Finsler, teacher of religion in the gymnasium of Basel. It has been incorporated into the *Corpus Reformatorum* as Volumes LXXXVIII. and successors, and so Zwingli takes his place in this authoritative collection next to Melanchthon and Calvin. The edition was long preparing and is a great improvement upon its predecessor. It began to appear in parts in the fall of 1903. With the second volume a different publisher begins his work, but otherwise there was no change. That was soon to come. Egli died on December 31, 1908, within eight days of his sixty-second birthday. His successor is Walther Köhler, who also succeeded him in the university.

The last part of the second volume appeared in October 1898. The next part to appear was the first of the seventh volume, for very wisely it was determined to do as Schuler and Schulthess did and interrupt the succession of the treatises with a portion of the letters to and by Zwingli. For the collection of these letters Egli had especially exerted himself and had much increased their number by diligent search on every hand, both in and out of Switzerland. It would have been a particular delight for him to have seen his labours in print, but it was not to be.

The correspondence in the Schuler and Schulthess edition

---

[1] It has two title-pages. Thus of Vol. I Corpus Reformatorum | Volumen LXXXVIII | Huldreich Zwinglis | sämtliche Werke | Band I | [device] | Berlin | C. A. Schwetschke und Sohn | 1905. | and on the opposite page: Huldreich Zwinglis | sämtliche Werke | unter Mitwirkung | des Zwingli-Vereins in Zürich | herausgegeben | von | Dr. Emil Egli | Professor an der Universität in Zürich | und | Dr. Georg Finsler | Religionslehrer am Gymnasium in Basel | Band I | [device] | Berlin | Verlag von C. A. Schwetschke und Sohn | 1905. | (It has the Asper portrait of Zwingli, and a Zwingli medallion between the title-pages.)

Of Vol. II Corpus Reformatorum | Volumen LXXXIX | Huldreich Zwinglis | sämtliche Werke | Band II | [device] | Leipzig | Verlag von M. Heinsius Nachfolge | 1908. | (The other title-page is identical with the above except the name of the publisher and the date.)

Preface

fills volumes seven and eight, and in the new edition the same numbers will be given to them. Volume seven was finished on December 31, 1910.[1] Another change in the order of publication was made, and now volume three is appearing alternately with volume eight. Nothing seems to be lacking to give this edition scholarly completeness. Each of its contents is provided with a special introduction; it is then studied philologically and bibliographically, and in the case of the German treatises, because of the difficulty of reading the Swiss German, provided with a glossary at the foot of the page. Besides, each treatise has adequate notes giving information on all appropriate points. The contents are arranged chronologically. All of these editions are found in the library of Union Theological Seminary, in New York City.

Most of the translations which appear in this volume were made years ago from the Schuler and Schulthess text for the publication I then contemplated, but circumstances, among which was the fact that there had been announced a new edition of the originals, led me to postpone the enterprise and then I became absorbed in other work and could not attend to it. When I was at liberty to do so the new edition had made considerable progress. Happily the translators were

---

[1] Corpus Reformatorum | Volumen XCIV | Huldreich Zwinglis | sämtliche Werke | Band VII | [device] | Leipzig | Verlag von M. Heinsius Nachfolger | 1911. |

Opposite: Huldreich Zwingli | sämtliche Werke | unter Mitwirkung | des |Zwingli-Vereins in Zürich | herausgegeben | von | Dr. Emil Egli † | professor an der Universität in Zürich | D. Dr. Georg Finsler | Religionslehrer am Gymnasium in Basel | und | D. Dr. Walther Köhler | Professor an der Universität in Zürich | Band VII | [device] Leipzig | Verlag von M. Heinsius Nachfolger | 1911. |

To this volume there is a third title-page: Zwinglis Briefwechsel | Gesammelt, erläutert | und unter philogischer Mitwirkung der Professoren | Dr. Hermann Hitzig und Dr. Albert Bachmann | bearbeitet von | Emil Egli | herausgegeben von | Georg Finsler | Band I | Die Briefe von 1510–1522 | mit einer Abhandlung von Prof. Dr. P. Kalkoff: | Erasmus von Rotterdam und seine Schüler Wilhelm Nesen und Nicolaus | von Herzogenbusch im Kampfe mit den Löwener Theologen | [device] | Leipzig Verlag von M. Heinsius Nachfolger | 1911. | (The volume has the portrait and a biographical sketch of Elgi.)

willing to revise their translations with the new text in hand. These translators are Mr. Henry Preble of New York City, who has done all the Latin treatises, and Lawrence A. McLouth, Professor of German, New York University, and Walter Lichtenstein, Ph.D., librarian of Northwestern University, who have made the renderings from the German.

When the present volume was undertaken, I asked permission of the editors and publishers to be allowed to use such portion of their notes and introductions as suited my purpose. They have generously given me permission and so my readers will share with those who use the new edition, in the original, a considerable part of their learning.

I desire here to thank these editors, publishers and translators for their generosity and manifestation of interest in this enterprise. By this combination of Swiss and American labours, Zwingli is properly presented to the English-speaking public, as he would not be without it.

Those familiar with my *Selections from Zwingli*,[1] published by the University of Pennsylvania in 1901, will notice that in this and the volumes which, I trust, are to follow, the contents of that volume appear. For permission to reprint that matter I am indebted to the courtesy of the Department of History of that University, and I here express my grateful thanks.

[1] Selected works | of | Huldreich Zwingli, | (1484-1531) | the Reformer of German Switzerland. | Translated for the first time from the originals. | The German works by Lawrence A. McLouth, Professor of German in New | York University, and the Latin by Henry Preble, New York City, | and Professor George W. Gilmore, Meadville, Pennsylvania. | Edited | with general and special introductions and occasional notes | by | Samuel Macauley Jackson, | professor of church history in New York University; editor of "The Heroes of | the Reformation," and author in that series of the life of Huldreich Zwingli. | Philadelphia: University of Pennsylvania. | 1901. | Sold by | Longmans, Green & Co., | 91 and 93 Fifth Avenue, New York. | [1901.]

The volume contains the translation of the following articles: Visit of the Episcopal delegation to Zurich, April, 1522 (same as the letter of Zwingli to Erasmus Fabricius in this volume); The petition of eleven priests to be allowed to marry, July, 1522 (in this volume); the Acts of the first Zurich Disputation, January, 1523; Zurich marriage ordinance, 1525; and Refutation of the tricks of the Catabaptists, 1527.

Preface

In this volume, will be found, in English translation, all the matter from Zwingli given on the first three-hundred and twenty-seven pages of the edition of the originals now appearing, and by way of introduction, and as far more interesting than anything I could write, the original life of Zwingli, written by his bosom friend, Oswald Myconius. This is, I believe, its first appearance in the English language in modern times, but, as the special introduction states, it was first translated in the sixteenth century.

I have also inserted a treatise attributed to Zwingli in the Schuler and Schulthess edition, but which was really by Erasmus and Thomas Blarer, because it is alluded to by Zwingli in his *Suggestio*, which will appear in Volume III of this series. The grounds for its inclusion by Schuler and Schulthess are thus stated in their special preface:

"When Zwingli learned that the papal anathema was upon the point of being launched against Luther, he went to his friend Wilhelm von Falk, who in the absence of the legate Ennius was fulfilling his functions towards the Federation, and tried to persuade him to dissuade the Pope from putting forth the condemnatory Bull, on the ground that nothing could be more surely foreseen than that the Germans would treat both the Bull and the Pope with contempt. Reporting this to Myconius in a letter[1] Zwingli said, 'That the same fate awaits myself seems exceedingly likely; I am ready, and in such event shall not lack for consolation.' But the warning was altogether too late. And now Zwingli published this writing without the name of the author or of the place of printing, the edition coming out in the late summer of 1520.

"Simler gives in his collection (Vol. IV.) two Latin editions, one written in Latin letters, the other in German letters (one sheet folded in quarto), and a translation of the same period, with the title 'Consilium hominis ex animo satisfactum cupientis et Romanae sedis dignitati et Christiani orbis

[1] In the new edition, VII., 343, 4.

paci' ('Advice of a man who from his heart desires that both the dignity of the Roman See and the peace of the Christian world be fully safeguarded'). 1521 (a sheet and a half folded in quarto). The Latin edition in German letters is characterized by many errors, several omissions, and bad punctuation. There is an appendix with the title, 'Apologia Christi dni nostri pro Martino Luthero ad urbem Rhomam,' ('Christ Our Lord's defence of Martin Luther before the city of Rome'). Cratander, printer at Basel, sent this writing to Von Watt on March 8th with the *Acta Lovaniens* ('Louvain Proceedings') against Luther, remarking that he recognised in both the pen of Erasmus. The inference was correct in regard to the 'Proceedings' but not in regard to the 'Advice,' etc., for Von Watt in the copy preserved in the Library of the monastery at Zurich has made a note in his own hand that Zwingli was the 'Advice' suggester.[1] The 'Defence' is also without mention of its author: only the fact that it is appended to the 'Advice' makes it seem probable that it is the work of one and the same author."

It is proposed to follow this volume with others, until all the Latin treatises of Zwingli, all the letters to and by him, and much of the matter now in German, including both the First and Second Disputations, shall have been published. It is not expected to include his commentaries on the Bible. The volumes will necessarily vary in size, but will probably average five hundred pages each. This initial volume is unfortunately much smaller than those which follow, but circumstances have prevented its enlargement.

Since work was begun by me on this volume there has come into my hands the Rev. Dr. Beresford James Kidd's *Documents illustrative of the Continental Reformation*. (Oxford, at the Clarendon Press, 1911.) It is a first-class source book. The headings to the sections are admirably done and present a remarkably concise history of the period covered. Most of

---

[1] Wirz, *N. Hist. eccl. Hebr.*, I., 194, 5; 184, 5.

Preface

the selections are in Latin, but there are also translations from the German, and some of the matter is in its original English. The section devoted to Zurich affairs is to be highly commended. Almost all the Latin matter will be found in this and subsequent volumes, translated, while in English Kidd gives the items from Egli's *Actensammlung* relative to the punishment of those who broke the Lenten fast in 1522, the street fighting which ensued, and the defence of Froschauer before the magistrates, all of which are referred to in this volume's special introduction to the sermon "On the choice of foods." But much other illustrative material will be welcomed by the student.

SAMUEL MACAULEY JACKSON.

NEW YORK,
May 20, 1912.

CONTENTS

	PAGE
PREFACE	iii
ORIGINAL LIFE OF ZWINGLI	1

I A

THE FABLE OF THE OX. A COMMENTARY ON THE PRESENT (AUTUMN, 1510) COURSE OF AFFAIRS, BY HULDREICH ZWINGLI OF THE TOGGENBURG, IN CRUDE CENTIMETRE FORM 27

I B

THE FABULOUS POEM OF THE PRIEST ZWINGLI CONCERNING AN OX AND MANY OTHER ANIMALS, REFERRING TO CURRENT (AUTUMN, 1510) EVENTS 31

II

ACCOUNT BY HULDREICH ZWINGLI OF THE ENGAGEMENTS BETWEEN THE FRENCH AND THE SWISS HARD BY RAVENNA AND PAVIA AND IN OTHER PLACES, AND OF THE CONVENTION AT BADEN IN SWITZERLAND, IN THE YEAR 1512 35

III

THE MISSING DIALOGUES 48

IV

THE LABYRINTH 50

V

TRANSCRIPT OF THE PAULINE EPISTLES 55

xiv   Contents

                              VI   PAGE

A CHRISTIAN SONG WRITTEN BY HULDREICH ZWINGLI WHEN
    HE WAS ATTACKED BY THE PESTILENCE (1519) .   .   56

                             VII

ADVICE OF ONE WHO DESIRES WITH HIS WHOLE HEART THAT
    DUE CONSIDERATION BE PAID BOTH TO THE DIGNITY
    OF THE POPE AND TO THE PEACEFUL DEVELOPMENT OF
    THE CHRISTIAN RELIGION   58

                            VIII

1. WHAT ZWINGLI SAID AND PREACHED AT THIS TIME
    (1521) AGAINST THE MERCENARY SERVICE OF THE SWISS.
   2. WHAT ZWINGLI PREACHED AT THIS TIME (1521) .   68

                             IX

CONCERNING CHOICE AND LIBERTY RESPECTING FOOD—CON-
    CERNING OFFENCE AND VEXATION—WHETHER ANYONE
    HAS POWER TO FORBID FOODS AT CERTAIN TIMES—
    OPINION OF HULDREICH ZWINGLI   70

                              X

LETTER OF HULDREICH ZWINGLI TO ERASMUS FABRICIUS
    ABOUT THE PROCEEDINGS, ON THE 7TH, 8TH, AND 9TH
    OF APRIL, 1522, OF THE DELEGATES SENT TO ZURICH BY
    THE BISHOP OF CONSTANCE   113

                             XI

A SOLEMN WARNING BY HULDREICH ZWINGLI, A SIMPLE
    PREACHER OF THE GOSPEL OF JESUS CHRIST, ADDRESSED
    TO THE HONOURABLE, WISE, STEADFAST, SENIOR CON-
    FEDERATES AT SCHWYZ, THAT THEY SHOULD BEWARE
    OF, AND FREE THEMSELVES FROM, THE CONTROL OF
    FOREIGN LORDS   130

                             XII

PETITION OF CERTAIN PREACHERS OF SWITZERLAND TO THE
    MOST REVEREND LORD HUGO, BISHOP OF CONSTANCE,

Contents

THAT HE WILL NOT SUFFER HIMSELF TO BE PERSUADED TO MAKE ANY PROCLAMATION TO THE INJURY OF THE GOSPEL, NOR ENDURE LONGER THE SCANDAL OF HARLOTRY, BUT ALLOW THE PRIESTS TO MARRY WIVES OR AT LEAST WOULD WINK AT THEIR MARRIAGES . . 150

XIII

A FRIENDLY REQUEST AND EXHORTATION OF SOME PRIESTS OF THE CONFEDERATES THAT THE PREACHING OF THE HOLY GOSPEL BE NOT HINDERED, AND ALSO THAT NO OFFENCE BE TAKEN IF TO AVOID SCANDAL THE PREACHERS WERE GIVEN PERMISSION TO MARRY . . . 166

XIV

DEFENCE CALLED ARCHETELES, IN WHICH ANSWER IS MADE TO AN ADMONITION THAT THE MOST REVEREND LORD BISHOP OF CONSTANCE (BEING PERSUADED THERETO BY THE BEHAVIOUR OF CERTAIN WANTONLY FACTIOUS PERSONS) SENT TO THE COUNCIL OF THE GREAT MINSTER AT ZURICH CALLED THE CHAPTER 197

The Original Life of Zwingli

[The life of Huldreich Zwingli by Oswald Myconius, written in Latin in 1532, and dedicated to Agathius of Bern, put into modern English from Neander's edition of the lives of the Four Reformers,—Luther by Melanchthon; Melanchthon by Camerarius; Zwingli by Myconius; and Calvin by Beza (*Vitæ quatuor Reformatorum*, Berlin, 1841)—on the basis of the version by Henry Bennet, published in London in 1561, and revised by Mr. Henry Preble. This is the first life of Zwingli to be written.]

I.—Introduction.

YOU have asked me, my dear friend Agathius, for a thing as worthy of execution as it is far beyond the compass of my skill. For great things require great powers. My training has been such as to make me creep upon the ground so far, and nature implanted a sort of instinctive lowliness in me at birth. And is it not indeed an arduous task to sketch the life of Zwingli? I do not say to write it fully, and you very wisely do not ask this, being well aware of what is to be demanded of the humbly endowed. The person properly fitted for that [*i. e.*, for writing a worthy life of Zwingli] were not so much a Plutarch as a Cicero: so great is he in the estimation of his friends, and in reality, though so small in the eyes of his enemies, and you say yourself, that Zwingli has been spoken of in your ears as God, while there are those who disparage him so much that you wonder that the earth does not open and swallow them. For this cause, you say, you long to become acquainted with the man from some one well acquainted with his life and conversation: and this particularly on account of the books so solidly composed, which he left. For you want these to have the greatest influence possible. I will not deny that I knew Zwingli intimately, both as my highly valued patron, and as the most beloved of advisers: that, therefore, I am his debtor to no slight degree. But what can I give?—so barren am I of appropriate expression! If you had not asked me I might have forgotten my indebtedness, but now that you press me I will do what I can. And I can say simply, and truly, and briefly things that, I think, will give satisfaction to your soul, for whom alone I would have what I am about to say written.

II.—Zwingli's parentage and birthplace. His precocity. At ten years of age sent to Buenzli, the schoolmaster at Basel. His literary and philosophical studies at Bern and Vienna.

He was born, then, of worthy parents, his father [Huldreich] Zwingli, his mother Margarita Meylina [Meile], about the year 1487 [correctly January 1, 1484], in the village of the Toggenburg called Wildhaus, at a height which is almost equal to that of any mountain in Switzerland. I have more than once thought, in my simple-mindedness, that he drew something of divine quality directly from the heavens near which he lived, and surely there has not for many years been seen among men anything so nearly approaching the divine. His father was distinguished for his holiness of life and for having attained to the highest dignity his neighbours could bestow, for he was chosen Ammann [chief magistrate]. Seeing signs of promise in his little boy, he committed him at a very tender age to his brother, a priest, to see if there were the making of a scholar in him. The boy soon gave such satisfaction that he was sent to a school-teacher under whom he learned so quickly that he found all the things he was taught too easy to give his clever intellect due exercise. Therefore he was sent to Basel, being then about ten years old, and placed under the teacher, Gregory Buenzli, a good man, learned and wonderfully gentle. Here, forthwith, he made such progress in character and letters that in the disputations, which were then customary, he carried off all the honours from all the boys and youths of the school, on which account he incurred the greatest hatred on the part of the older boys. His proficiency in music was beyond what is expected of his years, as is apt to be the case with those especially gifted by nature in any particular art. His studies were recognised by Buenzli, who loved him dearly, as not congruous with such joyous and pregnant wit.[1] Wherefore, sending him home, he counselled that measures should be taken for his education in accordance with the excellence of his abilities. So it came about that he was sent to Bern, and came under Heinrich Lupulus, a remarkably learned man, and famous also as a poet, who was the first to teach the classics in Switzerland. Introduced by him into the secrets of classical learning, he acquired elegance of diction, and the knowledge and discernment of things. He also learned the theory of poesy, so that he could compose verses himself, and felicitously criticise those composed by others. In somewhat less than two years, he had laid the foundation for the study of philosophy. So he went next to Vienna [1500], and there embraced in his studies all that philosophy embraces, turning it to good account, for the increase and embellishment of his learning.

III.—Return to Basel; teacher of the classics in the school attached to St. Martin's church; mitigates the severity of his studies with the delights of music.

After several years thus spent, he was recalled home. Then in order not to put off longer the practical application of his learning, he went to Basel [1502], where he poured forth for the benefit of others, what he had been taught, for being the head master of St. Martin's school he taught the humanities to the great advantage of the boys. Meanwhile, he more closely studied philosophy, and followed carefully the trifling of the sophists with no other intention than that, if

[1] That is, he had outgrown Buenzli's school.

he should ever be fighting against them, he might know his enemy. He mingled wit and pleasantry with these serious studies: for he was sunny in disposition, and agreeable in conversation to an extraordinary degree. Afterwards, he devoted himself to the theory and practice of all kinds of musical instruments, with no other purpose than to refresh his mind, when wearied by severe study, and be able to return to such study with renewed vigour. I am well aware, Agathius, what occurs to you in connection with this, namely that his enemies have turned his devotion to music against him, asserting that music is rather the handmaid of voluptuous pleasure than a help to study. And I confess that I have often heard far more abominable things about him, especially from the priests living in concubinage: but then, what is anywhere so holy that it escapes the besmirching of foul tongues! I know whereof I speak, and do not care what carping critics say. Is it not a most solid argument for the truth of what I affirm, that he not only cultivated music in this way himself, but earnestly advised all students of letters to cultivate it on the same grounds? For since there is nothing that so harmlessly cheers the mind of man, however disturbed by sorrow, or clears it more happily, however clouded by perplexities, why should he not have given such advice?

IV.—Becoming Master of Arts, 1506, he is elected pastor of Glarus, and gives himself up entirely to theological studies.

Now when he had for some time sweated over his studies, both of the liberal arts, and of philosophy, he received the Master's degree, the customary reward in the schools of such labour; yielding more to the general opinion of men, who judge those only learned who bear these glittering titles, than to his own feeling. Then, because the regular course of things demanded it, he paid diligent heed to theology in the scholastic form, but he quickly perceived what a waste of good time it involved, since it was such a jumble of worldly wisdom, philosophy, God, inane loquacities, barbarities, vainglory, and things of that description, that no sane doctrine could reasonably be hoped from it. Nevertheless, he continued in the enemy's camp, like a spy as it were, until the Glareans chose him as their pastor, although he had not yet been ordained. Then, truly, what had been begun by others, he was compelled to complete. He became a priest, devoted himself to studies, especially to theological studies, for henceforward he made little account of the heathen classics, unless they assisted him in the sacred things, and in preaching. With this end in view, it should be said in passing, that for the sake of the illustrations he committed Valerius Maximus to memory, and did not forget him. He saw how many things he ought to know, to whom the office of teaching the flock of Christ had been entrusted, but more especially, the indispensable knowledge of God, as well as the eloquence, through which • he could expound everything rightly and profitably, in such a way that anybody could understand him. What he thought should be done, he did. He pored over the Old and New Testaments, studied orators and their orations to find out their secret, and found it: he put it into practice, however, not after the fashion of Cicero, but so as to profit us both in speaking and in forming opinions. So he made such progress that he was considered by learned and virtuous men to have the Sacred Scriptures at ready command. But he was so far from being satisfied with this, that he desired to add to it a knowledge of the sacred tongues: by which he knew he would be able to fill up what he still lacked. Wherefore, he gave himself first to the Greek tongue, by the help of lexicons and translations. He copied Paul's Epistles [in Greek],[1] and committed them to memory, so that it finally came to this, that he understood the Greek better than the Latin. Afterwards, he dealt in the same way with all the books which make up the New Testament. Having learned subsequently from Peter that

[1] This is a mistake. The transcript was made at Einsiedeln in 1517, as he states himself.

the Scriptures are not of private interpretation, he looked up to heaven, seeking the Spirit as his teacher, and supplicating with prayer that He would bestow that by which the meaning of the Divine mind might be as perfectly elucidated as possible. And lest he should deceive either himself or others, by a false representation of the Spirit, he compared Scripture with Scripture, and elucidated the dark by the clear, so that no one should fail to perceive that the Spirit and not a man was the teacher, whenever he expounded Scripture. Oh fact divine! Thus it came about that knowledge of heavenly truth, which lay hidden a long time, to the detriment and perdition of souls, was happily restored to us. He felt about the orthodox writers [the Fathers?] as they felt about themselves, that they should be read with discrimination, and tested by the canonical Scriptures as by a touchstone: for they were generally speaking too much adulterated by philosophy and human reasoning to make it right to grant them the authority of Scripture, as had been done hitherto nevertheless. What he had thus learned he turned to practical account in this way. He began to fight according to the precept of Christ against the most pernicious abuses, above all against the pensions (as we call the presents of princes, which used to be given to certain men for the sake of their help in hiring soldiers and making war), which it was his fixed determination utterly to root out so that the country might return to its pristine virtue. For he saw that there would be room for the heavenly doctrine only when the fountain was cleansed of all evil. There is no reason, Agathius, why you should say to yourself, "Zwingli while yet a papist thought thus of the gospel?" Believe me, twenty-seven years ago, on account of this very thing, and because he had not condemned the theses of John Picus of Mirandola concerning those matters which he [Picus] had once vainly set up at Rome in order that he might debate them, he was secretly spoken of by certain blockheads as a heretic. Hence odium, impudence in speech, outcry, wily working of the children of the world against Zwingli took their beginning, and increased as his virtues increased. On the other hand, the man was so loved by those who favoured the right and the good, among them the elders and the virtuous among the people, also priests of a less corrupt life, that they were encouraged to hope that he would restore the ancestral righteousness. Meanwhile he preached gospel grace without alluding at all or very cautiously to the abuses of the Church of Rome. He wanted the truth acknowledged by his hearers to do its good work in their hearts, for by truths perceived and understood we are able without difficulty to distinguish the false. Nor did the time permit anything different, for the truth would have been wholly lost amid so great a wantonness and evil-mindedness of mankind sooner than the abuses of religion would have been done away. It is true that I cannot clear him while a young man of all stain of sin, but his regard for purity, and especially for his holy office, constantly restrained him from weakening the influence of the heavenly teachings by a bad example. Such was Zwingli at Glarus.

V.—He removes to Einsiedeln, 1516; by reason of his increased acquaintance with Christ and the Greek literature, he comes to perfect understanding of both the Old and New Testaments.

An opportunity was offered to remove to Einsiedeln, which for the time being seemed an eminently sensible thing to do. Theobold Geroldseck [von Hohengeroldseck], a baron, and a doctor of theology, a man equally devoted to learning, to the learned, and to true piety, administrator at that time of the Hermitage of the Holy Virgin, called him. The concourse of men from almost all parts of mankind, so celebrated was the name of the place, attracted him, as it gave such a favourable opportunity to preach Christ and his truth in regions varied and remote; and also by reason of his greater leisure he could prosecute the study of Greek, which he had not unpromisingly begun, until he attained, as it were, to the summit. Nor was his hope wholly disappointed, for Christ began to be known more soundly, and he carried forward his Greek studies until he attained a perfect knowledge of both Testaments.

VI.—Called to the first parish in Zurich, he entered upon his service on Christmas day, 1519.

At this juncture the church at Zurich lacking a pastor in its first parish [the pastor primarius] was blest with men among its members who laboured day and night to get him chosen instead of any one else. He knew nothing of this himself until, happening to go to Zurich, he was asked by a canon of Zurich, whether he would be able to take charge of the people at Zurich in the matter of preaching the word of the Lord? He replied that he was able, and if in so celebrated a place Christ's grace was preached and received it could scarcely be that the other Swiss cantons would not follow its example, and so a return to sense be made. Although he knew that he should not receive as much salary as he relinquished, still if they offered him the service he would reply in accordance with their wish, for he would not offer himself as a candidate. Not long after I was secretly directed, I, I say, Agathius, at the time of election, after many had personally canvassed for the place, to put Zwingli's name in nomination for the office of pastor. I consented, the thing went through, he was called, to the very great satisfaction of the good. A little while after this in the very first meeting with the canons he declared in person what and how he proposed to teach the people, to wit, the history of Christ the Saviour as Matthew the Evangelist describes him, nor should his honour be longer obscured, whose excellence had now for a long time been hidden to the detriment of the Divine glory and of souls. The same, however, he would expound not according to human reason indeed, seeing that he was sworn to no interpreter, but according to the purpose of the Spirit, which through diligent collating of the Scriptures, and through fervent prayers from the heart, he doubted not that he should be given to understand. On hearing this some mourned, and some rejoiced, just as there had been difference of opinion previously among his electors. What, therefore, he promised he began on Christmas day, 1519, and thenceforward prosecuted with good omens.

VII.—The fame of Luther is noised abroad. Zwingli commends his writings. He inveighs powerfully against the pensionaries, oppressors of the poor, and the idle rich.

While this was taking place the name of Luther from day to day became more celebrated as his books were more and more sedulously thumbed by all. Zwingli himself kept away from them, but he faithfully exhorted his flock, even from the pulpit, to buy and read them. See, I beg of you, his idea. He wished that the people, hearing and reading them, after they learned that he himself had abstained from reading them, should perceive the parity in spirit between himself and Luther, yea, their unity, both drawing out of the Divine Scriptures, and so would more freely adhere, and be obedient unto the truth, however much it might seem at variance with what they were used to. In this way marvellous success was attained in a short time. The method of his teaching bore away the palm, for by means of it the simple learned equally with the most intelligent and acute. It was adapted to the norm of the common mind. Therefore it was not possible that any one attending his preaching could go away without being better informed and enriched in divine learning. Thus while he taught the light of truth clearly and most zealously, no one ever spoke more sharply against vice: and especially did he inveigh heavily against the pensionaries, the oppressors of the poor, and against those wasting their lives in luxury and idleness. He exercised an authority in rebuke such as I have seen in no other person. While with burning words he thundered against idleness and pensions, he always added, in order that worthy persons who were accounted as of the same rank and class as the reprobate might not be disturbed, "Good man, this is not meant for you. You have no personal interest in what I am saying, so pay no attention to it." Sometimes he pressed his theme too far, especially at moments when things had happened in consequence of which he made remarks or digressions. This was why in the beginning vicious schemes, either of priests or of persons abusing their power, were formed against the course he advocated. For when it had come to pass that by far the better and more numerous part of the people believed the truth, he sometimes used these "digressions" against those things which were less to be borne within the Church. On this account not an hour passed in which either from the laity or the priests there was not brought out some most insidious plot against this champion of the good and the true. But perhaps there will be an opportunity to expatiate upon this in another place. Now let us return for a little while to his studies.

VIII.—His studies and scheme of life.

In the midst of these anxious labours he never omitted his reading of the Greek authors, but went through Homer, Aristotle, Plato, Demosthenes, Thucydides, and in lighter vein Lucian, Theocritus, Hesiod, Aristophanes, and others. And because his studies required it, and just then Andrew Boschenstein, learned in the Hebrew language, came to Zurich to open a school, he became his very diligent pupil. These studies at once pleased him: wherefore after he obtained from the Senate [the Great Council] a gymnasium [a high-school] of good learning in which the Latin, Greek, and Hebrew tongues should be taught, he urged strongly that James Ceporinus, a young man proficient in the three languages, should be called: under him it was that Zwingli acquired whatever pertained to grammar. Then, having collated the Septuagint with the translation of Jerome with the assistance of Leo Jud, who had previously made some progress in these labours and studies, and of Felix Manx, afterwards branded with the marks of Catabaptism, never to be gotten rid of, he ventured dexterously to expound Isaiah and Jeremiah, those most excellent prophets. He carried on all his studies standing up, setting apart certain hours for them, and nothing but dire necessity compelled him to omit them. From early morning to 10 o'clock he gave himself to reading, exegesis, theology, and writing, as time and occasion required. After dinner [the usual hour was 10 A.M.] he attended to those who wished to talk with him or get his advice or he conversed or walked out with his friends till two o'clock; then he returned to his study. After supper he walked about a little, then generally wrote his letters, which occupation sometimes kept him up till midnight. Moreover, as often as business compelled he was at the command of the Senate.

IX.—Machinations of enemies. Successful disputation of Zwingli with Francis Lambert on the intercession of the Saints; other disputations with others follow. The Pope's [Adrian VI.'s] letter to Zwingli.

Just at this place, Agathius, if it pleases you to hear about the labours of Zwingli against the enemies of the truth, and the machinations of the wily workers against this man of God, it is necessary to go back a little. To be sure Francis Lambert, a Minorite of Avignon, whose name was familiar to the French and German nations, is not to be reckoned among his enemies. Nevertheless, because he was among the first to bring on the attacks on Zwingli, he should not be passed over. Leaving the monastery, he came to Zurich [1522], not having doffed his Franciscan robes, and immediately joined with Zwingli in a public disputation upon the intercession of the Saints. I do not know what moved the man, whether it was merely the truth or because he really did it only to keep up appearances, but after a pretty long speech he yielded readily and thanked God that by means of so excellent an instrumentality God had plainly and clearly granted him knowledge of the truth. Not long after he was followed by John Faber, Vicar General of Constance, and Doctor Martin Blansch, preacher at Tübingen, who were sent by Hugo, Bishop of Constance, at the request of the Zurichers. Although they had nothing in their orders beyond hearing the causes of the differences—so they reported—and studying how they might be ended, yet one word led to another and they fell into discussions concerning the gospel, the intercession of the Saints, the constitution of man, and I know not what else, so that the day passed in this manner, and not unprofitably, for all the multitude, whose number was about six hundred, came to realise that earthly things are nothing in comparison with heavenly things. The Bishop did not satisfy himself with sending the aforesaid delegation, for not long after his suffragan came to Zurich to persuade them to believe in the intercession of the Saints and the sacrifice of the Mass, which also he attempted in his book so highly praised by many scholars. But in this he had his labour for his pains, for a man noble both in blood and spirit on being asked what the vicar-general had done replied, "the vicar-general drove away the sow; we drive the litter." Then it was, these things having fallen out thus most favourably to religion by the grace of God, Huldreich [Zwingli] was first compelled to write, but what books, and what useful books—for they present sound doctrine in a way at once simple and profound such as no other books do with which I am acquainted—he left behind him it is not necessary even briefly to describe or even to write their titles, as they are all accessible, and bear amplest testimony to themselves.

While these things were occurring, somehow the report of Zwingli reached even to the Roman Pontiff, who sent to us a legate with a letter to him in these words:

"Adrian, Pope, Sixth of the name, to his dear son

sendeth salutations, and the Apostolical benediction. We send the venerable brother Ennius, Bishop of Verulam, our domestic prelate and nuncio of the Apostolic See, a man distinguished for prudence and fidelity, to that unconquerable nation most completely linked unto us and to the Holy See, in order that he may treat with it respecting things of the highest importance to us and the Holy See, and to the entire Christian commonwealth. Although he is enjoined to treat of these with your nation collectively and in public, yet because we have a special knowledge of your distinguished merits, and deeply love and prize your loyalty, and also feel particular confidence in you, we have commissioned this bishop, our nuncio, to hand over our letter to you in private and manifest our heartiest good-will toward you. We exhort your devotion in the Lord, to have all confidence in him, and with the same disposition in which we are inclined to remember your honour and profit, to bestir yourself also in our affairs, and in those of the Apostolic See. For which you will earn no small thanks from us.

"Given at Rome at St. Peter's under the ring of the Fisherman, January 23, 1523, the first year of our pontificate."

X.—Zwingli begins to reform the Church. Rise of the Catabaptists. Disputation of Baden, 1526. Plots contrived against Zwingli. False accusations brought against him.

I wanted you to know this letter from the Pope so that you could see plainly that if Zwingli had preferred the grace of man to the grace of God he might have had all he wanted in this life. For the Pope did not only write to him as above but also to the excellent Doctor Francis Zinck, that he should gain the man for himself and the Apostolic See. When I asked Francis what the Pope had promised for Zwingli's support he replied seriously, "Everything except the papal chair." After this because the gospel strongly showing its strength was esteemed as the truth from heaven by the greater part, and especially had been received by the Senate of Zurich, and the Council of Two Hundred, the man began to plan how he could put things into a better state, and that everything might be done in order, whatever changes seemed especially to pertain to the furtherance of the gospel were made at the earliest opportunity. The number of the priests and monks had for some time seemed greater than was required for the usages of religion. Therefore the Senate decreed on the persuasion of Zwingli's celestial spirit that it should be reduced to the number necessary for the ecclesiastical offices. Not that any one was to be ejected or deprived of his benefice, but was to hold it during life, but when death had made a vacancy it was to remain unfilled. The three orders of monks were collected into one place, their cowls being taken from them. They were at liberty to go out as they pleased to work, to marry, to study. And those who did not take kindly to the sound doctrines were permitted to migrate whithersoever they desired, so careful were they not to offend any one's conscientious scruples. The revenues of the Church were employed upon either the ministers of the Church or the teachers of good learning or the religious and monks who were left or on the poor. There were found among them promising youths, not a few to whom the study of piety was attractive; these being retained were supported for the benefit of the whole seigniory of Zurich, and when the necessity arose were employed. A man most devoted to good letters and sacred learning, Zwingli instituted among them a school, which if he had lived there is no doubt would have been second to none. Moreover he made the Senate depute some to judge cases of conjugal difficulties, and persuaded them that the worship of images must be abolished, the Mass utterly done away with, and the Lord's Supper restored. Meantime, good God, what a pestilence had crept in!—the heresy of the Catabaptists, prohibiting the baptism of infants, and rebaptising themselves, then rushing with wild spirit into all the heresies that ever were. At first when he became aware of the thing, because the leaders were both friends and scholars, both citizens and parishioners, he tried in a familiar way to dissuade them, but when, promising in his presence, they began on leaving to deny, to lie, to gather disciples, to disrupt the Church, to set up a new one, he was forced to go against Satan with all his strength, and make open war upon him. Believe me, Agathius, I was present at nine friendly conferences and earnest disputations. If it were my task to treat of the matter at considerable length I should certainly have something to say. They foamed at the mouth with palpable blasphemies and abuse, and in a word whatever revelation of evils John[1] makes they piled upon Zwingli. This plague, the more the efforts to repress it, the more fiery it became. Therefore the Senate was at length compelled to assail it with imprisonment, exile, and death, not as Catabaptists but as perjurers, disobedient and seditious persons, unless it (the Senate) wished to give the impression of advocating the false rather than the true, sedition rather than peace, the bad rather than the good. Yet it was not possible in this way to avoid the necessity of forewarning the good by published books so that they might not be led away by deceits. Doctor Balthasar Hübmaier was the head of the Catabaptists, not long before a friend and companion in the gospel, but a little while after a most violent foe. He first broke out in writings and then after he had escaped from Waldshut, a town on the Rhine, and had secretly entered into Zurich, being apprehended, he resisted by word of mouth in the court-house in the presence of the deputies only. Then he requested the Senate that he be permitted to confer with Leo Jud, Sebastian Hofmeister,[2] and me. His wishes were complied with a second time. We laboured with this man so that he promised to recant the next day. Therefore in this mind coming the day after into the church from he court-house, he ascended the pulpit after Zwingli was come down and confirmed all he had taught before, moved thereto he pretended because he (Zwingli) had

[1] In the Revelation.   [2] Myconius uses his Latin name, Œconomus.

put so much stress upon constancy, the miserable man judging that his pertinacity was constancy! Returned to prison he was altogether hidden until by the kindness of Zwingli he was secretly sent away, not without a guide and travelling money, and came to Constance, where he so loaded the man [Zwingli] with abuse that he was forced to apologise to the brethren. But enough of the Catabaptists.

You desire to know about the disputation at Baden as your letter shows, and especially why the Senate of Zurich refused to permit Zwingli to go to Baden. These matters have all been committed to writing and published, and I would rather that you should investigate them there. That you may not, however, say that you have never heard about them, behold here is the letter of the Zurichers to Doctor John Eck in which they invite the man to them. Here also is the letter of safe conduct for the same and solemn promise of all good men bidding him to come and examine and expound from both Testaments on an even footing with Zwingli (whose errors and heresies he had taken upon himself of his own accord in two letters to the delegates of the Confederacy to refute publicly anywhere), the truth of God, to the common profit of the whole Church. By reading these you will understand that Eck cared nothing for what they wrote; so you will easily perceive why the Zurichers kept Zwingli at home. And yet the same matter has been most truthfully defended also by him in several works against Faber. I wish much that I had a copy of the disputation to send you. You would see how beautifully he expresses himself in his famous style. But Zwingli laboured more in running about, cogitating, watching, counselling, warning, writing both letters and books which he sent to Baden than he would have done had he taken part in the disputations even in the midst of his foes, particularly against a chief so unskilled in the truth. I have for my part desired nothing more earnestly in my life than that he had been permitted to take part personally. The Five Cantons would have seen where truth and where falsehood ruled. But the place was not favourable to Zwingli.[1] When this was found out, and afterwards at Bern, Murner, Eck, four bishops, and certain principal monks had first been courteously and honestly invited by the Senate, did he not go thither willingly and rejoicing for the truth? Nevertheless, he was conducted by two hundred armed men through the commonwealths of the Confederacy. He made also the long journey to Marburg, to the colloquy with Luther and Melanchthon upon the Lord's Supper. He feared nothing there, for the place was suitable. What tremendous difficulties he laboured under in all this I believe you must know already. Certain scholars had called him a dogmatist in teaching, principally because of his doctrine of the Eucharist. I do not doubt if ever they could have read sympathetically and weighed faithfully what he wrote to the German princes assembled at Augsburg many would have judged him differently. I refer you also to that document that I may not waste time in writing to no purpose.[2] What can you do with a man who refuses to learn from it the truth about the Lord's Supper?

So much for his labours in behalf of the truth. I will now tell briefly to what perils he was exposed for its sake. When priests and monks had been degraded from their positions (so to speak) and a mandate had been issued against the pensioners as we call them, the enemy turned to plots to try if by any means they might destroy the man. I will be silent about the secret plots that may be known to me, and will tell you about those known to people in general. Some one came to his house after midnight and prayed him to come to a man at the point of death. The deacon replying for the master of the house that he would do whatever was necessary himself (for Zwingli was not to be disturbed during the night because of his daily duties), the visitor objected so strongly that the suspicions of the deacon were aroused that he had some plot on foot. The deacon therefore, going as if

---

[1] Baden in Switzerland, 14 miies North of Zurich.
[2] In English translation by Jacobs in his *Book of Concord*, ii,. 159–179, and reprinted in Jackson's *Life of Zwingli*, pp. 452–484.

he would tell his master all about it, frustrated the marauder by closing the door and leaving him outside. In the morning the facts were discovered, that he was to have been gagged and carried away secretly in a boat. Shortly after a horse was got ready to be used for the same purpose.

Again we saw a waylayer (it was said he was from Zug) in the city girded with the longest kind of sword openly wandering about without a cloak watching for a favourable opportunity to run across the man and kill him. The man was reported and taken into custody, and disappeared.

Two Zurichers under the influence of liquor—I will not mention their names though I know them—threw stones one night against Zwingli's house and breaking his windows behaved so cruelly, basely, and inhumanly with their shouts and curses and blows that none of the neighbours dared to protest even through the windows. So they kept on till they had used up their stones, their words, and their strength. The tumult was reported to the mayor in the morning, the gates were shut and armed men searched for the offenders in vain in every nook and cranny of the city until certain prostitutes who knew about their hiding places, not being adepts in concealing, unintentionally betrayed one of them; the other had already escaped. The fellow was dragged from the wine cask of a certain priest and taken to prison by the enraged crowd. After many trials he was condemned to perpetual imprisonment, and for some weeks he lay in captivity until he was released by request of Bern.

Zwingli sometimes dined away from home with friends or entertainers. Therefore returning he was almost always escorted, without being aware of it, by good citizens, lest evil should befall him on the way. And the Senate in this perilous time placed watchers around his house at night. See, I beseech you, what unjust accusations were brought against the man that he should have to be protected in this way! They called him "a pensionary" because not knowing it was wrong he received at one time an annual pension from the Roman pontiff. He himself indeed excused this offence to his Germans thus: "The dealings which I once had with the Pope ceased years ago. I thought then it was allowable to receive a pension from the pontiff to defend his way. But having realised the sin of it, I gave up the whole business. Therefore the deputies (factores), as they are called, accuse me of wrong in the matter, and being angry at my giving up the pension, impute to me what I have done as a sin because they persuade men that by receiving the pontifical pension they serve God." And to Berthold Haller and Caspar Megander, he thus writes of the gifts of princes: "I esteem the glory of Christ and if you prefer mine own also more than all the wealth of all the princes, not to mention the moderate munificence of one king. In times past I have learned what gifts meant, so that in old age desire after them is not possible."

For the rest they not only called him thief and heretic and adulterer, so blackening his name and doctrine, but they cried out against him publicly with asinine clamour. But when these miserable and insane men saw that nothing was accomplished by all these assaults, either against the word of the gospel, or against the servant of God, they turned themselves with their whole strength against those obedient to the Word, if perhaps tired out they might feel disgust with the one who caused them to feel another's scorn. They calumniated him, made him of no account, publicly and privately jeered at him to such a degree that the Zurichers began to consider how they might avert this evil. It would require a volume if any one would know this affair fully or write exhaustively about it.

To sum up it came about there were formed new alliances for the defence of the doctrine of Christ, the old ones being left unmolested not without great exertions and planning by Zwingli, not surely that anything was attempted against his country (this was impossible in such a fosterer of his country), but because in accordance with the course once begun he had resolved to eradicate vices and establish the evangelical doctrines thus to the praise of God and the advantage of all

Switzerland, nor because he aimed at protecting the things of God in this way, but because he desired nothing more than that all nations might confess the Lord, and that the extent of the alliance might terrify the minds of the ungodly, and so more easily win them to Christ.

XI.—Two civil wars, called the Cappel Wars, in which Zwingli participated; in the first (1529) he was in the midst of the deliberations, in the second (1531) he was chosen chaplain.

And so it came even to war, but what kind of war as far as our hero and the men of Zurich are concerned? The kind that Zwingli himself described in the following words to his friends [at Bern, in *Works*, Schuler and Schulthess ed., vol. viii., 290, dated 1529]: "What I have written to you before I repeat again and again that you may be steady and not afraid of the war. For that peace which some urged so strongly is war not peace, and the war upon which we are entering is peace not war, for we thirst for no man's blood, neither do we propose to shed it even if a disturbance takes place, but we want to cut the sinews of the oligarchy. If this is not done, neither gospel truth nor the gospel ministry will be secure among us. We are meditating nothing cruel; on the contrary all we do is friendly and fatherly. We desire to save some who are perishing through ignorance. We are engaged in the preservation of liberty. Therefore do not turn away in abhorrence from our counsels. They are milder and fairer than they have been represented to you. To all who report us falsely you yield ready credence, whereas you have always thus far had experience of our reliability but of their inconstancy, not to say mendacity. Stand fast therefore in this, that in fidelity to God and man you come up to our promise. Why should I say more? Fear nothing, for we shall so conduct ourselves through the goodness of God and the alliance of all that you will be neither ashamed nor apologetic for us." Thus far he. I have transcribed his words the more willingly because they testify to you, Agathius, in the most convincing manner how entirely unjust it is to represent Zwingli as sanguinary. He was indeed a brave man in danger, intrepid and wise, but it was as far from him to thirst for the blood of even the most inveterate enemy as it should be from every wise man and every minister of Christ. The liberty of the country, the virtues of the fathers, and most of all the glory of God and of Christ were both foundation and aim of all his plans, whatever all the enemies of Zwingli in all nations say, whatever they shout, whatever they maintain. Behold, I speak the truth before you and God.

He therefore took part in the two civil wars, each of which is named the Cappel War from the monastery called the Chapel. To the first he went of his own motion, so that he might be present at the deliberations lest anything might occur contrary to what was true and right. Most happily things fell out and it was concluded without bloodshed. About it he often related to me that in it he had encountered more malice and perverse counsel than in his whole life he had learned from experience or from books. In the second war he was elected chaplain, and although he told himself as well as others that he would not go, nevertheless he went. His divining mind saw what the future had in store. The cause of war never met his approval, *i.e.*, the cutting off of provisions [from the Forest Cantons], for he knew what kind of counsel famine gives. Albeit, to speak frankly, after this plan [to cut off provisions] had been once accepted by the reluctant Zurichers (for others whom we know well had taken it up in no bad spirit since they thought by consultation and discussion a way would be found meanwhile for pacificatory measures even though the Zurichers had preferred a war), Zwingli was not pleased, since he feared that a change would only bring them into greater contempt with their adversaries, although he did not so very strenuously oppose it.

XII.—Zwingli perishes in the Second Cappel War. He left Zurich for the front early on Oct. 11, 1531; and was killed that afternoon.

Also within fourteen days before his departure he said from the pulpit in my hearing, amid the general excitement, "I know, I know what all this means. It means my death, everything is done to put me out of the way." So also the comet which was seen for many weeks he whispered into friendly ears would be fatal to him and also to one other person. We always had understood it meant Œcolampadius. In no really military style, then, the Zurichers sallied forth (whenever I think of the undisciplined affair I am pierced through as by swords), for there was no order, no plans, no direction, so much difference of opinion, so many persons running with scared faces here and there, before and behind the banner, for I cannot say "soldiers" except of a few of them. A very small number in all indeed (five thousand were summoned, not four thousand five hundred were present) against so well prepared a multitude. So the Zurichers set out, Zwingli following in the rear on horseback and armed according to our custom. When I saw him, I could scarcely stand for sudden pain of heart presaging the worst. We passed the day [in Zurich] in continual sighs and prayers to God. But He had appointed a different thing, for us, not against us, as I certainly interpret it in all piety. For be it said in passing, we have learned to advance more cautiously. We hold the gospel in higher estimation, we reverence God more devoutly, and they are more manifest who all this time have been adversaries to the gospel of Christ.

As, then, I saw them going out in the morning, so at night I heard the news,—the fight had been sharp yet unsuccessful, and our Zwingli had perished. It was reported that three times he had in the shock of arms been prostrated, but each time he had struggled to his feet; a fourth time he was struck under the chin by a spear, and, fallen upon his knees, said,

"What evil is there in this? They are able, it is true, to kill the body but not the soul." And having so spoken he fell asleep presently in the Lord. After the defeat, during the leisure given to the enemy (for our soldiers had retired into a well guarded place) the body of Zwingli was sought for (and who told them so quickly that he had been present in the battle or had fallen?), was found, tried and condemned, cut into four parts, thrown into the fire, reduced to ashes. The enemy having retired after the third day, friends of Zwingli went to see if they could perchance find any remains of him, and lo! (strange to say) his heart presented itself from the midst of the ashes whole and uninjured. The good men were astounded, recognising the miracle indeed, but not understanding it. Wherefore, attributing everything to God, they rejoiced because this supernatural fact had made more sure the sincerity of his heart. A man whom I knew very well, in fact very intimately, came to me shortly afterwards asking whether I desired to see a portion of Zwingli's heart which he carried with him in a casket. Because a sort of horror on account of this sudden remark pervaded my whole body I declined. Otherwise, I could have been an eye-witness of this thing also.

This, then, is the course of Zwingli's life, this the way of his death which the loyalty of his soul to his country and the devotion of his heart to the Republic of Christ brought upon him, horrible, indeed, in the eyes of men, precious in the sight of God, such a death as awaits all teachers of the divine righteousness unless the Lord in His singular grace prevent and save them. I think I have fulfilled your request, Agathius. What I promised I have given, truth and brevity; bound to no elegance of diction, I have indulged in none. I hope there may appear in the future some one who for the use of the studious pious shall put the finishing hand upon all these things, making his narrative as attractive as possible while in accordance with truth, and giving it the elegance which is worthy so excellent a man.

Farewell to you and interpret this my compliance [with your request] without prejudice.

At Zurich in the year MDXXXII.

The Works of Huldreich Zwingli

I A

THE FABLE OF THE OX. A COMMENTARY ON THE PRESENT COURSE OF AFFAIRS, BY HULDREICH ZWINGLI OF THE TOGGENBURG, IN CRUDE CENTIMETRE FORM

(Autumn 1510)

[The first publication of Zwingli was a poem. It is in two forms, of which the Latin is the original. Zwingli wrote them both, but has made the German form different in various particulars from the Latin, as well as longer. The Latin form has been translated by Mr. Henry Preble, the German by Walter Lichtenstein, Ph.D., librarian of Northwestern University, Evanston, Ill.

The Latin form has the caption: Huldrici Zwinglii Toggenburgii ineducatum bovis fabulosum centimetrum currentium rerum commenticium.

("The fable of the Ox, a commentary on the present course of affairs by Huldreich Zwingli of the Toggenburg in crude centimetre form.")

In Schuler and Schulthess ed., iv., 145-7. In Egli and Finsler ed., i., 10, 12, 14 (being put opposite to the German form).

The German form has the caption: Ulrichen Zwingli, priesters, fabelisch gedicht von eim ochsen und etlichen tieren ietz louffender dinge begriffenlich ("The fabulous poem of the priest Zwingli concerning an ox and many other animals, referring to current events"). In Schuler and Schulthess ed., ii., 2., 257-62. In the same volume, pp. 264-8, is a rhymed translation into modern literary German. In Egli and Finsler ed., i., 11, 13, 15, 17, 19, 21, 22 (being put opposite to the Latin form as far as the Latin extends).

Egli elaborately explains the circumstances of the time which are alluded to in the poem, and to this long preface (i., 1-7) the reader is referred. Suffice it here to say that, partly by what Zwingli himself has furnished, we may identify the various characters mentioned in the poem with familiar personages. Thus the Ox is the Swiss, the Cats are the agents of foreign powers who tried to hire, and frequently did do so, the Swiss to fight in foreign wars because they had made a reputation for themselves as soldiers. Zwingli, like all other lovers of his country, deprecated such conduct, and here he vigorously protests against it—a display of zeal which later cost him his place. The other animals are the Dog Lycisca, a name borrowed from Vergil (Eclogues, iii., 18: "loud barking Lycisca"), who here stands for the wide-awake patriotic clergy, the Lion is the King of the Romans, from the House of Habsburg; the Leopard is the French; the Fox is Venice; the Herdsman is the Pope; and the Ram, another borrowing from Vergil (Eclogues, ii., 64, "the playful goat follows the lucerne-bloom"), is Graubünden or Schaffhausen. The pasture of the Ox is Switzerland.]

THERE was a garden spot hedged about on one side by high mountains, on another by gurgling streams, and in it roamed, cropping the green blades of grass, a fine fat bullock of ruddy hue, with widespread horns and on his brow rich waving hair. His chest was broad, and an ample dewlap marked his chin. Anon he would take a long-drawn breath and quaff the cool waters, generously endowed as he was in animal attractions, and without an enemy save envious Fortune who mingles gall with all things sweet. She gave him cunning keepers at whose nod the simple-hearted beast should do all things as though directed by Medusa's eye. To his flank clung inseparably the dog Lycisca, giving notice of hostile snares, so that the ox, with the aid of the Fauns that he delighted to call to mind, might be more cautious, and foreseeing blunt the attacks of the beasts. Then though lions with their terrible roar and many another wild beast might charge upon him, they would retire with hardly a wound given, and the rough ox would rise ever unconquered, and thus victorious.

But when they accomplished nothing by either talk or onslaught, they turned to other means, and arranged to deceive him with cunning. They promised cats all sorts of rich things (for cats delight in what is rich), birds and fish withal, that they might induce the ox to leave the cliffs and garden spot, and make for lands outside (whereby were greater glory). And first the variegated leopard approached with mighty winning ways, and presently began to lure on the cats with a rich bait. When they had been caught, the poor ox was taken with the same coin, though Lycisca barked long and loud but without avail. When the goad-bearer(?) began with persuasive words and baleful craft, he led the sluggish ox where he would and where he would not. And it had not been usual to bury the dung before the unaccustomed food eaten and the altered stomach had discharged droppings more offensive than garlic (?). Then they were ordered to let up on the richer viands, that the excrements might not smell as badly as horse dung which had first been turned over. The cunning keeper never let up on the tidbits, but evaded the order with clever words, hiding the dung in a ditch, so that the ox might not be offended by the odour and would cease to find fault with the feast,[1] but he could lead the poor beast as before. Thus persuaded the ox ran upon drawn swords, devoured blades, and incurred all sorts of dangers to enrich the mighty cunning leopard, and nourish a serpent.

When the lion saw this, he became envious of the clever fellow's pile, and approaching the ox with drooping tail and dishevelled mane, begged him to enter into a holy and righteous league with him. This the simple-hearted ox presently whispered in the ear of the whiskered cat, who, answering without delay, rejected the proposal (that he might not lose the bounteous gifts of the leopard), adding: "It is not safe to trust to the lean beast (though he be king and lord supreme), for when he lacks food, he may make a savage attack upon you to satisfy his gnawing hunger." The ox listened to the suggestions and scorned the friendship of the lion, than which the excellent lion scarcely ever met with anything worse, and furious said to himself, "I'll get even with the perfidious rascal." Straightway he flies to the leopard's cave (from whom he had suffered hundreds of frauds and contemptuous indignities) and complains, and implores his powerful aid. Presently the lion and the variegated one strike an adamantine league to make all the animals tremble.

Presently they charge upon a timid fox, and biting at the beast soon reduced to despair, try to do him up with every kind of snare, but, torn and limping upon three legs, he crawls to a herdsman who happened to be nearby, and telling of his deep wounds and his bruised head, begs him

---

[1] The Latin of this savoury passage is so obscure even with the emendations of Schuler and Schulthess that I do not feel sure of its meaning.—H. P.

piteously to help him and (such is the astuteness of the animal) promises to return immediately all the fowls that he may have carried off. Then the shepherd has pity for him, though before he has seen through his little wiles, and, forgetting these, proceeds to help the little animal, and addresses himself to the ox directly with these words: "You are not unaware how lively a sense of the tried worth and faithfulness of your father and godfather I have ever had. Contemplating that, I come to warn you now not to let me find you inferior to them. You know how the lion and the leopard are mangling the herd. They plunder the sheep, and murder them cruelly, tearing them asunder and getting them away stealthily under the aspect of simplehearted lambs. I want to anticipate their wiles and thieving expeditions and under your initiative make the herd whole." Lycisca barks in joy at these pleasant words and advises the ox not to abandon his friend the herdsman, under whose guidance he can easily escape the jaws of the threatening conspirators. This gnaws the vitals of the cats, and they cast glances at the cunning fellow often meditating flight. When the ox in his growing sluggishness sees this, he turns his head a little, but goes on as though driven by a goad as before. When the brethren, the lion and the terribly cunning one, behold this, they break forth in rage, howl, and, grinding their sharp teeth, declare bloody war upon the ox, unless he renounces his agreements and abandons the herdsman. Thus is the life of the ox kept in doubt and trouble.

There had been a goat present at these proceedings, and he says to himself: "I rather think the ox will get a fine beating now, unless he is saved by the protecting staff of the herdsman, or unless the leopard and the lion fall out, or the variegated one brings gifts of reconciliation, but then the herdsman will be angry. The net drawn on all sides can be sundered only by arms, but so much the better for me. I shall crop the luxuriant clover and scorn their gifts. Let those take the gifts who prefer to live in dishonour."

I B

THE FABULOUS POEM OF THE PRIEST ZWINGLI CONCERNING AN OX AND MANY OTHER ANIMALS, REFERRING TO CURRENT EVENTS

(Autumn 1510)

I SHALL tell you of a garden fenced in and protected by a strong hedge, having high hills in one place, and in another are heard rivers flowing by. Here dwells a stout ox of beautiful red colour, a hairy, fine forehead, a broad chest, and large horns. From his neck hangs down the fine flesh. This ox feeds on the green grass from the garden, and if he becomes thirsty he drinks the cold water, and thus in beastly fashion is well provided for. He is hated only by blind fortune, which enviously desires nothing sweet to be without bitterness. It ordered cats to join themselves to this ox, and they are the sly keepers of the ox and by them alone is he led in all matters (thus there were at one time three sisters, who between them had only one eye, and this Medusa possessed). By the side of the ox there is always present also a faithful dog, by the name of Lycisca, who makes known to the ox the treacherous plans of the animals, in order that he might the more readily frustrate the plans with the aid of the Fauns, whom rightly he honoured in his heart, whereby he always remained in good health. Even though the lion attacked him and roared cruelly, and many other animals, both large and small, he attacked them all boldly, so that badly gored they were hardly able to regain their lair. Thus the ox came out of every battle unconquered. Since then the other animals could do nothing with blows or with words. We shall see how then this ox was duped. Soon the leopard slyly, according to his wont, came to the ox. He praises the deed of the ox and the glory of it and says that were the ox to make a reputation for himself also in a foreign land no one else would equal him. He bribes the cats with large presents (the highest aim of the cats), that they might not cease until the ox had entered into an alliance with the leopard. Then the dog protested loudly, but without avail, for the ox is drawn by the cats. When then the leopard had brought the stupid ox by means of deceit into his league, he leads him now here, now there, far, far away. Thus the poor ox was betrayed by the cats, so that he considered it his duty to aid the leopard by his strength and diligent labour. He receives small and great injuries, blows, sword-strokes, in short acts as an anvil, and that the leopard may become wealthy, he is even ready to nourish a serpent. When the lion perceived the good fortune of the leopard, he hurried to the ox and addressed him, first having put aside his tail and mane. He tells the ox how anxious he is to enjoy his company, and asked him in friendly fashion to join him of his own free will and not forced thereto. The ox immediately told this to the cats. The latter said: "Comrade" (in order that they might not lose the favour and bribes of Sir Leopard), "have patience; for it is an uncertain matter to trust that chap, though he is a king and great lord; but rather remove yourself far from him. If he should ever be in need of food he would attack you. You see his lean face and hungry mouth; therefore be warned in time and let him be." The ox was obedient and informed the lion that he would not accept his alliance. This angered the lion and he went about roaring, raging, and thinking how he might harm this ox. He bethinks himself that no friendship can flourish which is founded on selfish interests. Since then the leopard had won the ox over for selfish reasons, he would speedily let him go again if it suited his purposes. Therefore the lion goes to the lair of the leopard and complains to him and relates his trouble. He requests aid from the leopard, though the latter had always despised him and had often injured him by robbing women and the like. This all should now be forgotten, providing their league would have a good reason. Soon the alliance was made and soon all animals were to be frightened. They soon came to the quarters of the fox and with their sharp claws wounded him badly, and their desire was to drive him away entirely from all his dens. The fox went to the keeper, limping along on three legs, and complained to him of his deep wounds and of the robbery, and he begged favour on condition that he would return all the fowls which he had ever taken treacherously from him; therefore he asked favour. The herdsman, though he had been injured on several occasions by the fox, forgets all this, and promises him aid and comfort in putting an end to the anger of the leopard and the lion. He hurries to the ox and asks him in mild fashion for aid, and says that he is suffering from the allies of the ox, that they were attacking his cattle and sheep and, dressed in lamb's clothing, were butchering everywhere. He does not mention the fox at all, of whom perhaps he was thinking most. After much exhortation the ox willingly bows to the wish of the herdsman. The dog barks for joy. He was greatly pleased at this turn of affairs, which gnawed at the heart of the cats and caused them great pain. Often they looked mournfully in the direction of the leopard. When the ox noticed this, he turned about slightly again; but hurrying along he put an end to the delay. When the allies perceived this, they at once declared that they would make war against the ox, unless he immediately gave up his alliance with the keeper; their object being to draw down upon the ox even the hatred of the keeper, so that the ox deserted by all would be lost and would be devoured by them.

There was present a ram, who had a lock of hair on his chin, and hence assumes the position of a learned and wise man, though in reality he has little of learning or wisdom. He says: "I believe the ox will be ruined on account of the way he acts; unless the herdsman protects him with his staff, or the league of the leopard and lion is dissolved, or the leopard again gives presents. But in the latter case the shepherd is to be feared. The net is spread and everything prepared. I shall be taught by the fall, to eat the green herbs and to resist all bribes and presents; for where bribes have free play, there liberty cannot continue to exist. Liberty is such a blessing that one reads the Spartans said to Hydarnes[1] that they would fight for it not only with spears but also with axes. But where bribes besiege the hearts of animals, all friendship, liberty, and faithful alliance is despised."

MEANING OF THIS POEM.

By herdsman I mean the Pope, by dog the clergy, while by lion I mean the Roman king; the French king is represented by the leopard, and the common people by the ox. Who were the cats?—Well, whoever is angry should await his opportunity.

[1] The general of Xerxes in the third war of the Persians against the Greeks.

II

ACCOUNT BY HULDREICH ZWINGLI OF THE ENGAGEMENTS BETWEEN THE FRENCH AND THE SWISS HARD BY RAVENNA AND PAVIA AND IN OTHER PLACES, AND OF THE CONVENTION AT BADEN IN SWITZERLAND, IN THE YEAR 1512

(Autumn 1512)

[De gestis inter Gallos et Helvetios ad Ravennam, Papiam aliisque locis, et conventu apud Thermas Helveticas anno 1512 relatio Udalrici Zwinglii. Autumn 1512. In Schuler and Schulthess ed., iv., 167–72. In Egli and Finsler ed., i., 30–7. Translated by Mr. Henry Preble. The Baden alluded to was in Canton Aagau, and only 14 miles north of Zurich.

The "Account" was sent in October 1512 to Joachim Watt, then in Vienna, by the hand of Zwingli's brother James, who was about to enter the Scotch monastery there (it was so called because founded by the Irish monks who came to the Continent under Columbanus in the sixth century). The "Account" was one of those exhibitions of Latin composition made by Humanists for their scholarly friends. They were often declared by their authors to be poor affairs and written at great haste, so that their faults must be forgiven —whereas they may have spent much time in elaborating them and were the best they could do. This particular "Account" was derived from such reports as had come in Zwingli's way, especially from parishioners who had come back from the war. The Swiss had been the allies of the Pope. Opposed as Zwingli was to the mercenary service, and to war in general, he thought at that time that it was even commendable to aid the Pope. He changed his mind later. In 1513 and 1515 he was in Italy as chaplain of the Glarus contingent.

Immediately preceding the "Account" in the editions is the following letter to Vadian, written because he had not acknowledged it:

Huldreich Zwingli to Joachim Watt, the philosopher, greeting:

I could not have wondered enough at the tardiness of your writing, my dear Joachim, if I had not known the interruptions to which you are subject and the press of business under which you labour. For my affection for you is of such a character that it thirsts for as many letters from you as the Danube has drops of water; and if they are not forthcoming it pants continually as with a burning fever. I have sent to you a certain report [the "Account"] roughly drawn up and hastily written, which you will make allowance for as you know I wish. For you know that I belong to that kind of men whom you destroy if you do not make allowance for them. For poor and worthless trifles are set down at their first suggestion and with no polishing, just as they fall.

I beseech you to be as kind to my brother [James] and to the other, Valentin [Tschudi], as you can, if they are with you. Another one also is sent, Ludwig Roesch, by his brother, pastor of the parish of Wye [St. Gallen], [he is] the grandson by his daughter of my little old chaplain; and he is commended to your sound judgment. Whatever kindness you do him you shall receive a return for; it shall not be in vain.

If you wish to know what news there is with us, there is a good deal going on, but all is uncertain. Every day we receive messengers from the Pope or Cæsar [the Emperor], the Milanese, the Venetians, the Savoyards, and the French, and send others to them. I will attempt to write you these in such good shape (if I only can) as not to greatly disgust you, I trust, although my workshop brings forth nothing except what belongs to the moment.

I am applying my ignorant self to the study of Greek and Latin. So take good care that your toil and labour do not come to naught. What is to be taken in hand after the "Introduction" of Chrysoloras [so he calls, as was usual, the "Erotemata," *i. e.*, interrogatives, which was the first Greek grammar in use in the West, and whose earliest edition appeared in Venice in 1484. The author lived c. 1355–1415] is done? I do not know who has stirred me up to the study of Greek unless it is God; for I do not do it on account of glory, for which I do not look, but solely for the sake of sacred literature. I commemorate Arbogastus [Strubius] with my little praises without conceit. If the laurel pinches the hair, soften it with a laurel cake, *i. e.*, a trifle (try something easier in the same line), for Henry Loreti of Glarus has been crowned with the poet's wreath by the Emperor [Maximilian] at Cologne.

From our house, Feb. 23, 1513.]

SINCE the defamation of our Brothers-in-arms[1] is constantly flying abroad on swift wing, and since that which the event itself stamps with approval as rightly and justly done is undergoing most unfair distortion through the slanderous words of wrangling detractors, I have determined to sketch for you with laconic brevity and thus all the more vigorously the true position of our commonwealth. Let me pass by, therefore, the terms under which a treaty was entered upon and concluded between the Most Blessed Vicar of Christ, Julius Second, and our allied forces; I call them Brothers-in-arms and Allies all the more gladly because it is reported that some fool or worthless wretch (a Pytha-

[1] The Swiss.

The Italian Campaign of 1512   37

gorean ferule ought to be laid upon him for his early ripe impertinence in thus venturing to wag his tongue) has stated that we should more strictly be denominated traitors and conspirators than allied forces. I might throw a morsel to this snarling cur and, since he is pleased to draw inferences from the individual to the general and universal, I might say: "Does it follow that because a certain man has shown himself the assassin of his mother country, all his townsmen are or ought to be called matricides?" Could anything more ridiculous be said?

But be it enough to show how the King of the French[1] (who, having laid siege to the Church of Christ, has been most incontinently flattered all this while with the honorary title "Most Christian") has worried and subdued the Venetians in a protracted war of many battles, and those no child's play either; how he has ravaged or taken away their cities, and has crowned his reckless insolence by engaging in hot encounter with the Most Blessed Head of Christendom, setting up an antipope[2] at the instance of the Devil, as they say, and taking away Bologna, that mother of learning and nurse of pontifical law, as well as various other noble cities.

Last Easter His Most Excellent Majesty, the King of Spain[3] (whom they now style "Most Christian King"), seeing that the bark of St. Peter was being tossed by the waves to the danger point, took pity upon the Church to such a degree that he hurriedly got together the best army he could and sent it forthwith to reinforce the troops of the Pope, which were still tarrying in the middle of Italy as during their winter quarters. This force—such is the delight as well as the skill of the race in war—made straight for Ravenna. When the lord of the French discovered this, he immediately gathered together the great forces that he had in the field against the Spaniards and their allies, the Venetians, and sent them to Ravenna. As soon as the

[1] Louis XII.
[2] This was a mistake. It is true, however, that a French ecclesiastical council in 1510 resolved to refuse obedience to the Pope.
[3] Ferdinand the Catholic.

Spaniards got sight of them, they eagerly accepted battle and their courage was raised all the higher by the cunning of an engineer whose cleverness was worthy of Archimedes or Dædalus. He devised some light carts armed with scythes, and upon each of these he placed a small cannon, and they pushed these carts ahead of them by their hands or feet.

The French army was commanded by a Grand Master[1] (a dignitary among the Lombards), who stationed the lancers [German mercenaries, Lanzknechts] in the van with the Swabians and Gascons next them, and flanked them with an imposing body of horsemen. He remained in the rear with the reserves.

The Spanish army was smaller than the Venetian, for they had been battered in many conflicts and few were left, but they were united with a force of brave young warriors. Made one army, the two numbered thirty thousand men. Pushing their cannon forward when the signal for battle was given, they touched them off and rained forth a shower of balls. Thereupon, as the enemy's lancers hesitated, they say the Grand Master cried out: "What are you waiting for? Are you put there to be imbedded with iron balls like a target? O that you were now that unflinching band of allies who at sight of the foe roar like savage lions and charge with a rush. Up, soldiers, up; refuse not victory, ye who have so long been wont to conquer and have not learned defeat! Rout the lines so often put to flight, break their ranks, give them swords and lances and javelins for their shot!" The rain of balls had now let up a little, and the Frenchmen began to advance on the double quick. The Spaniards lighted their rolling cannon and pushed them down with all their might into the midst of the enemy, inspiring the greatest terror in the lancers and hope of victory in themselves. Thus they came into close quarters so compactly and with such fire and valour that, though neither line yields, each is forced to stop frequently to take breath. Again and again they withdraw the wearied ranks and replace them with

[1] Gaston de Foix, Duke of Nemours and nephew of Louis XII.

The Italian Campaign of 1512

new ones, and so, giving and taking wounds, accompany the sun from his rising to his going down.

Seeing how stubborn a fight it is to be, the Spaniards dash in so savagely that the contest becomes forthwith one of swords hand to hand where the battle is hottest. They maim and slash and butcher the Gascons and the cavalry—for of the lancers the larger part had already fallen, while a few had escaped by flight—till eight thousand men are slain. At this sight the Grand Master, raising his eyes to heaven, ground his teeth and cried: "Either this day shall be my last or I will not suffer the Spaniards thus to win a bloodless victory." Then, putting spurs to his horse and followed in a mass by the reserves, he charged so recklessly upon the foe that he was overwhelmed and fell fighting nobly. The rest, pitted against an enemy now thrown out of order and fearing nothing less than a fresh army, put him to flight and, winning the victory and the town, shut out the Spaniards and Venetians, who had gone forward some distance in their onslaught. Night put an end to the battle. Hannibal did not inspire the Romans and Italians with greater alarm after the disaster of Cannæ, such were the lamentations on all sides at the French supremacy hanging over their heads, and such the prayers for mercy and help and comfort.

Accordingly the allied forces, contemplating the situation of the Mother of Christians, thought it would be a bad and dangerous precedent if they should allow the first best monarch to rage so far as to trample with impunity upon the common mother of the Faithful of Christ. With sudden zeal they began to hold meetings and determined to repair energetically the damaged affairs of Italy and the Church. The Cardinal of Santa Potentiana [Matthias Schinner[1]]

[1] Matthias Schinner, here mentioned, was born in Mühlebach, in Upper Valais, Switzerland, in 1456, educated at Zurich and Como and became bishop of Sian (Sitten) in 1500. In 1509 Pope Julius II. appointed him legate in Switzerland, and he induced the Swiss to send troops to the Pope. But he subsequently lost their favour and was compelled to leave the country For his services the Pope made him a cardinal in 1511. He belonged to the fight-

(legate *a latere*) attended the conference and with entreaties and protestations urged them in the name of their compact to take the field at once. He had only money enough to give a pound to each soldier, yet, incredible as it seems, an army of twenty thousand of the choicest infantry was enrolled in six days and hastened under arms through the Tyrol, over the Adige (for passage had been granted by the Emperor, but secretly, because he was anxious to have the remainder of the agreement of Treves duly carried out), and past its bluffs and fortifications (they call them enclosures) to Verona, occupied as it was by the French and the lancers alike. The French abandoned the city before the Brothers-in-arms reached it. Thus the Emperor casually, yet in accordance with his purpose, paid the King of the French, through the flight of his men, the two hundred dollars—crowns they call them—which he had borrowed. Going in search of the enemy the army receives with great honour the Cardinal of Santa Potentiana (he is bishop of Sion), and there they take counsel, having learned what had befallen the army of the Venetians. Presently these arrive with seven hundred cuirassiers and nearly five hundred light-armed foot-soldiers. They were Rascians, a Venetian tribe, and at sight of our forces showed such joy that it was a sort of premonition of success. Onward they marched, therefore, to a river (its name I did not hear and so do not know it),[1] across which could be seen a formidable French encampment. The banks, of different elevation, were joined by a bridge, and the farther bank, Valleggio by name,[2] had three very strong towers at the head of the bridge filled

---

ing parsons, even as the Pope did, for he led the Swiss in person in the battle of Marignano in 1515, which was a bad defeat to the Swiss, and the Allies against the French in 1521, which resulted in the defeat of the French. In the early days of the Reformation he was on friendly footing with Luther and Zwingli, but like so many other prelates who had yielded intellectual assent to the theology of the Reformers, he could not bring himself to leave the Old Church, and in course of time advocated violent measures to suppress the Reformation. He died in Rome on September 30, 1522.

[1] It was the Mincio.   [2] 15 miles south-west of Verona.

The Italian Campaign of 1512

with armed men, while a neighboring height, strengthened by a solid and strongly garrisoned castle, still further secured the camp. There a shower of projectiles was kept up for some time from both sides until the cannon of the Venetians proved superior. The French were driven from the castle and towers and camp and our soldiers were supplied with an abundance of provisions.

Marching on from there they came to a place called Pontevico[1] [French Pontevin] and found it occupied by the French. A castle in the middle of the stream[2] is connected by a double bridge with the two banks. The storming of the place had been made difficult by the cutting down of the bridge on the side where the army was approaching. Thereupon (so vigorous for any kind of task is the youthful band of the Brothers-in-arms) they make a feint of swimming across in sight of the enemy and building a bridge under cover of the Venetian cannon. Then some of the best of them climb down the bank and, finding no one to prevent them, swim across, launch the enemy's boats, and cross over the bridge thus extemporized. But the enemy had already fled and they caught only such as they reached with the cannon from afar. After this place I understand that another was captured, strong enough in men but not in courage. For, having an unjust cause, the French easily lost heart and furthermore had been deprived of the support of the Germans.[3] They knew, too, with what sort of enemy they had to deal provided they should come down to battle.

Seeing no chance to trust themselves safely to the open field anywhere, they shut themselves up in Pavia,[4] to try what the chances of fate might bring, and began to collect there all the supplies possible. Then the most vigorously impetuous of the allied forces intercepted a great number of their fatted oxen and furnished the whole army with fresh

[1] 19 miles south-south-west of Brescia.
[2] The Oglio.
[3] The Lanzknechts had been ordered by the Emperor Maximilian to return home.
[4] On the Ticino, which joins the Po 3½ miles south-south-east of Pavia.

meat for many days. Huldreich von Sax, leader of the army of the Brothers-in-arms, a man as universally prudent as courageous, determined to lay siege to the city since to storm it seemed impracticable. They had already reached the bank of the Po[1] when the French made a second attempt to prevent their crossing. But no obstacle is insurmountable to him who really works. I must describe here an episode which, though hard to believe, is still true as well as amusing. There were among the French eight hundred of the Lancers, survivors of the disaster of Ravenna. When some of our men swam across the Po[1] to fix the first supports for a bridge on the farther bank, these Lancers rushed out to stop the undertaking. Meanwhile all the youthful band of Brothers-in-arms, being practised swimmers, runners, and jumpers, had thrown off their clothes and, clinging to their spears, were swimming naked across the Po,[1] to engage with the foe, who seemed to be given them by God for constant practice in the art of war. For they always burst forth into a war-like laugh whenever they have to engage with the Lancers, not because these are unwarlike and defeated without effort, but because they have much oftener defeated them than been defeated by them, and yet it is always part of that force that is sent to confront them. The Lancers took to their heels and got themselves back into the town, though they saw the shining whiteness of our bodies. Thus the Po[1] was crossed without hindrance, and they made vigorous preparations to besiege the city. After a few days' siege it was captured in the following manner. A few challenges indicate to their unsuspecting minds how things are likely to turn out. Six Frenchmen at once challenge four of the Brothers-in-arms and are slain, then two call out one—pleasant news to hear—and that a man of Glarus. He, being used to hunting the wild beasts of the mountains, carried an arquebuse on his shoulder, and having made the battle equal by killing one of his antagonists with the bullet from his gun, attacked the other with his sword. Then, as

---

[1] It should be the Ticino, a branch of the Po.

The Italian Campaign of 1512   43

they fought, another Brother came up and finished the almost conquered Frenchman. Then the French, losing confidence in their defences, their forces, and their courage, begin to meditate a retreat as soon as a fit opportunity offers, and see that it can be accomplished by means of the lancers. They address them in these words:

"You see, excellent fellow fighters, that either by chance or by the hand of fate, the fortune of our French arms is growing daily worse. Therefore we must take measures for our escape, since we cannot for victory. You see there is no hope left. You see nothing remains to us short of death save flight alone. Ah, how vigorously you have laboured in these days to have the palm of victory bestowed upon you! Add valour to your valour now, though the day be your last. Let us heavy-armed and light-armed infantry guard the way as long as the part of the city that looks towards the Mincio[1] is free from the foe, that the means of getting out may not be cut off, and that we may all be restored to safety together. Be it enough for those who could not win to save their lives, in order (I use an expression of Demosthenes) to win another day. We leave all the engines of war in your hands, that none may think himself betrayed; for in them is our best hope of safety."

The unsuspicious Lancers suffered the French to retire with whatever they chose, thinking that they would make good their words by their deeds, but they no sooner got across the Mincio[1] than, plunging into full flight, they abandoned the Lancers. When the people of Pavia saw this, they began to promise a month's pay to both the soldiers of the Venetian army and the Brothers-in-arms, on condition of not being plundered. Our soldiers were possessed with a desire to fight with the Lancers, and some of them got thereby all they wanted. The cannon had been posted in the zoölogical garden outside the city. A hundred men from the differ-

[1] It should be the Ticino.

ent divisions were detailed to watch these, and it was not yet noon when the women and old men, whom the Lancers had not viewed with the least suspicion, began to slip out first. They set up ladders against the walls and signalled to our soldiers to enter. The hundred who had been set to guard the cannon run up rashly enough, mount the ladders with a few others, leap the walls, and form themselves in line within the city unknown to the whole army, for eagerness for battle kept every one busier fighting than spreading news. Thereupon they would have all been cut down to a man had not the chance to fight been taken from the Lancers as well as from themselves by the very narrowness of the streets. They had their cannon, while the invaders had nothing but the weapons in their hands and their fiery courage, and they were often forced to dodge into some corner as the balls went flying about. They devote their special energies to capturing some piece of ordnance. Presently they succeed in turning about two, all ready to light, and, firing them into the enemy, drive them back more and more. Then some one scaled the wall and cried out: "Victory! The city is ours!" But the army refused to believe the soldier, and forbade approaching nearer the wall. "The day was lost," they said; "they were not aware there were any friends in the city." At length some, shaken by the stentorian uproar, mount the walls and crushing forward the vainly resisting Lancers drive them into the river. Only fifty of the eight hundred were taken alive. Meanwhile the Brothers-in-arms are let in through the gates. The Venetian cavalry dash swiftly ahead to see if they can come up with any stragglers among the retreating foe, but catch very few. Then a shout was raised in the whole town, proclaiming Julius and the Swiss victorious. The castle still held out, but was taken two days later and with it eight heavy cannon, ten long ones (so-called Dragons) and ten field-pieces, some of which had belonged to the Venetians. When they saw them they embraced them, wet them with their tears, and kissed the image of St.

Mark, so much to heart had they taken their long-suffered disgrace. The remaining cities that had not surrendered, sent envoys and surrendered themselves into the power of the Cardinal[1] and the Allies. Meanwhile the Spaniards took Genua by storm, and Asti begged suppliantly for peace, and surrendered to the Holy Alliance. Thus, freed by the Brothers-in-arms, all Italy, both the Ligurian coast and Lombardy, proclaimed that they owed as much to the allies as Greece set free once owed to Titus Quinctius.[2] All through the cities and towns and country trumpets were sounded, bells were rung, teachers, monks, and orators mounted the platform to publish the Allies as God's People to punish the enemies of the Bride of the Crucified Lord. The nobles flock together from all sides to see the victorious army, and send gifts of wine and grain, and all the world shows great gratitude with dancing and merry-making. The victorious army remained several days at Pavia and put to rest an insurrection that had begun to raise its head. I refrain from describing it since it ended thus quietly. Then envoys were sent from both sides to settle the affairs of the Milanese. Three hundred of the Florentines who were with the French obtained from the Cardinal and Huldreich von Sax permission to depart unmolested after the French had disappeared in scattered flight over Mont Cenis, but afterwards, having got a glimmer of hope that they were going to renew hostilities, they turned to follow them in contravention of their oath, and were captured by the Venetians, who were in friendly alliance with the region. Several strongholds are still occupied by the French garrisons, which it is hoped will be driven out in a few days, when they see that no confidence is to be placed in their monarch.

A convention was ordered to assemble at Baden,[3] the general municipal headquarters of the Allies. Here there came

[1] *I. e.*, Schinner.
[2] Flamininus, the conqueror of Philip of Macedon in the second Macedonian War, 197 B. C., and "the liberator of the Greeks."
[3] In August–September, 1512.

together the envoys of His Holiness the Pope, Julius II., the Emperor, the Cardinal of Santa Potentiana [Schinner] (Delegate *a latere*), the King of Spain, the King of the French (but that was kept secret), the Duke of Savoy, the Duke of Lorraine, the Venetians, and the Milanese, each with their special demands. There you might see the caution and cunning of mankind, how some twine one thing into another and get at their object indirectly, others say the opposite of what they mean, because the earlier words of another lord seem likely to hinder them from blocking him off. The Emperor himself caused the greatest confusion of all, for when it had been agreed upon in secret that Maximilian, the son of the banished Duke Louis Sforza, should be restored to the throne, he declared, to the great astonishment of everybody, that Lombardy, as an imperial province, ought not to receive a ruler from any one but the Empire. This the Allies took very ill, declaring that the Emperor had promised to send cavalry but had kept only the letter of his promise; the brunt of the war had been borne by themselves and the Pope and the Venetians. The Emperor now wanted to swallow up what he had contributed nothing to win. These controversies did not, however, degenerate into conflict. Another delegation arrived from the Holy Father Julius and the Cardinals, saying that the Brothers-in-arms had been included in the book of Rescuers of the Church.[1] His Holiness was grateful and would grant whatever they wanted. The majority, nay all, ask for the right to carry on their banners the picture of the Crucifixion; the Men of Glarus, the picture of the Resurrection. In final assembly it was decreed that Maximilian, son of Louis, be restored to his father's throne, etc.

I should have written more (for this is not a hundredth part of the whole), beloved Joachim, had not urgent matters called me to other things. I hope you will read in

---

[1] A reference to the papal Bull *Etsi Romani* in which the Swiss are called "Rescuers of the Church." A German translation of the Bull is in W. Oechsli, *Quellenbuch zur Schweizer-Geschichte*, i., 259 *sq.*, and of the *Account*, here given, pp. 255–259.

the same spirit that I have written, and grant me indulgence, for in the space of three hours it certainly was not vouchsafed unto me to write more elaborately and more fully.

III

THE MISSING DIALOGUES

REFERENCES in the Zwingli Correspondence show that Zwingli wrote at least two Dialogues which were passed among his friends in manuscript, and which were perhaps intended by him for publication. But there is no evidence that they were ever put in print, at all events no copy either in manuscript or print is extant. Of the nature of the first we cannot even conjecture. In the letter of Johannes Dingnauer to Zwingli, dated Dec. 6, 1514, occur these words: "But what the learned among us think of your Dialogue, and especially that unique most learned specimen of all learned men, Erasmus of Rotterdam, you will hear when we meet." (In Schuler and Schulthess ed., vii., 9; in Egli, Finsler and Koehler ed., vii., 20 sq.) Five years later we have several allusions to a Dialogue entitled "The Pest," and which was suggested by Zwingli's experiences with that scourge. The first reference occurs in the letter of Kaspar Hedio to Zwingli, dated Dec. 10, 1519: "The second question that you ask relates to 'The Pest.' The word 'pest' was of evil significance till you made it a word to which a good meaning can be attached, for the 'pest' which wretchedly distresses miserable mortals is indeed bad, but 'The Pest' of Zwingli is good." (In Schuler and Schulthess ed., vii., 100; in Egli, Finsler and Koehler ed., vii., 237 sq.). The second reference is in Zwingli's letter to Oswald Myconius, dated Dec. 31, 1519: "As to my 'Pest' about which you wanted to be informed (in your second letter, I think)—I

The Missing Dialogue 49

wish that it and every sickness mentioned in it were extinct. When Hedio wrote me he said that Nepos was going to write to me about it; as yet no one has written, neither Nepos, nor his son-in-law, nor his father-in-law. He was at Rhenanus's in Selestadt. I hear that it is commonly reported that the learned approve it but fear for me because it is too bitter. But I could have wished that it [the plague itself] had been sweeter to me at the time when it was slaying me. For what are called 'plagues' therein by me have no less an evil effect upon me than that one which threatened to send me to Orcus." (In Schuler and Schulthess ed., vii., 103 sq.; in Egli, Finsler and Koehler ed., vii., 245.) The last allusion to this lost production is in the letter of James Nepos to Zwingli, dated April 17, 1520: "I had sent your Dialogue, most cultured Master, by the lame bookseller before I went to see my friends. Send it back, if you think best (as I said to you in person). I will see that it is put into print." Nepos was a proofreader of Froben, the great printer of Basel. (In Schuler and Schulthess ed., vii., 130; in Egli, Finsler and Koehler ed., vii., 301.)

IV

THE LABYRINTH

(Spring 1516)

[Der Labyrinth. In Schuler and Schulthess ed., ii., 2, 245-51; in modern literary German, pp. 251-6. In Egli and Finsler ed., i., 53-60. Translated by Walter Lichtenstein, Ph.D., librarian of Northwestern University, Evanston, Illinois.

This poem is a great improvement upon its predecessor. It is a fruit of Zwingli's humanistic studies, and tells in a pleasing manner one of the most familiar classical tales. He has given us himself the moral he wished to draw, and there is no evidence that he had any other design. But others, as for instance Schuler and Schulthess, disregarding Zwingli's own statement, have considered it an allegorical poem like that about the Ox and so have made this table of identifications: The one-eyed lion is Spain—Aragon; the crowned eagle is Maximilian; the winged lion is Venice; the cock is France; the ox is the Swiss; the cats are those who entice the Swiss to become mercenaries; the bear is the abbot of St. Gall; the ring is the law of Schwyz and Glarus; the dogs are the allies of the Swiss cantons.]

IF you are surprised at this construction, hearken and immediately the whole affair will be described; it is known as the Labyrinth and was first thought of in Egypt, later it became known in Italy, Lemnos, and Candia. It was builded very neatly, as you will see, in accordance with the plans of Dædalus of Athens, in Crete (now known as Candia). The expense of construction was borne by Minos, who wished to hide therein the shame of his wife, Pasiphaë, who, having had intercourse with a bull, gave birth to a monstrosity, which from head to waist was human, while the rest of its body resembled that of a strong bull. This terrible creature had to be fed on human beings. Minos imprisoned the Minotaur in the Labyrinth and gave him only human beings to eat, especially Athenians, whom he punished in this fashion for having slain his son, Androgeos, without cause. All this Theseus learned when he came to his father Ægeus. This young hero, who had already slain the robber Sciron, the murderer Corynetes, and others, besides capturing the Marathonian bull, was accompanied by Heracles. The anger of Theseus was aroused by the means Minos took to revenge himself, and he determined to put an end to this disgrace to the fair name of Athens. Therefore he sailed to Crete in order to battle valiantly. When Ariadne, daughter of King Minos, saw him, she fell in love with him and sent secretly to him, and when he came she spoke: "Theseus, do not fear. Though you are compelled to fight this monster, you will not be conquered. Remember well, however, the entrance to the Labyrinth, and do not allow yourself to be made insane by the dreary horror of the place. For this terrible battle take along this roll of thread, which unroll behind you, in order that you may regain the entrance; otherwise after the battle with the monster is over you will die miserably in the solitary place." Theseus took the thread and his club, and boldly hurried to the entrance of the Labyrinth. First he opened the creaking door and then entered the cave. It must be understood that the Labyrinth was so constructed that the sound of one vault re-echoed in all the others, and the sound broke in upon the stillness as if the bull was bellowing near by. But Theseus did not allow himself to be frightened, and he soon became accustomed to this sound. Then again the dreariness frightened him, the cave, so curiously constructed, had now a long walk, then suddenly sharp corners and narrow passageways, changing soon after to chambers with high ceilings, so that he could feel the air, and then again he had to crawl through sand. There were many doors and unexpected windings, as well as descents, hallways, blind passages, and the like. Furthermore the walls were disfigured with images of cruel animals of all kinds. Thus he saw the image of a terrible lion, single-eyed, which would have frozen his heart with fear; but he bethought himself in time to examine this deception, and he soon discovered that the lion was merely a figure on the tapestry. This greatly encouraged him. A little later he caught sight of a picture, which seemed to him very terrifying. It was a crowned eagle looking in all directions, with its mouth wide open and having terrible claws and large wings and tail. He reflected, however, that the crown signified virtue rather than anger, and confidently passed on. Then he came to a cock, whose comb stood upright in elegant fashion as if he were afraid of no animal, be it large or small, and looking as if he wished to fight all. The cock had attracted a large number of hens and was showing them food, and in the middle of them all the cock himself was sitting. Theseus did not permit this to worry him, but concluded that these animals after wandering about for some time had lost their way and had been unable to regain the exit alive. Therefore Theseus, thread in hand, continued on his way. Suddenly he saw another image, which frightened him greatly. It was a terrible winged lion, who closed the path; Theseus wondered whether it was a griffin, but approaching closer, he bethought himself that wings are intended for flight, not for standing still, if the animal is attacked; he recognised it to be a lion non-ferocious, but full of deceit. He was intermixed with the birds lest he be recognised as a beast-of-prey and he could never escape unattacked. Boldly advancing he saw an intelligent, beautiful ox, led by many cats, each of which fancied he was able to lead him according to its desire, so that it might jump upon him. Some drew him this way, others that way; in front, behind, and everywhere walked on the reckless crew, so that Theseus recognised easily how much they were annoying the ox; but since they were so roguish, he let them be in order to pass on. Thus he soon saw an ugly representation, which frightened him greatly. It was a bear, an untamed animal, in order that it might terrify all the more. But since he thought it a mere picture he approached and saw that an iron ring passed through the bear's nose and in front some one was beating and

The Labyrinth

taming him. Theseus cast all fear aside, thinking the bear would be tamed in due time. Thus he passed on unharmed and soon went through another door, where he saw a large number of dogs, which he despised, for he saw they were mere images, since they were motionless. Soon thereafter he heard the monster pawing and roaring in terrible fashion. Therefore he strengthens himself against fear, saying to himself: "If you overcome this monster, you will bring fortune to yourself and great honour; also you will release the people of Athens from this onerous tyrant. Forward then; fortune favours the brave. If fortune does not smile, but deceives you, it is still something for one to have attempted the great deed. For he alone dies bravely, who perishes while attempting to do a brave deed."

Thus he came to the beast, who, pleased, raised itself and launched itself against Theseus, thinking first to throw the hero to earth and then devour him. But Theseus defended himself bravely and threw the roll of thread into the mouth of the beast, so that it could not readily open its jaws. Then fighting bravely he gave the monster so many blows that it finally was weakened and at last was tamed by death. Then Theseus took out the thread. Thus retribution always comes in the end to all who are presumptuous. God does not forget, however long He delays.[1]

Now you shall learn that this Labyrinth signifies the worry and work of this world; but Theseus, the bold hero, stands for the strong, good man of honour, who always does right and sacrifices himself for his native land. The monster signifies shame, sin, and vice; but the thread, intelligence, which teaches us to follow the straight path of duty if we

---

[1] [The sentiment of the German rhyme is familiar through the English of Longfellow, in his poem "Retribution," a translation of one of the *Sinngedichte* of Friedrich von Logau (see *Complete Works of Henry Wadsworth Longfellow*, Cambridge edition, ed., H. E. Scudder, Boston, 1908, p. 616):

"Though the mills of God grind slowly, yet they grind exceeding small;
Though with patience he stands waiting, with exactness grinds he all."
W. L.]

But the German poet echoed Greek poets.

wish to cover ourselves with glory. The maiden Ariadne signifies the reward of virtue, which no one ever regrets.

Now look at men, how without reason they wander around in the Labyrinth without the thread; therefore they will hardly be able to come to the light again. I fear that they have decided to dwell here forever with their following, though we are only guests here, strangers, exiles, sufferers, and wanderers; thence when we think ourselves to be well settled our souls are taken from us. In us there is no love of God, which would turn aside from as much evil, and would lead us to despise all earthly treasures, in order to gain God more easily. The world is so full of deceit that we have no more the image of Christ than the heathen. Yea we are worse; for the heathen do all deliberately, so that repentance and misery does not come over them. We, on the other hand, in our conceit hurry all matters along thoughtlessly. Therefore we are all in trouble. Whoever commits crime and murder is considered a bold man. Did Christ teach us that? "Greater love hath no man than this, that a man lay down his life for his friends." [John xv., 13.] See how for a little gain we barter away our lives; thus we plague our neighbours, and injure all natural right with wars, quarrels, and other matters, so that we might think the hellish furies to have broken loose. Tell me what have we of Christians more than the name? No one shows patience or wisdom. Most of all the princes have learnt nothing except to pursue their own desires. As soon as a notion enters their heads, everything else must cease. But when God allows peace to shine upon us, men become beasts. In order, however, not to stir the fire (for men are very angry, when abused), I have bethought myself of the pleasant fashion of a series of fables, which you can easily understand. I shall tell how each animal wandered up and down the Labyrinth and shall request them all to acquire better manners.[1]

[1] The promise was apparently unfulfilled.

V

Transcript of the Pauline Epistles

IN Egli and Finsler ed., i., 61 (the page is really not numbered), mention is made of Zwingli's transcript of the Pauline Epistles made from Erasmus's Greek Testament, which appeared from the enterprising house of Froben in Basel in 1516,—the first Greek Testament. There is no evidence that Zwingli owned a copy of this edition—so his transcript was made from the copy in the library of the monastery at Einsiedeln. The transcript was finished in March, 1517, and is still extant, being in the Zwingli Museum in Zurich. It has numerous marginal annotations, many of them doubtless of a much later date. These have been copied and will appear in the volume of Egli, Finsler and Koehler ed., devoted to Zwingli's exegetical writings. The transcript is very neatly done. Zwingli boasted that he had committed these Epistles in Greek to memory! He was very fond of showing off his attainments in Greek, frequently in rather an amusing fashion. But then he always follows his quotation of a Greek word, or at most a clause, with a translation, so the reader is helped out. In my biography of Zwingli (2d ed., 121 sq. and 135 sq.) is much information about this transcript, including a special excursus and a photographed facsimile of one of its pages. Dr. Philip Schaff in his *Church History*, vii., 31, gives the text and a translation of the last lines which Zwingli wrote as the colophon of his transcript.

VI

A Christian Song Written by Huldreich Zwingli when he was Attacked by the Pestilence

(End of 1519)

[Ein christenlich gsang, gestelt durch H. Z., als er mit pestilentz angriffen ward. In Schuler and Schulthess ed., ii., 2, 270-2. In modern literary German, translated, pp. 272-4. In Egli and Finsler ed., i., 67-9. Translation reprinted from my life of Zwingli, pp. 132-4.

This is the most successful of Zwingli's preserved poetry. It was the memorial of his serious illness from the plague which in 1519 carried off nearly half of the population of Zurich. Though unadapted to singing it has been given a tune and is found in many hymn-books of the 15th and 16th centuries, published in Zurich.]

I.—At the Beginning of the Illness.

Help, Lord God, help
In this trouble!
I think Death is at the door.
Stand before[1] me, Christ;
For Thou hast overcome him!
To Thee I cry:
If it is Thy will,
Take out the dart,
Which wounds me
Nor lets me have an hour's
Rest or repose!
Will'st Thou however
That Death take me
In the midst of my days,
So let it be!
Do what Thou wilt;
Me nothing lacks.[2]
Thy vessel am I;
To make or break altogether.
For, if Thou takest away
My spirit
From this earth,
Thou dost it, that it[3] may not
  grow worse,
Nor spot
The pious lives and ways of
  others.

[1] In the sense of "protect."
[2] The words may also mean equally well, "nothing shall be too much for me."
[3] "It," *i.e.*, my spirit.

Song Written when Attacked with Pestilence

II.—*In the Midst of his Illness.*

Console me, Lord God, console me!
The illness increases,
Pain and fear seize
My soul and body.
Come to me then,
With Thy grace, O my only consolation!
It[1] will surely save
Everyone, who
His heart's desire
And hopes sets
On Thee, and who besides
Despises all gain and loss.
Now all is up.
My tongue is dumb,
It cannot speak a word.
My senses are all blighted.
Therefore is it time
That Thou my fight
Conductest hereafter;
Since I am not
So strong, that I
Can bravely
Make resistance
To the Devil's wiles and treacherous hand.
Still will my spirit
Constantly abide by Thee, however he rages.

III.—*During Convalescence.*

Sound, Lord God, sound!
I think I am
Already coming back.[2]
Yes. if it please Thee,
That no spark of sin
Rule me longer on earth.
Then my lips must
Thy praise and teaching
Bespeak more
Than ever before,
However it may go,
In simplicity and with no danger.
Although I must
The punishment of death
Sometime endure,
Perhaps with greater anguish
Than would now have
Happened,[3] Lord!
Since I came
So near;[4]
So will I still
The spite and boasting
Of this world
Bear joyfully for the sake of the reward
By Thy help,
Without which nothing can be perfect.

---

[1] "It," *i.e.*, Thy grace.
[2] *I.e.*, to health, to myself.
[3] *I.e.*, if I had died this time.
[4] *I.e.*, to death's door.

VII

ADVICE OF ONE WHO DESIRES WITH HIS WHOLE HEART THAT DUE CONSIDERATION BE PAID BOTH TO THE DIGNITY OF THE POPE AND TO THE PEACEFUL DEVELOPMENT OF THE CHRISTIAN RELIGION

(Late summer of 1520)

[Consilium cuiusdam ex animo cupientis esse consultum et pontificis dignitati et Christianæ religionis tranquillitati. Translated by Mr. Henry Preble. In Schuler and Schulthess ed., iii., 2–6. But its authors were Erasmus, and for the "Defence" Thomas Blarer. See Egli and Finsler ed., i., 434, n. 1. See preface to this volume.]

IT is the part of a Christian spirit to be heartily devoted to the Vicar of Christ, and to desire that his authority remain intact. On the other hand, it belongs to the pious duty of the Pope to hold nothing of his own so dear as not gladly to exalt above it the glory of Christ his Lord and the general peaceful development of the Christian religion. And those who are devoted to the authority and glory of the Pope, should show wisdom in their devotion. This they will do if they champion them by means which are approved by even the unspoken judgments of the pious and good. Otherwise no one does injury to the Papal dignity more than they, who would have it guarded and defended by no other safeguards than human fear and rewards. Therefore the more zealous a man is for the Christian Religion, the more deeply he is pained by this disturbance that has arisen at the hands of certain persons[1] who have embittered Luther into writing somewhat unre-

[1] Allusion to Tetzel, Wimpina, Prierias, and many others.

strainedly, and have goaded the otherwise gentle heart of the Pope[1] into dealing with Luther more severely than is perhaps expedient for the peace and quiet of the Republic of Christ. The character of Luther's writings I am not at present considering, but only suggesting that we take into account not only what befits Luther but what makes for the peace of the Church. For often and openly have offences been ignored, that greater disturbance might not arise.

In the first place it is distinctly enough admitted that the thing started from bad beginnings. It sprang, no doubt, from hostility to the good literature now springing up even among the Germans, and hostility to the languages now showing new life everywhere. For those who thus far, without being fortified by these things, have been held to be teachers of consummate learning, think their own influence is being overshadowed by the brilliancy of them. Certain persons, therefore, have left no stone unturned to crush them, differing greatly in this from the Roman Pontiff, who has the highest respect for these studies. Furthermore, as to Luther, the largest part of this evil must be laid at the door of those who have preached and written about indulgences and the power of the Roman Pontiff things which no educated and religious ear could bear, so that as far as the beginning of this disturbance is concerned Luther may fairly seem to have been influenced by devotion and zeal in the cause of the Christian Religion. Moreover, those who do not excuse his beginning afterwards to write more bitterly, yet make allowance for it, saying that he was not altogether without reason angered by the exceedingly bitter hectoring and taunts of certain persons. Without having yet read his books, they raised among the people the cry of "Heretic, Antichrist, Schismatic," before the Pope had made any public interposition of his authority in the matter at all. Nobody admonished or confuted him, though he declared himself, as he even now declares himself, ready for discussion with any one—they only damned him. For

[1] Leo X. (1513–21).

the answer of Prierias the Augustinian[1] even those who obtained the Bull against Luther do not countenance.

When the proposition of Eck had been entrusted to the decision of the School of Paris, the Schools of Cologne and Louvain, though nothing had been entrusted to them, came forward and simply damned Luther. And though they did this by common consent, they do not agree on certain points, and those vital ones. Furthermore, the personages by whom the matter has been managed so far are such as may fairly be looked on with suspicion, for their own interests were involved. Nor is their life or teaching such that their judgment ought to have any great weight, especially in so important a matter.

The method of procedure against Luther is, therefore, rightly discountenanced by all the best and most learned, even though Luther had written things clearly heretical. Nor does one, if he discountenances the course and the method of the proceeding, on that account side with Luther, any more, by heaven, than if one suggests that a murderer ought not to be punished unless he has been convicted and condemned by due process of law. And, in fact, the Bull which is promulgated rather mercilessly against Luther[2] displeases even those who are devoted to the dignity of the Roman Pontiff, because it savours more of the impotent hate of certain monks than of the mildness of him who represents the gentleness of Christ, or than of the spirit of the Holy Father, Pope Leo, than which until now nothing has seemed more merciful and kindly. Hence a great suspicion arises that there are people who abuse his natural gentleness and kindliness to serve their own individual passions.

And yet, by as much as the authority of the Roman Pontiff is more sacred than all other, by so much should the more watchful care be taken to prevent anything ema-

---

[1] This is a mistake. He was a Dominican.

[2] Issued June 15, 1520. A translation is given by H. E. Jacobs in his life of Luther (N. Y., in "Heroes of the Reformation" series, pp. 413-435).

Advice on the Pope and His Authority 61

nating from him which may seem unworthy of him to those unspoken judgments of good men that no potentate, however great, can afford to disregard. Besides, the more widely this matter extends and the more dangerous it is, the more carefully should one avoid setting forth any decision without due consideration.

Every one knows that the Christian life, through the tendency of things gradually to deteriorate, has fallen off sadly from the pure gospel teaching of Christ, so that everybody admits there is need of some marked official renovation of regulations and customs. Therefore, while nothing ought to be attempted wantonly, neither should those be wantonly snarled at who offer suggestions with honest purpose, even if they seem to do it too freely. And even though it were beyond all controversy that Luther had quite wandered from the truth, yet it were the part of theological comity, first to give the man brotherly admonition, then to refute him by sound reasoning and by the testimony of the Holy Scriptures, and, if when thus refuted he would not return to wisdom, to treat him as we are wont to treat a lost member. Those who advise this course are not advocates of Luther, but of theological propriety and of the Papal dignity, if, peradventure, Luther might in this way be utterly done away with, cast out first from the minds of men and afterwards also from the libraries. As it is, by the burning of his books he is, perhaps, to a certain extent, plucked from the libraries, but meanwhile his opinions become fixed in the minds of a greater number of people, since they see that these are not refuted.

The better endowed minds of the laity have an opinion of their own, as well as the clergy, and opinions, even in the case of the learned, are apt to take their start from a man's natural temperament. There are so many learned as well as good men, who, though most purely and tenaciously devoted to the truth of the gospel, yet find no cause of offence in Luther's books! Minds of this kind desire to be taught; they neither wish nor ought to be driven by force.

It is the mark of a donkey to yield to force only, and the mark of a tyrant to use force. Surely it is most becoming to theologians to teach with all gentleness, and not to work with taunts or benefits or secret banding together.

Nor must we consider here what befits Luther only—I am not sitting in judgment upon him now—but what at the present crisis is best for the peace of the Republic of Christ.

We see that Luther is respected by all for the uprightness of his life, and that he has thus acquired a firm hold upon the hearts of men, especially of the Germans, though among other nations also, the people of the soundest judgment, that is, the people farthest removed from things which are wont to corrupt the judgment, are all most favourably inclined to Luther.

Every one acknowledges that he has derived benefit from that preacher's books, even if some things in them, perhaps, fairly deserve disapproval.

We know the feelings of the Germans, we see the persistency of Bohemia for all these years, and the not very different state of things in the neighbouring regions. We hear daily serious complaints from many quarters declaring that the yoke of the Roman See can be borne no longer. And this burden they do not perhaps lay so much to the charge of the Papal authority as to that of those who abuse the authority of the Pope to further their own tyrannical doings.

Thus if things are managed in a spirit of hatred and violence, anybody of much discretion will readily foresee what an upsetting of things may arise from this. For we see that the most dangerous dissensions in the world have often sprung from rather trifling beginnings.

Nay even, the world seems utterly weary of the old theology with its tendency to slip overmuch into the hair-splitting of the sophists. It thirsts for the fountains of the teachings of the gospel, and seems likely to burst in to reach them, unless the doors are opened. Thus even if Luther be altogether obnoxious, yet the theology of the schools ought to be reformed.

Since, therefore, the difficulty arose from a bad beginning in the first place, and there seem to have been errors on both sides, first on the side of those who by their wicked denunciations roused the anger of Luther and then embittered him more and more by their hate-inspired and ungoverned uproar, and especially since they seem in this matter to be working for their own private gain, while no such suspicion can fall upon Luther content with his modest position, it seems desirable that this whole case be settled by a commission of persons who are absolutely free from suspicion of partiality.

But cognisance of matters of faith belongs in an especial degree to the Roman Pontiff, and his prerogative must not be taken from him. Yet for the general good he will suffer this matter to be entrusted to others, men of pre-eminent learning as well as of known honour and integrity, upon whom no suspicion can fall either of a desire, from fear or hope, to toady to the Roman Pontiff as against the truth of the gospel, or of advocating the opposite side through general devotion to humanity.

These commissioners shall be nominated, one each from his own nation, by three princes themselves entirely beyond suspicion, the Emperor Charles, the King of England,[1] and the King of Hungary.[2] After having carefully read through Luther's books and examined Luther orally, they shall give their decision and it shall be binding. And Luther now convinced, will frankly acknowledge where he is wrong and will see to the publishing of his works in another edition with the errors corrected by himself, that a rich harvest of gospel gain may not be lost on account of some few mistakes. For many men regard it as unfair and unprofitable that on account of a number of slips such as belong to human affairs the parts that are right should also be condemned. For in the books of St. Augustine there still exist and are read

[1] Henry VIII.   [2] Louis II.

answers of heretics taken down by the stenographers that are full of impiety and blasphemy.

But if Luther shall even after this persist in the things that have been condemned by the commissioners, it will be necessary to go to heroic treatment. Thus no one will side with Luther if thus beaten, and if he returns to wisdom the matter will be settled without disturbance of the Republic of Christ.

Nor will the authority of the Roman Pontiff be impaired by this course, but the suspicions of men will be met, with whom the decision of the Pontiff himself is likely to have less weight in this case, because he might seem to be favouring his own side in the matter of indulgences and the primacy. On the contrary, he will be the more commended by all men for devotion to his sacred duty in having given up something of his prerogative for the truth of the gospel and the peace of the Christian world.

But if there are any to whom this plan is not acceptable, the next best thing seems to be to refer this case to a General Council to be called at an early date, and such a council seems for various other reasons to be demanded by the condition of the Republic of Christ, unsound as it is in many respects.

For it seems inopportune to treat so difficult a matter in a cursory sort of way, especially when such confusion reigns in the Emperor's affairs, and things are unstable enough, both in Germany and in Spain, to make it undesirable to add stuff for new disturbances. Besides, it is fitting that the inauguration of a new Emperor be carried through with favourable omens, and not be rendered sinister and unpropitious by hateful things of this kind.

I would not prejudice any one in favour of this plan. I have only said with singleness of purpose what it appears to me best to do, and I have been especially influenced to do so by invitation of men in the highest places both lay and clerical. I pray that the truth of the gospel may prevail and that all things may redound to the glory of Jesus Christ. Amen.

Advice on the Pope and His Authority

Νικησάτω ἡ τοῦ Χριστοῦ παιδεία καὶ ἀλήθεια (may the knowledge and truth of Christ prevail!)

Christ Our Lord's Defence of Martin Luther addressed to the City of Rome.

Thou summonest me to rise and judge my cause, as if thy cause were mine. Thou thoughtest in thy wickedness that I should be like thee. I will accuse thee and will set before thy face, will set before thy face, I say, those things which I myself and afterwards Peter, first priest appointed by me, and Paul, chosen of me, taught thee, to wit, humility, gentleness, frugality, and peace, not arrogance, not tyranny, not extravagance, not wars. Show me in all of thee a single one of those virtues which Paul taught. Show me that thou art free from a single vice of those which Peter and Paul denounce. Thou sayest my Martin[1] bases his reviling of thee upon empty rumours. If the rumour of the tyranny of Count Jerome had been an empty rumour, nine husbandmen had lived the longer whom he ordered strangled for one hunting dog, and Florence would have been free from treason. If the rumour concerning Brother Peter, Sixtus's cardinal, and his pomp and luxury had been an empty rumour, thou hadst not deserved these verses against thee on his account:

> "Holy Rome had put him into an unavailing hat.
> This urn of snowy marble holds Peter.
> Sylvetus mourns, Syrasia mourns and the lamb.
> It will be pander, she harlot, he catamite."

The rumour concerning the vices and virtues of Cæsar Borgia is not vague; rather all the world heard of his life and that of his father, Alexander Sixth, as not such as I taught, and strangers from all nations and kingdoms saw him at the Jubilee with a seraglio such as was especially unbecoming to my vicar. But greater and more dreadful things John Francis Sutanus set forth against thee in his unadorned speech. And there are people who proclaim openly the doings of Julius,[2]

---
[1] Martin Luther.   [2] An allusion to Julius II., Pope, 1503-13.

his lust and the youths who are said to have danced before His Holiness with stark naked girls. You quote the words of my prophets. I have also other prophets, one of whom thundered: "Woe unto you that join house to house and lay field to field till there be no place! Will ye dwell alone in the midst of the earth? Woe unto you that rise up early in the morning that ye may follow drunkenness and drink till night! And the harp and the lyre and the tabret and pipe and wine are in your feasts, and ye regard not the work of the Lord."[1] And another of my prophets cried: "Where are the princes of the nations who find their sport in the birds of heaven, who lay up treasures of silver and gold in which men trust, and there is no end to their acquisition thereof."[2] Thou mightest long since have returned to reason in consequence of other teachings and revilings from friends of mine who have castigated thy vices in these latter days. Thou mightest read Sermon 85, Francis Petrarca, John Campanus, Bernard, Ludolph, John Pico della Mirandola, Philelphus, Raphael Maffejus, Pace's Speech at the Death of Innocent VIII., Baptista of Mantua's Sylvæ, Fasti, Calamitates, First Parthenice, Eclogæ, and various passages of Platina.[3] Hast thou never had pity upon captive Constantinople to restore her to me, though in thy Bulls of Indulgences thou hast for many years made frequent mention of the crucified capital and of casting out the enemies of my faith by the

---

[1] From Isa., v., 8, 11, 12.

[2] Latin Vulgate of Baruch, iii., 16-18.

[3] By "Sermon 85" is probably meant the 85th homily in the collection of Paulus Diaconus, which was the most familiar Homiliarium of the period. It is taken from Ambrose and is upon Luke iv., 28, 29—the story of the expulsion of our Lord from Capernaum—an appropriate passage here. It will be found in Migne's series of the Latin Fathers, xv., 1629.

To facilitate reference to the works of the Humanists whose names appear above, their names are here arranged alphabetically according to the form of the names as given in the catalogue of printed books in the British Museum: *Bernardus*, Sylvester; *Campanus*, Joannes Antonius; *Filelfo*, Francesca; *Ludolphus*, de Saxonia; *Maffejus*, Raphael Volaterranus; *Pace*, Richard; *Petrarca*, Francesco; *Pico*, della Mirandola, Giovanni Francesco; *Sacchi*, Bartholomæus, de Platina; *Spagnuoli*, Baptista, Mantuanus.

alms taken from the poor and humble of my fold? For what purposes has the money been disbursed that thou hast raked together or received from thy agents meanwhile? Where is the treasure left by Paul Second[1] and Julius Second?[2] Where the vast mass of money which at every moment thou has been wont to gather in gratifying all sorts of men? For thou refusest nothing if there is gold in it. Thou shalt give account some day of thy dealings. Thou shalt not escape me. Thou shalt not elude my judgment, even though thou dost triumph in thy arrogance over the simple-mindedness of my children.

[1] D., 1471.   [2] D., 1573.

VIII

1. What Zwingli Said and Preached at this Time against the Mercenary Service of the Swiss

(1521)

[Zeugenaussage und Predigtworte zu den Soldverträgen mit dem Ausland. In Egli and Finsler ed., i., 73. Translated by Walter Lichtenstein, Ph.D., Librarian of the North-western University, Evanston, Ill. The first text is taken from Zürcher Staatsarchiv, A. 225, 1 (Frankreich); the second from Heinrich Bullinger's Reformationsgeschichte, herausgegeben von J. J. Hottinger und H. H. Voegeli, 1 Bd., Frauenfeld, 1838, p. 51, reprinted in Schuler and Schulthess ed., ii., 2, p. 350. They prove that Zwingli's early disapproval of the Swiss entering the mercenary service, except that of the Pope, as shown in his poem "The Ox," had now no exception, for he exclaimed against the Pope as well. He does not appear to have published any tract on the subject, but satisfied himself with pulpit and private utterances. Very largely in consequence of Zwingli's stand, the Canton of Zürich forbade all mercenary service.]

A WOMAN told him that in a certain house here in Zürich several people—he did not know whether or not they were natives of Zürich—sat together and wondered whether if the Swiss Confederacy considered Kiburg, Grüningen,[1] and the Lake of Zürich as separate, thus making of the city and dependent territory four independent members [of the Confederacy], they would also have joined the French league.

2. What Zwingli Preached at this Time

Zwingli preached frequently at this time against the practice of accepting money; and showed how such practice

[1] Two dependencies of Zürich.

Opposes Mercenary Service of Swiss

would dissolve and overturn a worthy Confederacy. He also opposed alliances with princes and lords for if once entered into every honest man would hold that what had been promised would have to be carried out. Therefore one should contract no alliances, and if God had once helped a people to be rid of alliances one should beware and not enter upon new agreements which would cost much blood. "And I could wish," said Zwingli, "that one would declare the alliance with the Pope null and void and would send the treaty back with the messenger." He also said: "Against a wolf one raised the hue and cry, but no one really opposed the wolves who destroyed most people." It was fit and proper that these latter wore red hats and capes; for if one shook them ducats and crowns would be scattered round about; if they were wrung out, the blood of your son, brother, father, and good friend would flow. In short, though Zwingli was accused by divers persons of having winked at the papal enlistments, influenced by the imperialists, nevertheless the fact was that there was nothing he opposed so vigorously. The papal partisans in fact did not love him so dearly, nor he the papists that they were at all likely to have any confidential conferences.

IX

Concerning Choice and Liberty Respecting Food—Concerning Offence and Vexation—Whether Anyone has Power to Forbid Foods at Certain Times—Opinion of Huldreich Zwingli

(April 16, 1522)

[Von erkiesen und fryheit der spysen. Von ergernus und verböserung. Ob man gwalt hab die spysen zu etlichen zyten verbieten. Meynung Huldrichen Zuinglis. Translated by Lawrence A. McLouth, Professor of German, New York University. In Schuler and Schulthess ed., i., 1-29; in Egli and Finsler ed., i., 88-136.

This is, as Egli has demonstrated, the expansion of a sermon Zwingli preached on March 23d, 1522, together with an appendix addressed to the chapter of the Great Minster, Zwingli's church, on the question whether any one had authority to forbid flesh at any particular time. It was the first of Zwingli's publications in the interest of the Reformation. It shows the practical order of his mind.

The Roman Catholic Church has enjoined that in strict fasts there should be only one meal a day and that at it no meat and no product of animals used as food, such as milk, butter, cheese, eggs, should be eaten. The "choice of foods" here spoken of was between allowed foods such as fish, including shell fish, animals which lived on fish, as otters and beavers and certain water fowls, but not wild duck or wild goose. The drink must be of such things as quench thirst, as water, wine, beer, coffee, tea, lemonade, but not fluids which are foods under another form, such as milk and soup. The Church regulations as to fasting were in Zwingli's day in Zurich enforced by the civil authorities.

Zwingli had come to the conclusion that whatever practice lacked Biblical support was not of obligation. He had previous to the Lenten fast that year maintained that it lacked Biblical support, but he did not himself disobey the city regulation. Some of his parishioners were more bold and consistent and ate meat. The chief offender was the printer Froschauer, who, under plea that he had an unusually large amount of work to do during this Lent, ate meat with his work-people, and when Zwingli called upon him

Liberty Respecting Food in Lent 71

offered some to Zwingli! Zwingli declined, but could not deny that Froschauer was entirely within his rights as a Christian man. The authorities thought differently and cited Froschauer before them. It was then that Zwingli preached this sermon in which he maintains the eating of meat during Lent was not forbidden in the Scriptures. The magistrates were thereby influenced to refrain from punishing Froschauer, and to repeal the ordinance the following year.

Egli, in his *Actensammlung zur Geschichte der Zürcher Reformation in den Jahren 1519–1533*, gives in No. 234 the defence which Froschauer made before the civil authorities. Disputes as to the Scriptural warrant for the Lenten regulations caused street fighting. The *Actensammlung* takes account of these breaches of the peace (No. 232), and records the trials of the offenders (No. 233). [See preface to this volume.]

To all pious Christians at Zurich, I, Huldreich Zwingli, a simple herald of the Gospel of Christ Jesus, wish the grace, mercy, and peace of God.

DEARLY Beloved in God, after you have heard so eagerly the Gospel and the teachings of the holy Apostles, now for the fourth year, teachings which Almighty God has been merciful enough to publish to you through my weak efforts, the majority of you, thank God, have been greatly fired with the love of God and of your neighbour. You have also begun faithfully to embrace and to take unto yourselves the teachings of the Gospel and the liberty which they give, so that after you have tried and tasted the sweetness of the heavenly bread by which man lives, no other food has since been able to please you. And, as when the children of Israel were led out of Egypt, at first impatient and unaccustomed to the hard journey, they sometimes in vexation wished themselves back in Egypt, with the food left there, such as garlic, onions, leeks, and flesh-pots, they still entirely forgot such complaints when they had come into the promised land and had tasted its luscious fruits: thus also some among us leapt and jumped unseemly at the first spurring—as still some do now, who like a horse neither are able nor ought to rid themselves of the spur of the Gospel;—still, in time they have become so tractable and so accustomed to the salt and good fruit of the Gospel, which they find abundantly in it, that they not only avoid the former darkness, labour, food, and yoke of Egypt, but also are vexed with all brothers, that is, Christians, wherever they do not venture to make free use of Christian liberty. And in order to show this, some have issued German poems, some have entered into friendly talks and discussions in public rooms and at gatherings; some now at last during this fast—and it was their opinion that no one else could be offended by it—at home, and when they were together, have eaten meat, eggs, cheese, and other food hitherto unused in fasts. But this opinion of theirs was wrong; for some were offended, and that, too, from simple good intentions; and others, not from love of God or of his commands (as far as I can judge), but that they might reject that which teaches and warns common men, and they might not agree with their opinions, acted as though they were injured and offended, in order that they might increase the discord. The third part of the hypocrites of a false spirit did the same, and secretly excited the civil authorities, saying that such things neither should nor would be allowed, that it would destroy the fasts, just as though they never could fast, if the poor labourer, at this time of spring, having to bear most heavily the burden and heat of the day, ate such food for the support of his body and on account of his work. Indeed, all these have so troubled the matter and made it worse, that the honourable Council of our city was obliged to attend to the matter. And when the previously mentioned evangelically instructed people found that they were likely to be punished, it was their purpose to protect themselves by means of the Scriptures, which, however, not one of the Council had been wise enough to understand, so that he could accept or reject them. What should I do, as one to whom the care of souls and the Gospel have been entrusted, except search the Scriptures, particularly again, and bring them as a light into this darkness of error, so that no one, from ignorance or lack of recognition, injuring or attacking another come into great regret, especially since those who eat are not triflers

Liberty Respecting Food in Lent 73

or clowns, but honest folk and of good conscience? Wherefore, it would stand very evil with me, that I, as a careless shepherd and one only for the sake of selfish gain, should treat the sheep entrusted to my care, so that I did not strengthen the weak and protect the strong. I have therefore made a sermon about the choice or difference of food, in which sermon nothing but the Holy Gospels and the teachings of the Apostles have been used, which greatly delighted the majority and emancipated them. But those, whose mind and conscience is defiled, as Paul says [Titus, i., 15], it only made mad. But since I have used only the above-mentioned Scriptures, and since those people cry out none the less unfairly, so loud that their cries are heard elsewhere, and since they that hear are vexed on account of their simplicity and ignorance of the matter, it seems to me to be necessary to explain the thing from the Scriptures, so that every one depending on the Divine Scriptures may maintain himself against the enemies of the Scriptures. Wherefore, read and understand; open the eyes and the ears of the heart, and hear and see what the Spirit of God says to us.

First, Christ says, Matthew xv., 17, "What goes in at the mouth defileth not the man," etc. From these words any one can see that no food can defile a man, providing it is taken in moderation and thankfulness. That this is the meaning, is showed by the fact that the Pharisees became vexed and angry at the word as it stands, because according to Jewish law they took great account of the choice of food and abstinence, all of which regulations Christ desired to do away with in the New Testament. These words of Christ, Mark speaks still more clearly, vii., 15: "There is nothing from without a man, that entering into him can defile him; but the things which come out from him, those are they that defile the man." So the meaning of Christ is, all foods are alike as far as defilement goes: they cannot defile at all.

Secondly, as it is written in the Acts of the Apostles,

x., 10, when Peter was in Joppa (now called Jaffa), he went one day upon the housetop at the sixth hour, and desired to pray. He became hungry and wished to eat; and when the servants were making ready, he fell into a trance and saw heaven opened and a vessel descending as it were a great linen cloth held together by the four corners and let down upon earth, in which cloth were all four-footed animals, wild beasts, and creeping and flying creatures. Then a voice spoke to him, saying: "Arise, Peter, kill and eat." But Peter said, "No, Lord, for I have never eaten forbidden or unclean food." Then again the voice spoke to him, saying: "What God has purified, shalt thou not consider forbidden or unclean." Now, God has made all things clean, and has not forbidden us to eat, as his very next words prove. Why do we burden ourselves wilfully with fasts? Here answer might be made: This miracle, shown to Peter, meant that he should not avoid the heathen, but them also should he call to the grace of the Gospel, and therefore material food should not be understood here. Answer: All miracles that God has performed, although symbolical in meaning, were still real occurrences and events. As when Moses struck the rock with his staff and it gave forth water, it was symbolical of the true Rock of Christ, from which flowed, and ever shall flow for us all, the forgiveness of sins and the blessings of heavenly gifts, but none the less was the rock really smitten and gave forth water. And so here, although this miracle was symbolical, still the words of God's voice are clear: What God hath cleansed, shalt thou not consider unclean. Until I forget these words I shall use them.

Thirdly, Paul writes to the Corinthians (I., vi., 12): "All things are lawful unto me, but all things are not expedient: all things are lawful for me, but I will not be brought under the power of any. Meats for the belly and the belly for meats: but God shall destroy both it and them." That is, to me are all things free, although some things are rather to be avoided, in case they offend my neighbour too much.

(About the troubling of one's neighbour, I shall specially later on). And therefore no one can take from me my freedom and bring me under his authority. Food is taken into the belly to sustain life. As now the belly and the food are both to be destroyed, it makes no difference what one eats or wherewith one nourishes his mortal body.

Fourthly, Paul says, I. Corinthians viii., 8: "But meat commendeth us not to God: for neither, if we eat, are we the better; nor, if we eat not, are we the worse." This word Paul speaks of the food which was offered to the idols, not now of daily food. Notice this, however, to a clearer understanding. At the time when Paul wrote the epistle, there were still many unbelievers, more indeed, it seems to me, than Christians. These unbelievers offered to their idols, according to custom, animals, such as calves, sheep, and also other forms of food; but at these same offerings, a great part, often all, was given to eat to those that made the offerings. And as unbelievers and Christians lived together, the Christians were often invited to partake of food or meat, that had been sacrificed to the honour of the idols. Then some of the Christians were of the opinion, that it was not proper to eat this food; but others thought that, if they ate the food of the idols, but did not believe in them, such food could not harm them, and thought themselves stronger in their belief, because they had been free to do this thing, than those who from faint-heartedness and hesitation did not venture to eat all kinds of food. To settle this difference, Paul uses the above words: "No kind of food commends us to God." Even if one eats the food of the idols, he is not less worthy before God, nor yet more worthy, than one who does not eat it; and whoever does not eat it is no better. Indeed that will seem very strange to you, not only that meat is not forbidden, but also that even what has been offered to idols a Christian may eat.

Fifthly, Paul says in the First Epistle to the Corinthians, x., 25: "Whatsoever is sold in the shambles, that eat, asking no questions for conscience' sake." These words are clear and need no explanation, except that they are among other words about the offence caused by the food of idols. But do not let yourself err. From the pulpit I shall speak sufficiently of giving offence, and perhaps more clearly than you have ever heard.

Sixthly, Paul also says, Colossians ii., 16: "No man shall judge you in meat or in drink, or in respect of a holy day." Again you hear that you are to judge no man either as good or bad from his food or drink; he may eat what he please. If one will, let him eat refuse. Here it should be always understood that we are speaking not of amount but of kind. As far as kind and character of food are concerned, we may eat all foods to satisfy the needs of life, but not with immoderation or greediness.

Seventhly, Paul says again, I. Timothy iv., 1: "Now the Spirit speaketh expressly, that in the latter times some shall depart from the faith, giving heed to seducing spirits, and doctrines of devils; speaking lies in hypocrisy; having their consciences seared with a hot iron; forbidding to marry and commanding to abstain from meats, which God hath created to be received with thanksgiving of them which believe and know the truth. For every creature of God is good, and nothing to be refused, if it be received with thanksgiving: for it is sanctified by the word of God and of prayer." These are all the words of Paul. And what could be more clearly said? He says that God's Spirit spoke this as a warning, that they might withstand this, who had no fixed strong belief, and who did not put trust in God, but in their own works which they themselves chose as good. And that such things are placed in them by seducing spirits and devils, that inspire men with hypocrisy, that is, with the outward form, lead men away from trust in God to confidence in themselves. And yet the same will always surely realise in themselves, that they act dishonourably toward God, and they always feel the pain of it, and know their disgraceful unfaithfulness in that they see only their own advantage or desire and greed of heart. Still they are willing to sell themselves, as though they did it not for their own sakes, but for God's. That is having a conscience branded on the cheek. Then he recounts what they will forbid to do as bad. They shall not enter into marriage or wed. Know too that purity so disgracefully preserved had its original prohibition from the devil, which prohibition has brought more sin into the world than the abstinence from any food. But this is not the place to speak of that. Likewise it is forbidden that one should eat this or that food, which God created for the good and sustenance of men. Look, what does Paul say? Those that take from Christians such freedom by their prohibition are inspired by the devil. "Would I do that?" said the wolf, as the raven sat on the sow's body. Now God placed all things under man at the head of creation, that man might serve him alone. And although certain foods are forbidden in the Old Testament, they are on the contrary made free in the New, as the words of Mark vii., 15, clearly show, quoted in the first article above, as also Luke xvi., 15. "For that which is highly esteemed among men is an abomination in the sight of God." The law and the prophets were only a symbol, or have lasted only to John.[1] Hear now, that which seemed great to men was detested by God (the word is *abominatio*), and as far as the law is ceremonial and to be used at court, it has been superseded. Hear then that whatever a man eats cannot make him evil, if it is eaten in thankfulness. Notice that proper thankfulness consists in this, that a man firmly believe that all our food and living are determined and continued by God alone, and that a man be grateful for it; for we are more worthy in the sight of God than the fowls of the air which he feeds: us then without doubt he will feed. But the greatest thanks is a conscientious recognition that all our necessities are provided by him. Of these words nothing further.

Eighthly, after Paul shows Titus (i., 15) that there are many disobedient, many vain talkers and deceivers, which

[1] Luke xvi: 16.

one must overcome, he adds: "Unto the pure all things are pure: but unto them that are defiled and unbelieving is nothing pure; but even their mind and conscience is defiled." Here you see again he did not desire Jewish wiles heeded; this is plainly shown by the words next preceding, where he says: "Wherefore rebuke and punish them sharply (of course with words), that they may be sound in the faith, not listening to Jewish fables and human commandments, that pervert the truth." But they desired to draw the new Christians into abstinence from food, pretending that some food was unclean and improper to eat; but Paul showed that they were wrong, and said: To those of a pure belief, all things are pure, but to the unbelievers nothing is pure. Cause: their hearts and consciences are defiled. They are unbelievers that think the salvation, mercy, and freedom of Christ are not so great and broad as they really are, as Christ chid his disciples, saying that they were of little faith, Matthew xvi., 8, and vi., 30. In these passages we are certainly taught that we are not only fed each day by him, but also controlled and instructed with fatherly fidelity, if we console ourselves confidently alone in his word and commands. Wherefore every Christian should depend alone upon him and believe his words steadfastly. Now if you do that, then you will not believe that any food can defile a man; and if you surely believe it, then it is surely so, for his words cannot deceive. Accordingly all things are pure to you. Why? You believe, therefore all things are pure to you. The unbeliever is impure. Why? He has a doubting heart, which either does not believe the greatness and freedom of God's mercy, or does not believe these to be as great as they are. Therefore he doubts, and as soon as he doubts, he sins, according to Romans xiv., 23.

Ninthly, Paul says to the Hebrews (xiii., 9): "Be not carried about with divers and strange doctrines. For it is a good thing that the heart be established with grace; not with meats, which have not profited them that have been occupied therein." In these words see first that we should not be carried about with many kinds of doctrines, also that without doubt or suspicion the Holy Gospel is a certain doctrine, with which we can console ourselves and on which we can surely depend. Accordingly it is best to establish the heart with grace. Now the Gospel is nothing but the good news of the grace of God; on this we should rest our hearts—that is, we should know the grace of the Gospel to be so certain and ready, and trust it, so that we may establish our hearts in no other doctrine, and not trust to food, that is, to eating or abstaining from eating (so also Chrysostom[1] takes these words) this or that food; for that such oversight and choice of food was not of profit to those that have clung thereto is clear enough.

These announcements seem to me to be enough to prove that it is proper for a Christian to eat all foods. But a heathen argument I must bring forward for those that are better read in Aristotle than in the Gospels or in Paul. Tell me which you think more necessary to a man, food or money? I think you will say that food is more useful than money, otherwise we should die of hunger with our money, as Midas died, who, according to the poets, desired that everything he touched be turned to gold. And so food is more important to preserve life than money; for man lived on food before money was invented. Now Aristotle says that money is indifferent—that is, it is neither good nor bad in itself, but becomes good or bad according to its use, whether one uses it in a good or bad way.[2] Much

---

[1] Be not carried about with divers and strange doctrines, "strange," that is, different from those ye heard from us; "divers," that is, of all sorts; for they have no stability, but are different one from another. For especially manifold is the doctrine of meats. "For it is a good thing that the heart be established with grace; not with meats." These are the "divers," these the "strange" doctrines: especially as Christ hath said, "Not that which entereth into the mouth defileth the man, but that which cometh out" (Matt. xv., 11.). Homily xxx., iii., on Hebrews, Eng. trans. "Works of St. Chrysostom," *Nicene and Post-Nicene Fathers*, vol. xiv., 516.

[2] Egli and Finsler ed. give the reference: *Nicomachean Ethics*, iv., 1, §3. The passage may be thus rendered: "Whatever has use can be used either well or badly. Money is one of the things which have use. Now he uses

more then is food neither good nor bad in itself (which I, however, for the present omit), but it is necessary and therefore more truly good. And it can never become bad, except as it is used immoderately; for a certain time does not make it bad, but rather the abuse of men, when they use it without moderation and belief.

No Christian can deny these arguments, unless he defends himself by denying the Scriptures: He is then, however, no Christian, because he does not believe Christian doctrine. There are nevertheless some who take exception to this, either to the times, or the fasting, or human prohibitions, or giving offence. All these I will answer from the Scriptures later with God's help.

At first then they object to the time: Although all things are pure, still they are not so at all times; and so during the fasts, quarter fasts, Rogation-day week, Shrove-Tuesday, Friday, and Saturday, it is improper to eat meat. During fasts also eggs, milk, and milk products are not proper. Answer: I do not say that these are not forbidden by men; we see and hear that daily. But all of my efforts are directed against this assumption, that we are restrained at this and that time by divine law. Let each one fast as often as the spirit of true belief urges him. But in order to see that according to the law of Christ we are free at all times, consider as follows:

First, Mark ii., 23, once when Christ was going through the cornfields, his disciples began to pluck the ears (and eat). But the Pharisees said to him: "Lo, what are thy disciples doing that is not proper on the Sabbath day?" And Christ said to them: "Have ye not read what David did when he had need, when he and they with him were hungry; how in the days of Abiathar, the high priest, he went into the house of God and ate the bread that was offered to God, which it was improper for any one to eat but the priests,

---

anything best who has the virtues which go with it, and so he will make the best use of money who has the accompanying virtues. He is the liberal man."

and gave also to those with him, saying to them, "The Sabbath was made for man, and not man for the Sabbath: Therefore the Son of man is also Lord of the Sabbath." Notice here that need is superior not only to human but also to divine law; for observing the Sabbath is divine law. And still the hunger of the disciples did not observe the Sabbath. Notice again that no place withstands need, and that David in need might go into the temple. Notice also that the matter of persons is not respected in need; for David and his followers were not priests, but ate the food proper only for priests to eat. This I show you now that you may learn that what is said of one circumstance is said in common of all circumstances in the Scriptures, if anything depends on circumstances or is deduced from circumstances. Circumstances are where, when, how, the person, or about whom. Thus Christ says, Matthew xxiv., 23: "Then if any man shall say unto you, Lo, here is Christ, or there; believe it not." See, this is the circumstance where, or the place. The meaning is that God is not revealed more in one place than in another. Indeed, when the false prophets say that, one is not to believe them. In this way you should understand the circumstance of time, and other circumstances, that not more at one time than at another God is revealed as merciful or as wroth, but at all times alike. Else he would be subject to the times which we had chosen, and he would be changeable who suffers no change. So also of the matter of persons; for God is not more ready or open in mercy and grace to a person of gentle birth than to the base born, as the holy Paul[1] says, Acts x., 34: "Of a truth I perceive that God is no respecter of persons." But we do not need this proof here, where we wish to prove that all time is free to men. For the words of Christ are of themselves clear enough, when he says: the Sabbath is made for man and not man for the Sabbath; the Sabbath is in the power of man, not man in the power of the Sabbath. In a word, the Sabbath and all time are subject to man, not man to the Sabbath. Now if

---

[1] It should be Peter, of course.

it is true that the Sabbath which God established is to be subject to us, then much more the time which men have imposed upon us. Indeed, not only the time but also the persons, that have thus fixed and established these particular times, are none other than the servants of Christ and co-workers in the secret things of God, not revealed to men. And these same co-workers should not rule Christians, commanding as over-lords, but should be ready only for their service and for their good. Therefore Paul says, I. Cor. vii., 35: "I say this for your good, not that I would put a noose about your necks"—that is, I would not seize and compel you with a command. Again he speaks, I. Cor. iii., 21: "All things are yours; whether Paul, or Apollos, or Peter, or the world, or life, or death, or things present, or things to come; all are yours." Here you see that all things are intended for men or for the service of men, not for their oppression, yes, the Apostles themselves are for men, not men for the Apostles.

O overflowing spring of God's mercy! how well Paul speaks when he says, that these things are known but through the Spirit of God. Therefore we have not received the spirit of this world, but the spirit that is from God, because we see what great things are given us by God. You know your liberty too little. Cause: the false prophets have not told you, preferring to lead you about rather as a pig tied with a string; and we poor sinners cannot be led to the love of God any other way but by being taught to summon unto ourselves the Spirit of God, so that we may know the great things which God has given us. For who could but be thankful to God, so kind, and who could but be drawn into a wonderful love of him? Here notice too that it is not the intention of Christ, that man should not keep the Sabbath (for us Christians Sunday is ordained as the Sabbath), but where our use or need requires something else, the Sabbath itself, not only other times, shall be subject to us. Here you are not to understand either the extreme necessity, in which one would be near death, as the mistaken theologists dream, but ordinary daily necessity. For the disciples of Christ were not suffering extreme necessity, when on the Sabbath day they plucked the ears, else they would not have answered Christ as they did, when he asked them, Luke xxii., 35: "When I sent you without purse and scrip, lacked ye anything?" For the disciples answered: "Nothing." From this we understand that Christ never allowed his disciples to fall into such dire extremity, but that the need, which they felt on Sunday, was nothing but ordinary hunger, as also the word "need" as we use it does not mean the last stages of necessity, but has the usual meaning; as when one says, "I have need," he does not refer to the last or greatest want, but to a sufficiency of that which daily need demands. Then as far as time is concerned, the need and use of all food are free, so that whatever food our daily necessity requires, we may use at all times and on all days, for time shall be subject to us.

Secondly, Christ says, Luke xvii., 20: "The kingdom of God cometh not with observation: neither shall they say, Lo! here, lo! there." This word observation, Latin *observatio*, has this meaning, as if one carefully watched over something that had its time and moment, and if one did not take it then, it would pass away, as fishermen and fowlers usually watch, because fish and fowl have certain times and are not always to be caught. Not thus the kingdom of God, for it will not come with observation of time or place. Since now the mistaken theologians say that we ourselves deserve the kingdom of God with our works, which we choose of our own free will and complete according to our powers, the words of Christ, who cannot lie, answer: if the kingdom of God cometh not with observation or watching (of time, or place, or of all circumstances, as is proved in the above paragraph), and if at any time the prohibiting of the food which God has left free is nothing else but observation, then the kingdom of God will never be made ready by the prohibition of food. Now it must be that abstinence cannot avail anything as to time, and you are always to understand that it is not our intention to speak here of amount, but only of kind, neither of the times which God hath set, but of those which men have established.

Thirdly, Paul writes to the Galatians (iv., 9): "But now after ye have known God, how turn ye again to the weak and beggarly elements, whereunto ye deserve to be again in bondage? You have expectation, or you keep day and month, time and year." Here you hear the anger of Paul at the Galatians, because after they had learned and known God (which is nothing else but being known or enlightened of God), they still returned to the elements, which he more closely describes in Colossians ii., 20. But since we must use these words later more accurately and must explain them, we shall now pass them over, satisfying ourselves with knowing what the weak elements are. In Latin and Greek the letters were called elements, for the reason that as all things are made up and composed of elements, so also each word was made of letters. Now the Jews and heathen have always clung closely to the letter of the law, which oppresses much, indeed kills, as Paul says.[1] Not only in the Old Testament, but also in the New, it oppresses much. Is that not a severe word which is found in Matthew v., 22? "But I say unto you, that whosoever is angry with his brother shall be in danger of the judgment." So it is, if taken literally, indeed impossible for us weak mortals to keep. And therefore Christ has given it to us that we might recognise our shortcomings therein, and then take refuge alone in him, who mercifully pitied our shortcomings when he said, Matthew xi., 28: "Come unto me, all ye that labour and are heavy laden, and I will give you rest."

But whosoever does not know and will not know this narrow way to the mercy of God through Christ, undertakes with his own powers to fulfil the law, sees only the letter of the law and desires with his might to fulfil that, prescribing for himself this and that chastisement and abstinence at certain times, places, and under other circum-

[1] II. Cor. iii., 6.

stances, and after all that he still does not fulfil the law, but the more he prides himself on having fulfilled the law, the less he has fulfilled it, for in his industry he becomes puffed up in himself. As the Pharisee, that boasted of the elements—that is, of the works which he had literally fulfilled, said, "I thank thee, O God, that I am not as other men are; I fast," etc.[1] Consider the over-wise piety that exalts itself at once above other men, from no other reason than that according to his advice or opinion, and powers, he is confident to have fulfilled the law; and, on the other hand, consider the publican hoping for nothing but the rich mercy of God, and counting his own works nothing, but only saying: "O God, be merciful to me, a sinner!" Is not, then, the publican considered more righteous before God than the Pharisee? From all this you see that the weak elements are nothing else than human wisdom and conception of happiness, for man either purposes to wish and to be able to keep the letter of the law or else prescribes for himself some work to do, which God has not commanded but left free, and therefore likes to think the works prescribed by himself to be a sure road to blessedness, and clings to his opinion to his own injury. And for just this reason Paul complains of the Galatians, that having been mercifully enlightened of God they turned again to their own devices, that is, to the weak elements, to which the Jews and heathen held, and had not so strong a belief in God, that they trusted alone in him and hoped alone in him, listened alone to his ordinances and will, but foolishly turned again to the devices of men, who, as though they desired to improve what had been neglected by God, said to themselves: "This day, this month, this time, wilt thou abstain from this or that," and make thus ordinances, persuading themselves that he sins who does not keep them. This abstaining I do not wish to condemn, if it occurs freely, to put the flesh under control, and if no self-confidence or vainglory, but rather humility, results. See, that is branding and injuring one's own conscience

[1] Luke xviii., 11, *et seq.*

capriciously, and is turning toward true idolatry, and is, as David says, Psalm lxxxi., 12, "walking in one's own counsels." But this God desired to prevent by the words of David, who says[1]: "Hear, O my people, I will testify unto thee, Israel (that is, he sees God and trusts him so thoroughly that he is possessed of him), if thou wilt hearken unto me; there shall no strange god be in thee; neither shalt thou worship any strange god. I am the Lord thy God, which brought thee out of the land of Egypt: open thy mouth, and I will fill or satisfy it. But my people did not hear my voice, and Israel (that is, that which should be Israel) did not hearken to me, and I left them to their own desires, and they will walk in their own counsels." O Christian of right belief, consider these words well, ponder them carefully, and you will see that God desires that we hearken to him alone! If now we are thoroughly imbued with him, no new god will be honoured within our hearts, no man instead of God, no feeling of our own instead of God. But if we do not hear the true warnings of God, he will let us walk according to the desires and devices of our own hearts. Do we not see that consolation oftener is sought in human hearts than in God; that they are more severely punished who transgress human laws than those who not only transgress but also despise and reject God's laws? Lo, these are the new idols which we have cast and chiselled in our hearts. Enough has now been said about these words of Paul, and it is authority enough to prove that we are as little forbidden by God to eat at certain times as we are now forbidden by him to eat certain sorts and kinds of food.

They will now raise as objections the fasts, or all fast days, saying that people will never fast if they are allowed to eat meat. Answer: Have you heretofore fasted because you were not allowed to eat meat, as naughty children that will not eat their broth, because they are not given meat? If any one desires to fast, has he not as much the power to do so, when labourers eat meat, as when they are forced to

[1] In the same Psalm, vv., 8–12.

fast with the idle, and are thus less able to do and to endure their labours? In a word, if you will fast, do so; if you do not wish to eat meat, eat it not; but leave Christians a free choice in the matter. You who are an idler should fast often, should often abstain from foods that make you lustful. But the labourers' lusts pass away at the hoe and plough in the field. You say, the idle will eat meat without need. Answer: The very same fill themselves with still richer foods, that excite more than the highly seasoned and spiced. And if they complain of the breaking up of the custom [of fasting], it is nothing but envy, because they dislike to see that considered proper for common men, for which they can well find a substitute without difficulty and without weakening the body, on the contrary, even with pleasure; for fish eating is surely everywhere a pleasure. You say that many cannot endure this liberty in eating, not from envy, but from fear of God. Answer: O you foolish hypocrites, do you think that there is danger and injury in what God has left free? If there were in it danger to the soul God would not have left it unforbidden. Likewise, if you are so concerned about others, as to what they should not eat, why will you not note their poverty and aid it? If you would have a Christian heart, act to it then. If the spirit of your belief teaches you thus, then fast, but grant also your neighbour the privilege of Christian liberty, and fear God greatly, if you have transgressed his laws, nor make what man has invented greater before God than what God himself hath commanded, or again I will turn out a hypocrite of you, if you are such a knotty block, twisted in yourself and depending upon your own devices.

Concerning the Commandment of Men.

Here the first difficulty will occur, when one speaks to those who complaining ask: Is one to let go the ordinances of our pious fathers? Where have the Fathers or the Councils forbidden the use of meat during fasts? They can show no Council, but they come forward with the fasts: referring to canonical law. *De Con. di.*, v., 40.

Is one not to keep the feasts? Answer: Who says or teaches that? If you are not content with the fasts, then fast also Shrovetide. Indeed, I say that it is a good thing for a man to fast, if he fasts as fasts are taught by Christ: Matthew vi., 16, and Isaiah lviii., 6. But show me on the authority of the Scriptures that one cannot fast with meat. Even if it could be shown, as it cannot, still you know very well that labourers are relieved of the burden of fasting, according to your laws. Here I demand of you to show me where meat is forbidden to him not under obligation to fast. Thus they turn away from the observance of the fast, and at last they all come to the canonical law, fourth chapter, "Denique," etc., and when you ask for a waggon, they offer you a chopping-knife. The chapter beginning "Denique" does not command you to forbid laymen to eat meat; it shows that at these same times the laymen fill themselves with meat on the Sundays in the fast more than on other days. You hear, more than on other days: Thus they eat meat on other days, but that they keep it up on Sundays till midnight, troubles Gregory[1]; still he says that they are not to be forced from this custom, lest they do worse. But the priests and the deacons he recommends to abstinence from meat, eggs, and cheese— read this well and with judgment and you will find this rather against you than for you. After that they come with Thomas Aquinas,[2] as though one single mendicant monk[3] had power to prescribe laws for all Christian folk. Finally they must help themselves out with custom, and they consider abstinence from food to be a custom. How old the custom is supposed to be, we cannot really know, especially with regard to meat, but of abstinence from eggs the custom cannot be so very old, for some nations even to-day eat eggs without permission from Rome, as in Austria and elsewhere.

[1] Gregory the Great, pope, 590–604.
[2] 1227–1274.
[3] He was a Dominican.

Milk food became a sin in the Swiss Confederation in the last century and was again forgiven. And since I have chanced upon this matter, I must show you a pretty piece of business, so that you may protect yourselves thus from the greed of the powerful clergy. Our dear fellow Swiss purchased the privilege of using milk food from the Bishop of Rome in the last century: Proof, the documents about it at Lucern.[1] Go back now before the time of these letters and think what our forefathers ate before the indulgence, and you cannot say that they ate oil, for in the Bull the complaint was made that people in our country are not accustomed to eat oil, that they ate the foods usual there, milk, whey, cheese, and butter. Now if that was a sin, why did the Roman bishops watch so lazily that they allowed them to eat these fourteen hundred years? If it is not a sin, as it is not, why did they demand money to permit it? Say rather this, I see that it is nothing but air, see that the Roman bishops announced that it was a sin, when it became money to them: Proof, as soon as they announced it as a sin, they immediately sold it for money, and thus abused our simplicity, when we ought fairly to have seen that, if it was sin according to God's law, no man can remit it, any more than that one might murder a man, which is forbidden by divine law, could be permitted by any one, although many distasteful sins of this kind are committed. From all these remarks you notice also that abstinence from meat and drink is an old custom, which however later by the wickedness of some of the clergy came to be viewed as a command. So if the custom is not bad or dishonourable, one is to keep it properly, as long and as thoroughly as the greater part of men might be offended by its infringement. Answer: This will take a longer time, therefore I shall speak now of offence or vexation.

Of Offence or Vexation.

Offence or vexation, Greek, *skandalon*, is understood

[1] See the Swiss editor's note in loco.

in two ways: first, when one offends others, so that they sin in judgment or decision, and become worse; and of these we desire to speak first; second, offence occurs, although not in the Scriptures, but here as accepted by us, when a man in himself becomes more sinful or worse, or when a whole parish is purposely brought into a worse condition.

First, Christian love demands that every one avoid that which can offend or vex his neighbour, in so far, however, as it does not injure the faith, of course you are to understand. Since the Gospel has been preached frequently in these years, many have therefore become better and more God-fearing, but many on the contrary have become worse. And since there is much opposition to their bad opinion and plans, they attack the Gospel, which attacks the good cannot endure but oppose. From which reason the bad cry out saying: "I wish the Gospel were not preached. It sets us at variance among ourselves." Here one should not yield for that reason, but should keep close before his eyes what Christ says, Matthew x., 32: "Whosoever therefore shall confess me before men, him will I confess also before my Father which is in heaven. Think not that I am come to send peace on earth (understand by this, peace with the godless or sinful): I came not to send peace, but a sword. For I am come to set a man at variance against his father, and the daughter against her mother, and the daughter-in-law against her mother-in-law. And a man's foes shall be they of his own household."

In these words Christ gives us strength not to consider the vexation of those who will not be convinced of the truth; and, even though they are our nearest and dearest, we are not to be worried, if they separate from us, as he says later, Matt. x., 37: "Whosoever loves father and mother more than me, he is not worthy of me; whoever loves his son or daughter better than me, he is not worthy of me, and whoever does not take his cross and follow me, he is not worthy of me." And also Luke xiv., 26. So wherever it is a matter of God's honour, of the belief or of hope in God, we should suffer all

Liberty Respecting Food in Lent

things rather than allow ourselves to be forced from this. But where a thing cannot harm the belief, but offends one's neighbour, although it is not a sin, one should still spare his neighbour in that he should not injure him; as eating meat is not forbidden at any time by divine law; but, where it injures or offends one's neighbour, one should not eat it without cause. One should make those of little faith strong in the faith.

But when one (thirdly) will not be referred to the divine truth and the Scriptures, when one says: "I firmly believe that Christ has never forbidden me any food at any time," and when the one of little faith will not grant it or believe it, although one shows him the Scriptures about it, then the one who believes in liberty shall not yield to him, although he should yield the matter of eating meat in his presence, if it is not necessary; but he should cleave to the Scriptures and not let the sweet yoke of Christ and the light burden become bitter, so that it may not be unpleasant to men or please them less, and thereby show that it is a human and not a divine prohibition. Thus a burgomaster gives an answer, in the name of the Council, and after the answer adds something harsh and hard, which the Council did not command him to say and did not intend. He says: "This I say of myself; the Council has not commanded it." This also, all those that teach in God's name should not sell their commands, ordinances, and burdens as God's, so that the yoke of his mercy should not become unpleasant to any one, but should leave them free. That I shall prove by the opinion of Christ: Matthew xxiv., 49, and Luke xii., 45, where he does not want one to trouble one's fellow servants—that is, one's fellow Christians. "But if that servant say maliciously in his heart, 'My Lord delayeth his coming,' and shall begin to beat his fellow servants and to eat in excess and to drink with drunkards, the Lord of that servant will come on a day when he looketh not for him, and at an hour when he is not watching, and will cut him in sunder, and will appoint the share of the bad servant to the Pharisees." Here open your eyes and see whether the servant, to whom it was given to pasture the sheep of Christ, has not now for a long time beaten his fellow servants—that is, fellow Christians; whether he has not eaten and drunk excessively, and, as though there was no God, run riot, and troubled Christians with great burdens (I speak of bad bishops and priests—take it not of yourself, pious man) so that the sweet yoke of Christ has become to all Christians a bitter herb. On the other hand, see how the Lord has come with his light and illuminated the world with the Gospel, so that Christians, recognising their liberty, will not let themselves be led any more behind the stove and into the darkness from which a schism has come about, so that we really see that God has uncovered the Pharisees and hypocrites and has made a separate division of them. Yes, in that case I venture to command you to fight against those who prefer to keep the heavy yoke of the hypocrites rather than to take the sweet yoke of Christ upon themselves, and in thus doing to be careful to offend no one, but, as much as is in them, to keep peace with all men, as Paul says.[1] Not every one can do this, or knows how far to yield or to make use of Christian liberty, therefore we will hear the opinion of Paul about offence.

Secondly, Paul teaches in the Epistle to the Romans xiv. and xv., how one should avoid giving offence; these words I translate into German and give more according to the sense than the letter. Him, he says,[2] that is weak in the faith, help, but do not lead him into the trouble of still greater doubt. One believes that it is proper for him to eat all things; but the other, weak in faith, eats only herbs. Now the one who is certain that he may eat all things, shall not despise him who does not venture to do such (understand, from little faith); and he who ventures not to eat all things shall not judge the eater, for God

---

[1] Rom. xii., 18.—"If it be possible, as much as lieth in you, live peaceably with all men."

[2] Rom. xiv., 1, *et seq.*

Liberty Respecting Food in Lent   93

has accepted and consoled him. You weak man, who are you that you judge another man's servant? He will stand upright or fall for his own master, still he will be supported or held up, for God can well support or hold him up. One man esteems one day above another, another esteems all days alike. Let every man be fully persuaded in his own mind, that he who regards one day above another may do so to the honour of God, and that he who regards not one day above another does the same to the honour of God (understand that he has so strong a faith that he certainly does not believe himself at any time freed from God's rule, for the greatest honour to God is to recognise him aright and those things which are given us by him: John xvii., 3, and I. Corinthians ii., 12); also that he who eats all kinds of food, does the same to the honour of the Lord, for he gives the Lord thanks, and he who does not eat, does it also to the honour of God, and is also thankful to God, for no one among us lives for himself or dies for himself. Whether we live, let us live for the Lord, or whether we die, let us die for the Lord; and therefore whether we live or die, we are the Lord's. For to that end Christ died, arose, and lived again, that he might be Lord of the living and the dead. But, you weak man, why do you judge your brother? Or, you stronger man who eat, why do you despise your brother? For we shall all stand before the judgment seat of Christ. For it is written in Isaiah xlv., 23: "As I live, saith the Lord, to me shall all knees bow, and all tongues shall confess me, who am God." Therefore shall each one of us render God an account. Thus let us not judge one another, but be this our judgment, that no one displease or offend his brother. I know and am taught in Jesus Christ that nothing is unclean of its nature, except that it is unclean to him who considers it unclean. But if your brother is offended or injured on account of food, you do not act according to love (that is, you do not give up the food which injured your brother before he has been correctly instructed).

Vex and injure and offend not with food your brother, for whom Christ died, and in return your goodness (that you do all things in your faith, you eat, you keep fast, or not) shall not be despised. For the kingdom of God is not food or drink, but piety, peace, and joy in the Holy Ghost. Whoever serves Christ in these things, is pleasing to God and approved before men. Let us then strive to do the things which lead to peace; and that we may edify one another (that is, properly instruct), do not make God's work (piety, peace, and joy, as is written above) of no avail on account of food. All things are clean, but it is bad that a man eat with vexation and offence as a result. It is proper and good that a man eat no meat and drink no wine, indeed eat nothing, whereby your brother is vexed or offended or whereby he is made ill. You who are stronger, if you have faith, have it in you before God. Happy is he who does not doubt that which he considers certain; but whoever doubts and, in doubt, eats the meat about which he doubts, he is condemned, for the reason that he did not eat from belief; for what is done not in belief, is sin. Also thus should we, who are strong in belief, be patient with the timidity of the weak, and not please ourselves, but each of us please his neighbour by edifying and doing him good; "for even Christ pleased not himself; but, as it is written, "'The reproaches of them that reproached thee fell on me.'"[1] All these are words of Paul, from which you will shortly conclude three things. First, that he who firmly believes that it is proper for him to eat all things, is called strong; and secondly, that one who has no belief is called timid or weak; thirdly, that the strong should not let the weak remain always weak, but should take him and instruct him, that he become also strong, and should yield a point to the weak and not vex him maliciously. How we are to yield a point to the weak, you shall hear.

Thirdly, Paul says of vexation, I. Corinthians viii., 1,

[1] Rom. xv., 3.

to those who were present: They might eat of that which had been offered to the idols, for this reason: they well knew they believed not in the idols, and therefore without soiling their consciences they might eat such food, in spite of those who were badly offended by it; indeed to them he speaks thus: "We know that we all have understanding or knowledge of the food which is offered to the idols. Knowledge puffeth up and maketh conceited, but love edifieth." Here Paul means, that you, although you, a man firm in faith, know you do not sin, when you eat the food of the idols, should, if you love your neighbour, favour him fairly, so that you offend him not; and when in time he is better instructed, he will be greatly edified, when he sees that your Christian love overlooked his ignorance so mercifully. After Paul has said that those well taught in the faith know well there is no idol but only one true God and one Lord Jesus Christ, it is further mentioned that not every one is so well taught as the first mentioned; for some eat the food of the idols in such manner that they still hold to them somewhat, and also that food does not commend us to God (as is shown above in the first part of the fourth division). Indeed after all that he says further: "See that your power or freedom does not vex the weak, for if one of them sees you sitting knowingly at a table where the food of idols is eaten, will not his conscience be strengthened or encouraged to eat the food of idols? And then your weak brother through your knowledge and understanding perishes, for whom Christ died." See how strongly Paul opposes wanton treatment of the weak. It follows further on that when you thus sin against your brethren, frightening and striking their weak consciences, you sin against Christ; therefore, if food offends my brother I will rather never eat meat than that I make my brother offend. Here notice that, although the foregoing words are spoken of the food of idols, they still show us in a clear way how we should conduct ourselves in this matter of food, namely, that we should abstain in every way from making to offend, and that he is not without sin, who acts against his brother, for he acts also against Christ, whose brother each Christian is. But you say, "What if my brother from stubbornness will not at all be taught, but always remains weak?" The answer will follow in the last part.

Fourthly, Paul writes in the above mentioned epistle, I. Corinthians x., 23: "All things are lawful for me, but all do not result in usefulness." Let no one seek his own good, let each seek, that is, strive for, the advantage of the other. Eat all that is sold in the shambles, not hesitating for conscience' sake; for the earth is the Lord's (as. it reads in Psalm xxiv., 1), and all the fulness of the earth, or all that is in the earth. If an unbeliever invites you and you want to go with him, eat all that is placed before you (that is, as far as the kind of food is concerned; otherwise he would be a faithless glutton, if he ate all) not doubting for conscience' sake. But if one said to you: "That is from the sacrifice to the idols," eat it not for the sake of him who thus points it out to you, and for conscience' sake. I say not for *your* conscience' sake but for the sake of *another's* conscience. For why is my liberty judged by the conscience of another, if I eat with gratitude? Therefore, whether you eat or drink or whatever you do, do it to the honour of God; do not offend Jews or heathen and God's Church, just as I endeavour to please all men, not regarding myself, but the many, that they be saved; they are my followers as I am a follower of Christ. Here you see, first, that we should avoid for the sake of another what otherwise would be proper; secondly, that all things are proper for us to eat, that are sold in the shambles, without violence to the conscience; thirdly, how one should act about eating forbidden food after the manner prescribed for the food offered to idols; for although our proposition and the one here in Paul are not wholly alike, still a good rule is to be derived therefrom; fourthly, that although your liberty cannot be judged according to another's conscience, nor you yourself condemned, still you should always consider the honour of God, which honour, however, grows the greater among men, if they see you for the sake of the honour of God not using your liberty; fifthly, that all things can take place to the honour of God, indeed the daily custom of eating and drinking, of working, trading, marrying, if a man cleaves to God in all his doings, and trusts that he is called to, and chosen for, the work by God. And do not let this idea, which may occur to you, trouble you: "Then I will blaspheme, gamble, commit adultery, do other wrongs, and think I am called to this by God." For such things do not please the man who trusts in God. The tree is now good, let it produce only good fruit. And if one lives not in himself, but Christ lives in him so thoroughly that, although a mistake escapes him, he suffers from that hour for it, he is ashamed of his weakness. But those who thus speak are godless, and with such words insult God and those who have the Spirit of God. Listen to a striking example. No respectable and pious wife, who has a good husband, can allow one to report that which is dishonourable to her husband or let a suspicion arise of a misdeed, which she knows is displeasing to him. So man, in whom God rules, although weak, still cannot endure to be shamefully spoken of against his will. But a wanton likes to hear the disgrace of her husband and what is against him. Thus also those, who speak thus, are godless; otherwise, if they had God in their hearts, they would not willingly hear such disgraceful words.

Fifthly, Paul had Timothy circumcised, although the circumcision was of no service, that he might not offend the Jews, who at that time still believed that one must keep the Old Testament with its ceremonies together with the New Testament; and so he had it done, as it is written in Acts xvi., 3.

Sixthly, Christ himself did not wish to offend any one; for, when at Capernaum Peter was asked, Matthew xvii.,

24, whether his master paid tribute, Peter answered, "Yes." And after they had entered the house, Christ anticipated Peter (who doubtless was about to ask him something about tribute) and said: "Simon, what thinkest thou? Do the kings of this world take tribute and custom of their children or of strangers?" Peter answered him: "Of strangers." Jesus said to him: "Then are the children free. But lest we should offend them, go to the sea and cast a hook, and the first fish that comes up take; and when thou hast opened his mouth, thou shalt find a coin (it was a penny, that could pay for them both, but was worth much more than the real tax pennies, wherefore I think it was a tribute which they collected from Christ), take it and give it for thee and me." Thus Christ did not desire to vex the authorities, but rather to do what he might otherwise refuse. This paragraph I would not have added, had not my opponents represented it thus: Christ, they said, desired himself to avoid taxation. For this article is more against them than for them; thus, if you spiritual teachers in the flesh are all so inclined to avoid vexation, why do you not then also help to bear the common burden, when you see that the parish is badly vexed about it and cries out: "You go lazily away from our work. Why do you not help us carry the burden?" Hear also that Christ gave the tribute money, in order not to arouse any one to anger. Loose the knot. There are more places still in the Gospel in which the word *skandalon* is written; but it means there either disgrace, or if it means offence, it is used in the following sense: disgrace and contempt, Matthew xviii., 7. "Woe unto the world because of offences"—that is, woe unto the world on account of disgrace and contempt, since one despises, refuses, and rejects the simple (who is, however, as much God's as the highest), which the following words mean, when he says: "Take heed lest ye offend one of the least of these." Thus it is also to be understood, Luke xvii., 1, which also is clear from what precedes about the rich man, who did not let poor Lazarus have the crumbs. Thus also Mark ix., 42. But *skandalon* or vexation, so taken, does not fit our purpose, therefore from the first I did not wish to divide it into three parts.

Of Avoiding Vexation.

From the above mentioned arguments one can readily learn that one should carefully avoid offence. But still I must think that, as one should forgive the weak, one should also in forgiving teach and strengthen him, and not always feed him with milk, but turn him to heartier food; for Christ says, Matthew xiii., 41: "The Son of man shall send forth his angels (that is, messengers), and they shall gather out of his kingdom all things that offend and them which are not God-fearing and do iniquity, and shall cast them into a furnace of fire." Are his angels to do that? Yes. Then it is better that we should do it ourselves; then it will not be done by God and punished so severely, as Paul teaches us, I. Corinthians xi., 31: "For if we would judge ourselves, we should not be judged." If we ourselves take the offence, it must not be taken with the judgment of God, to which now St. Paul arouses us.

First, Christ says, Matthew v., 29: "If thy right eye offend thee, pluck it out, and cast it from thee: for it is profitable for thee that one of thy members should perish, and not that thy whole body should be cast into hell. And if thy right hand offend thee, cut it off, and cast it from thee: for it is profitable," etc., as above. The same is also said in Matthew xviii., 8, except that he adds the foot. Who is now the eye, the hand, the foot, which, offending us, shall be cast away? Every bishop is an eye, every clergyman, every officer, who are nothing more than overseers; and the Greek word *episkopos* is in German an overseer, to which the words of St. Paul refer, Acts xx., 28, where he says to the bishops of Ephesus: "Take heed therefore unto yourselves, and to all the flock, over which the Holy Ghost hath made you bishops (that is, overseers or shepherds), to watch and feed the Church of God, which he hath bought with his own blood." Here you see briefly what their duty is: overseeing the sheep, feeding, not flaying and shearing too closely and loading them with unbearable burdens, which is nothing else than giving offence, pointing out sins that are not present, so that weak consciences are troubled and made to despair; this is offending God's little ones: Matthew xviii., 6. But you see yourself, according to the words of Isaiah lvi., 10, that his watchmen have become blind, all ignorant, stupid dogs, that cannot bark, taught in loose things, lazily sleeping and dreaming, indeed, preferring dreams to the truth, the most shameless dogs, which cannot be satisfied: shepherds which have no reason, each following his own way or capricious desires, all avaricious, from the highest to the lowest, saying: "Let us drink good wine and become full, and as we do to-day, so shall we do to-morrow, yea, still more." These all are the words of Isaiah, and little is to be added. Do you not see that such eyes offend men much, and, although Christ tells us to pluck them out, we suffer them patiently? Understand also hand and foot which are so nearly related to you, as your own members; indeed, even if they are necessary to you for support and strength as a hand or a foot, still one is to remove them if they abuse their superiority. Now this paragraph is placed here by me to prove that offence should be avoided, and that one should not always endure it, but that everything should take place with timely counsel and reason, not with any one's own assumption and arrogance. If they do not do that, who ought to do it? We should recognise that our sins have deserved of God this, that such blind eyes lead us, the blind, astray and rule us. Nehemiah ix., 30: "Thou hast warned them in thy spirit through thy prophets, and they have not followed, and thou hast given them into the hand of the people of the earth"—that is, into the hands of the unbelievers. Also Isaiah iii., 4:

"And I will give children to be their princes (note this well), and old women shall rule them."

Secondly, the words of Paul are to be considered, Romans xiv., 1, where it is mentioned above in the second article on giving offence, in which place he says: "Him that is weak in faith receive ye, but not to doubtful disputations." See you, the weak is not to be allowed to remain weak, but is to be instructed in the truth, not with subtle arguments, by which one becomes more doubtful, but with the pure, simple truth, so that all doubt may be removed. Therefore I could well endure that those who are considered steadier and stronger in belief, also understood how to make Christians strong in belief, and gave them really to understand what has been given and left to them by God; but they do exactly the contrary. If anything is strong, they wish to make the same again weak and timid. Woe to them, as Christ spoke to the Pharisees, Matthew xxiii., 13: "For they closed the kingdom of God to men, for they neither go in themselves nor let other people go in." By means of these words of Christ and of Paul, I think I have excused my arrogance, of which certain hypocrites accused me—that is, of having preached upon freedom concerning food on the third Sunday of this fast, when they thought that I ought not to do it. Why? Should I snatch from the hand of those who cling to the Scriptures, which I myself have preached, their means of defence, and contradict the Scriptures and say they lie? And should I have in my hands the key of God's wisdom, as Christ says, Luke xi., 52, and not open to the ignorant, but also close it before the eyes of the knowing? Do not deceive yourself that you have persuaded me to this, you vain, loose hypocrite. I will rather take care of my soul, which I have laden with enough other misdeeds, and will not murder it outright with a suppression of the truth.

Thirdly, it is true that Paul had Timothy circumcised, Acts xvi., 3. But on the other hand, as he says, Galatians ii., 3, he did not have Titus circumcised: "Titus, who was with me, did not want to be forced to circumcision. He had this reason: False brethren have slipped unseen among us, who are come into our midst to spy out our liberty, which we have in Jesus Christ, that they might make us again slaves and subjects, to whom we yielded not a moment, that the truth of the Gospel might continue with you." Those who protect the liberty of the Gospel put this up before the ceremonies as a shield and bulwark. If Paul circumcised Timothy, still he did not, on the contrary, have Titus circumcised, although much reproach came to him on that account. What is to be done with him? Is Paul inconsistent with himself? No. If he had Timothy circumcised, it was because he could not keep him from it on account of the great disturbance of the Jews who were Christians. But afterwards, those of the Jews who had become Christians were better taught, so that he was able to spare Titus and protect him without great uproar; and, although some demanded his circumcision, and, when it did not happen, were greatly offended at it, he considered the truth and Christian liberty more than any strife that arose against it from bad feeling. Notice also in these words from Paul how everywhere the false brethren had undertaken to take liberty from Christians.

Fourthly, Paul writes, Galatians ii., 12, that Peter ate with the Christians, who had become believers from heathendom; indeed, he ate with the heathen. But when some came from Jerusalem to Antioch who were also Christians but converted from Judaism, he fled from the heathen, so that the Jews might not be offended. Paul did not desire him to do that, but chid him in these words: "You teach the heathen to live as Jews, because you are a Jew by birth"; that is, if you flee from the heathen on account of the Jews, you raise a suspicion against the heathen, that they were not really Christians, or they would have to keep human fasts, as the Jews, or else sin. And about this he said: "When I saw that he did not walk uprightly, I withstood him to his face." At this place you find Paul, who teaches diligently, not offending, not caring if a few want to be offended, providing he could keep the greater multitude unaffected and unsuspicious. For if even the Jews, on whose account Peter fled from the heathen, became offended, still Paul gave them no attention, so that the heathen Christians (thus I call them that were converted fron heathendom) could remain free and would not be brought under the oppression of the law by Jewish Christians.

When Christ spoke to the Pharisees, Matthew xv., 11, "Not that which goeth into the mouth defileth a man," his disciples said to him: "Knowest thou that the Pharisees who heard these words were offended and angered?" Christ answered them: "Let them go, they be blind leaders of the blind." See that here Christ's meaning is, as it seems to me, that the disciples should let the Pharisees go and should live according to their liberty and custom in spite of them; for they were blind and saw not the truth of liberty; were also leaders of those who erred as they did. Since now in the above two articles, I have spoken enough of offence and of the doing away with offence, it seems to me good to bring together in short statements all that touches upon offence, so that each may know where he shall yield and where not.

I. What clearly affects the divine truth, as the belief and commandments of God, no one shall yield, whether one is offended or not. Psalm cxlv., 18; I. Corinthians ii., 2; Matthew v., 10: "Blessed are they which suffer for righteousness' sake." II. Corinthians xiii., 8: "For we can do nothing against the truth, but for the truth."

II. The liberties, which are given to man by God, touching the law of food and other such things, should be considered with regard to God and man.

III. When one speaks of the liberty now under discussion, that we are released by God from all such burdens, one shall not yield in respect to truth and belief, whether one offend or not. For Paul says: "All things are proper for me." (I Cor. vi., 12.)

IV. But when the practice of liberty offends your neighbour, you should not offend or vex him without cause; for when he perceives it, he will be offended no more, unless he is angry purposely, as when the Jews became angry at the disciples' eating with unwashed hands and on the Sabbath: Mark ii., 24.

V. But you are to instruct him as a friend in the belief, how all things are proper and free for him to eat. Romans xv., 1: "We who are stronger in the faith shall receive the weak"—that is, comfort and instruct them.

VI. But when forgiving avails not, do as Christ said, Matthew xv., 14: "Let them go."

VII. And use your liberty, wherever you can without public disturbance, just as Paul did not have Titus circumcised: Gal. ii., 3.

VIII. But if it causes public uproar, do not use it, just as Paul had Timothy circumcised: Acts xvi., 3.

IX. Gradually teach the weak with all industry and care, until they are instructed, so that the number of the strong is so large that no one, or still only a few, can be offended; for they will certainly let themselves be taught; so strong is the Word of God, that it will remain not without fruit: Isaiah lv., 10.

X. Take this same view in other things, which are only adiaphora: as eating meat, working on holy days after one has heard the Word of God and taken communion, and the like.

Of Being Offended at Innocent Customs.

On account of all this they complain very bitterly who have learned the acceptance of virtues rather from Aristotle than from Christ: saying that in this way all good works, as not eating meat, abstaining from labour, and other things which I shall not mention, are done away

Liberty Respecting Food in Lent 105

with. To these I answer as follows: Many mistakes are made as to the choice of good works, although we might well hear what St. James says, i., 17, that all good gifts and presents come from above from the Father of lights. From this we can conclude that all good which pleases God must come from him; for if it came from any other source, there would be two or more sources of good, of which there is however only one; Jeremiah ii., 13: "They have forsaken me the fountain of living waters, and hewed them out cisterns, broken cisterns, that can hold no water." Notice the fountain; notice the broken cistern. Thus Christ speaks to the young man who called him good, in order to do him eye-service: "God alone is good." If he alone is good, without doubt no good fruit can come from any source except from the tree which alone is good. Then notice the angels and you will find that, as soon as they depended somewhat upon themselves, they fell. Thus also man, as soon as he depended somewhat upon himself, fell into the trouble that still follows us. See, those are the bad, false, broken cisterns, which are dug and thrown up only by men, not real natural fountains. Thus they thought that that would seem good to God and please Him, which they had attempted and which resulted in great disadvantage to them, from no other reason, as I think, than that they had assumed to know the good or the right, and did not depend alone on God and trust alone in him. Not that I mean to say that abstinence from food is bad; indeed, where it comes from the leading and inspiration of the Divine Spirit, it is without doubt good; but where it comes simply from fear of human command, and is to be considered as a divine command and thus trusted in, and where man begins to please himself thereby, it is not only good but also injurious; unless you show me from the Holy Writ that our inventions must please God. I shall also not be worsted, if you say to me: "Still the assembly of a church may set up ordinances which are kept also in heaven." Matthew xvi., 19, and xviii., 18: "Verily I say unto you whatsoever ye shall bind on earth shall be bound in heaven; and whatsoever ye shall loose on earth shall be loosed in heaven." That is true, but the observance is not made by the whole Christian Church, indeed only by certain bishops, who had for a time undertaken to place upon Christians certain laws, without the knowledge of the common people. Also if you should say that silence is a form of consent, I answer: The pious simplicity of Christians has kept silence in many things from fear, and that no one has told them of their liberty coming from the Scriptures. For example, whom did it ever please that the Pope conferred all benefices on his servants? Indeed, every pious man everywhere has said, "I do not believe it is right." But the people kept still about it with much pain, till the Gospel truth gave forth light, when for the first time the mask was taken from it. Thus also here the clergy have taken a hand to control everything, after they have seen Christians willingly following them. Why? They fear us for the reason lest he who transgresses the command be obliged to give us money. Yet it all would have had no success, if such oppressive regulations were not given out as being divine. We sold them for that, and where the agreement was of that kind, after the truth had come to light, you can see what kind of an agreement it was. But we will hear what Paul says of works.

To the Colossians, ii., 16 (which passage I have quoted above), he writes: "Let no man judge you in meat, or in drink, or in respect of a holyday, or of the new moon, or of the Sabbath days: which are a shadow of things to come; but the body is of Christ. Let no man beguile you of your reward in a voluntary humility and worshipping of angels, intruding into those things which he hath not seen, vainly puffed up by his fleshly mind, and not holding the Head, from which all the body by joints and bands having nourishment ministered, and knit together, increaseth with the increase of God. Wherefore if ye be dead with Christ from the rudiments of the world, why, as though living in the world, are ye subject to ordinances (touch not, taste not, handle not: which things are all to perish with the using) after the commandments and doctrines of men? Which things indeed have a showing of wisdom in will-worship, humility, and neglecting of the body; not in any honour to the satisfying of the flesh." All these are the words of Paul, which in Latin are not at all intelligible, but in Greek are somewhat clearer. But that each may well understand them, I shall briefly paraphrase them.

No one shall reject you or consider you good on account of any food, or holyday, whether you rest or not (always excepting Sundays, after God's Word has been heard and communion administered). Let the new moon fast and the Sabbath go; for these things have become only symbolical of a Christian holiday, when one is to cease and leave off sinning, also that we, repenting such works, become happy only in the mercy of God; and, as Christ has come, the shadows and symbols are without doubt done away with. One thing more, notice as to the time: It surely seems to me (I cannot help thinking so) that to keep certain times with timidity is an injury and harm to unchanging and everlasting justice, thus: simple people think that everything is right, if only they confess the fasts, fast, enjoy God (*i. e.*, take the sacrament), and let the whole year pass away thus; whereas one should at all times confess God, live piously, and do no more than we think is necessary in the fast. And Christ says again, Matthew xxv., 13: "Watch therefore, for ye know neither the day nor the hour."

Further, he reminds them that they shall not allow themselves to be beguiled by those who pretend humility. What is beguiling but disregarding the simple meaning of God and wanting to find or show to the simple another shorter way to happiness, and to seek therewith wealth, name, and the reputation of a spiritual man? Therefore Paul advises against this and warns us that we should not allow ourselves to be beguiled—that is, not allow ourselves to be deceived. For the same hypocrites will falsely assert that angels spoke with them and revealed something to them, and will elevate themselves on that account. Listen, how well he paints them in their true colours, and yet we do not want to recognise them. Why do you dream here of the doctrines and ordinances which are chattered out at the pulpit in the cloisters? And why of the crows which nip the ears of some of you? Do you not now hear that all such things are suggested by the flesh, and not by the spirit? For the same depend not on the head of Christ, from which all other members being arranged, co-ordinated, and united, receive their nourishment or support of heavenly life, and progress in a growth that pleases God. Notice here in the spiritual growth and increase a different method than in the bodily. In the body all members grow from the sustenance of the belly, but in the spirit from the head of Christ. Consider now human doctrines: if they are like the opinion of the head, they are sustained by the head; if they are not like it, they come from the belly: O ventres, O ye bellies! But if we are dead with Christ to the rudiments of the world—that is, if Christ by his death made us free from all sins and burdens; then we are also in baptism—that is, in belief, freed from all Jewish or human ceremonies and chosen works, which he calls the rudiments. If we are now dead to the rudiments, why do we burden ourselves with fictitious human ordinances? Just as though God did not consider and think enough, did not give us sufficient instruction and access to blessedness and we make ourselves ordinances, which oppress us saying: "Touch not, taste not, handle not"; which touching or eating does not serve to injure or disturb the soul. For only for this purpose have the false teachers pretended that this was injurious, that with simple-minded people they might have the name of being wise and godly, indeed also with those who prescribe for themselves their own religion, saying: "Is not such abstinence and purification of the body a good thing? Is it not a good thing to prevent sin by good ordinances?" Hear how much weight Paul gives this folly. He says these things have only the form of the good. If they have only the form of the good, they are themselves not good in the sight of God, for they arise from *ethelothriskeia*. It is a Greek word, and means the honour or fear of God, which one has chosen for himself and to which he stubbornly clings: as, for example, many will not cut the beard on Friday and think they greatly honour God thereby; and, when they transgress this, they greatly sin in thus doing, and consider the rule that they themselves have set up so important, that they would three times sooner break their marriage vows, than to do anything against their reputation for wisdom. Indeed, deceive not yourself that things are with God as you have persuaded yourself; that is true superstition, a stubborn self-chosen spirit. Here in the words of Paul consider the greater part of the ordinances and rules, and you will find pretty things. Such are the most of human ordinances, of which Christ says, Matthew xv., 9: "But in vain do they worship me, teaching for doctrines the commandments of men." He says *licke*[1], Greek for impossible, in vain; that tells the very truth. Then this follows: But they are worth nothing, if you consider them according to the need and wants of the body. All food is created for the support of man; as far as it only affects bodily use it is of no moment, whether you eat this or that food. Go rather again to the clearer words of Paul and read them again, and they will be much clearer to you and worthier in your heart.

Pious servants of Christ, these are the opinions, which I have preached from the Holy Writ, and have again collected for no other purpose than that the Scriptures might be forcibly brought to the notice of those ignorant of the same, and as Christ commands that they might rather search them, and that you and your people may be less reviled by them. For as far as I am concerned, it was

[1] The text so reads in some editions, but the better text has *matin*. The words are synonyms.

entirely against my will to write of these things, for the reason that, even if winning by the aid of the Scriptures, as without doubt I shall win with God's help, still I have gained nothing, except that according to divine law no kind of food is forbidden to man at any time; although among the right and humbly thankful this writing of mine causes great joy of conscience, in which they rejoice in freedom, even if they never eat meat at forbidden times. And as a result I must have a worse time avoiding offence than if I had left the world in the belief that it was a divine ordinance, which, however, I could not do. You know that the Gospel of Matthew, the Acts of the Apostles, the Epistles to Timothy, to the Galatians, both Epistles of Peter, on which you all heard me preach, are full of such opinions. But one must clear the dear face of Christ of such spots, unseemly things, and of the foulness of human commands; and he will become again dear to us, if we properly feel the sweetness of his yoke, and the lightness of his burden. God bless this his doctrine! Amen.

What has been written above, I am responsible before God and man to account and answer for, and I also desire of all who understand the Scriptures, in case I have misused the same, to inform me of this either orally or by letter, not disgracing the truth by shameless clatter behind one's back, which is dishonourable and unmanly. I desire to be guided everywhere by the New and Old Testaments. But what follows, I only wish to view as submitted, still with proof from the Scriptures, and let each one judge of it in secret for himself.

Whether Anyone Has Power to Forbid Foods.

I. The general gathering of Christians may accept for themselves fasts and abstinence from foods, but not set these up as a common and everlasting law.

II. For God says, Deut. iv., 2: "Ye shall not add unto the word which I command you, neither shall ye diminish aught from it." And also xii., 32: "What thing soever I command you, observe to do it: thou shalt not add thereto, nor diminish from it."

III. If one could not and should not add to the Old Testament, then much less to the New.

IV. For the Old Testament has passed away and was not otherwise given except that it should pass away in its time; but the New is everlasting, and can never be done away with.

V. This is shown by the sanctification of both Testaments. The Old is sprinkled and sanctified by the blood of animals, but the New with the blood of the everlasting God, for Christ thus spake: "This is the cup of my blood of a new and everlasting testament," etc.

VI. If now it is a testament, and Paul, Galatians iii., 15, says it is: "Though it be but a man's covenant, yet if it be confirmed, no man disannulleth, or addeth thereto,"

VII. How dare a man add to the testament, to the covenant of God, as though he would better it?

VIII. Galatians i., 9, Paul curses what is preached otherwise concerning the Gospel, thus: "If any other gospel is preached to you than ye have heard, let him that preached it be accursed."

IX. Paul says, Romans xiii., 8: "Owe no man anything, but to love one another."

X. Again, Galatians v., 1: "Stand fast therefore in the freedom wherewith Christ has made us free, and be not entangled again with the yoke of bondage."

XI. If he is to be cursed who preaches beyond what Paul preached, and if Paul nowhere preached the choice of food, then he who dares command this must be worthy of a curse.

XII. If we are not bound by any law but the law of love, and if freedom as to food injures not the love of one's neighbour, in case this freedom is rightly taught and understood, then we are not subject to this commandment or law.

XIII. If Paul commands us to remain in the liberty of Christ, why do you command me to depart from it? Indeed, you would force me from it.

XIV. When Christ said to his disciples, "I have yet much to say to you," he did not say, "I have much yet to teach you how ye shall lay commands on men," but he spake of things which he held up before them and which they, however, scarcely understood. But when the Spirit of Truth shall come, it will teach you all the truth, that they will understand all things according to the light of the Holy Ghost—that is, providing they do not at that time understand, either from ignorance or trouble and fear.

XV. For if such commands are to be understood in this matter, then the disciples have sinned, in not having forbidden labour and the eating of meat, running to the saints, putting on cowls.

XVI. Finally, God spake to Peter, Acts x., 15: "What God hath cleansed, that call thou not common." And the Sabbath is subject to us, not we to the Sabbath, as it is written above.

These points have forced me to think that the church officers have not only no power to command such things, but if they command them, they sin greatly; for whoever is in office and does more than he is commanded, is liable to punishment. How much more then when they transgress that which is forbidden them; and Christ forbade the bishops to beat their fellow servants. Is it not beating, when a command is placed upon a whole people, to which command the general assembly has not consented? Therefore, in these articles I leave to each, free judgment, and still hope I have to those thirsting for Christian freedom made this clear, in spite of the enmity to me that will grow out of it. It is those who fear the spit [on which their meat roasts] will burn off. God be with us all! Amen. I have written all this hastily; therefore may each understand it as best he can. Given at Zurich, in 1522, on the 16th of April.

X

LETTER OF HULDREICH ZWINGLI TO ERASMUS FABRICIUS ABOUT THE PROCEEDINGS, ON THE 7TH, 8TH, AND 9TH OF APRIL, 1522, OF THE DELEGATES SENT TO ZURICH BY THE BISHOP OF CONSTANCE

(April 1522)

[Epistola Huldrici Zuinglii ad Erasmum Fabricium de actis legationis ad Tigurinos missae diebus 7, 8, 9, Aprilis 1522. Translated by Mr. Henry Preble. In Schuler and Schulthess ed., iii., 8-16; in Egli and Finsler ed., i., 142-54.

Beginning with denial of the Scriptural obligation of tithes, then passing to the denial of the Scriptural support of fasting in Lent, Zwingli had wrought up the people of Zurich to the point of rebellion against the Church upon two almost vital matters. It was high time for some action on the part of the Church. Hence the visiting delegation from the bishop of Constance, the ecclesiastical over-lord of the city, and canton of Zurich. It was ordered not to bring Zwingli in, much less to debate with him. So his name was not mentioned and if it had not been for his persistence the delegation would have met only the Small Council and gone away with merely an admonition. Zwingli forced it to listen to him and also exhibited the support he had in the Great Council. The letter is racy reading.]

HOW the Reverend Lord Bishop of Constance [Hugo von Hohenlandenberg], through his delegates, the suffragan Melchior [Fattlin], John Wanner (who, however, I know took part in the affair against his will), and N[icholas] Brendlin, dealt with Huldreich Zwingli, preacher at Zurich, before the Board of Ecclesiastics and the Senate[1] on the 7th, 8th, and 9th days of April.

[1] *I. e.*, City Council, hence the members in it are called councillors, but the Latin form Zwingli used has been allowed to stand. This body was in two parts: the Small Council, which contained only 50 members, and only half of these were on duty at any one time; and the Great Council, also called the Council of the Two Hundred, which included the Small Council. The Great Council was the deciding body on all legislative matters of importance, the

ZWINGLI TO ERASMUS FABRICIUS.

On the seventh day of April the before mentioned Fathers came to our city pretty early, and I, knowing that they were coming, was trying to discover what their design was, and yet could not until late at night, when our beloved assistant, Henry Lüti, came and gave me warning that the clerk, as they call him, was getting together the whole body of priests for a meeting early next morning at the usual place of assembly of the canons. I regarded it as a happy omen that the thing had been thus neatly set on foot by a courier both lame and without grace, and began to consider in my mind how they were likely to begin their job. At length I understood, as I thought, and when day dawned and we had come together the suffragan began in the fashion that will follow when I come to describe how the matter was carried on before the Senate. His whole speech was violent and full of rage and arrogance, though he took pains to hide the fact that he had any quarrel with me. For he avoided mentioning my name as scrupulously as if it were sacred, though meanwhile there was nothing that he did not say against me. When the tragedian had finished shrieking out his part, I stepped forward, feeling that it was unbecoming and disgraceful to allow a speech which might do so much damage to go unrebutted, especially as I saw from their sighs and their pale and silent faces that some of the feebler priests who had recently been won for Christ had been troubled by the tirade. Therefore I made answer upon the spur of the moment to the words of the suffragan, with what spirit or feeling the good men who heard me may judge. The general gist of what I said, however, you shall hear when we come to the proceedings before the Senate. The delegates abandoned this wing as routed and put to flight, and

---

Small was the executive committee, and both were representative bodies. The chief officer was the burgomaster, here called the President of the Senate. See my biography of Zwingli, pp. 42-44.

hurried quickly to another, to the Senate, namely, where, as I have learned from Senators, the same harangue was delivered and my name was avoided in the same way, and the Senate was persuaded not to have me summoned. For they said they had no concern whatever with me. After this the opinions varied for some time, but finally they decided that the Commons (that is, two hundred men called the Greater Senate) should meet in full assembly on the following day, and that the bishops[1] of the city, of whom there are three of us, should be warned not to be present. For nothing was going to be said in reply to our friends, no one could contradict so sound a speech, and so on. When I discovered this, I devoted all my energy to getting us admitted to the meeting of the Senate to be held on the following day. For a long time I turned every stone in vain, for the chief men of the Senate said it could not be done, inasmuch as the Senate had voted otherwise. Then I began to cease my efforts and to plead with sighs to him who heareth the groans of those in bondage not to abandon the truth, but to come to the defence of his gospel, which he had willed to have us preach. At length on the ninth the citizens assembled, and loudly vented their indignation at their bishops not being admitted, but they of the Senate which from its number is called the Less resisted because they had voted otherwise previously. The Greater Senate, however, compelled them against their will to put the matter to vote, and it was decided that their bishops should be present and hear everything, and if need be make answer. Thus, not, as Livy says,[2] did the greater part prevail over the better; for here both the greater and the better part prevailed. And this I have allowed myself to write, not for the sake of laying any blame upon the Lesser Senate, but to show what plotting and underhand action can accomplish. For what else were the delegates

---

[1] Zwingli uses this term of the people's priests or preachers of the three parish churches in Zurich, viz., the Great Minster, Minster of Our Lady, and St. Peter's. He explains it below. [2] *Lib.* xxi., 4.

of the Bishop of Constance after but to say without witnesses whatever came into their mouths before the simple-minded Commons? Thanks be to God. For when the delegates were brought into the Senate, we bishops of Zurich were also admitted, Henry Engelhard, of Our Lady Minster Abbey, Rudolph Röschlin, bishop of St. Peter's, and I, Huldreich Zwingli.[1] Then when they had been given permission to speak, and the suffragan had extended to the assembly greeting and blessing from his Most Illustrious Leader and Bishop (for this must now at least be admitted), he began with that wonderfully sweet voice of his, than which I have scarcely ever heard one sweeter in speech. Indeed, if his heart and brain were as good, you might say that he could excel Orpheus and Apollo in sweetness, Demosthenes and the Gracchi in persuasive power. I should like to set down his speech in its entirety, but I cannot, partly because he spoke in an involved and jumbled together style, without order, and partly because so long a speech could not, I think, be remembered even by a Porcius Latro.[2] But since I had my note-book at hand and took down the main headings, in order to be able to meet and answer them more fitly, I will first put down these headings and then subjoin what I said in reply to each of them.

With the manner of a consummate actor he said that (1) certain persons were teaching new, obnoxious, and seditious doctrines (in German wiederwärtig und aufrührig lehren), to wit: that (2) no human prescriptions and no ceremonials ought to be regarded. If this doctrine prevailed, it would come to pass that not only the laws of the state but even the Christian faith would be done away with,

[1] Henry Engelhard had been people's priest at the Minster of Our Lady since 1496. He had also been a canon of the Great Minster, but in 1521 resigned so that Zwingli might be appointed. This act of disinterestedness shows what a fine character he was. He remained ever one of Zwingli's friends. He died in 1551, a very old man. Rudolph Röschlin, people's priest at St. Peter's, was very slow in accepting the Reformation, was at the time of this episcopal visit an old man, and a few weeks after it resigned his place and was succeeded by Zwingli's bosom friend, Leo Jud.

[2] Teacher of Ovid.

The Delegation from Constance 117

although (3) ceremonies were a sort of *manuductio* or "leading by the hand" to the virtues, for he was pleased to use this word *manuductio* even before people who did not understand Latin, because, no doubt, the German term eine Einleitung, "an introduction," did not seem to him strong enough (or, if you will, fine enough). Ceremonials were in fact, he said, a source (ein Ursprung) of virtue, though he afterwards had the boldness to deny before all those witnesses that he used the word; (4) they were also teaching that Lent ought not to be kept, for certain persons in this city had ventured to withdraw from other Christians and from the Christian Church, though this statement also he afterwards denied with as much shamelessness as stubbornness. My lord Brendlin bore witness that he had not used that expression, though the whole Senate still bears witness that he used it. So persistently do these people fancy that they are free to say off-hand whatever they please and to deny off-hand what they have said, almost at the moment of saying it. He said (5) that they had eaten meat in Lent to the scandal of the whole republic of Christ; though (6) this was evidently not permitted by the Gospels, they yet ventured to declare that they might do it in accordance with the writings of the Evangelists and Apostles; they had violated (7) the decrees of the Holy Fathers and the councils, and (8) a most ancient custom which (9) we never could have kept so long if it had not emanated from the Holy Spirit. For Gamaliel in the Acts of the Apostles had said:[1] "Let them alone; for if this work is of God," etc. Then he urged the Senate (10) to remain with and in the Church, for outside of it no one had salvation. For (11) the things which were being taught so wrongheadedly were being taught without grounds. And not having satisfied himself in what he had said before about ceremonials, he fell (12) to speaking of them again, saying that they were the only means by which the humbler Christians were brought to the recognition of salvation, and that it belonged to the

[1] Acts v., 34–42.

duties of the people's priests (for that is the way bishops and preachers are named now-a-days by those counterfeit bishops, to keep their name sacred) to teach the simple-minded populace that there were certain symbols which denoted certain things, and that it was their function to explain and set forth the meaning and value thereof. At length, after the above turn in his speech, John[1] began to discourse (13) upon grounds of offence, not unlearnedly, I confess, only I wish that he had cited as happily the things against himself as those for him. He added that Christ enjoined with as much emphasis as he put upon any precept, that offences be avoided, for he added that most clear mark of indignation, "Woe!" "Woe to the world because of offences!"[2] Going back also to Paul, from whose epistles he had quoted many things before he discoursed upon "Woe," he called to witness (14) that in order not to offend the Jews he had suffered Timothy to be circumcised.[3] And what he ought to have said among his first remarks about seditious teachings, he talked on after everything else, saying (15) that no one ought to trust his own ideas; for that even Paul had been unwilling to depend upon his own notions, and had gone to Jerusalem to compare his gospel with the Apostles, etc.[4] And after a very beautiful peroration to his remarks he rose, and was on the point of going away with his allies, when I addressed them in the following terms:

"My Lord suffragan" (and in this I made an indiscreet and ignorant enough blunder; for they tell me I should have said "most merciful Lord," but being unskilled in polished ways I take hold like a clodhopper) "and fellow-ecclesiastics," I said, "wait, I pray, until I make explanation in my own behalf." For that my fellow-bishops allowed me to do. To this he said: "It has not been enjoined upon us to engage in discussion with anyone." "And I," said I, "have no intention of entering into discussion, but what I have thus far been teaching these excellent citizens

---

[1] "It should be Melchior (Fattlin), and not John (Wanner)."
[2] Matt. xviii., 7.   [3] Acts xvi., 3.   [4] Gal. ii., 1.

I would willingly and gladly set forth to you who are both learned men and delegates sent here, so to speak, with full powers; that the greater faith may be had in my teachings if you shall have voted them right, and if not, that the opposite may take place." "We have said nothing," said he, "in opposition to you, and therefore there is no need for you to make explanation." But I said: "Though you have refrained from mentioning my name, yet all the force and power of your words were aimed and hurled at me." For, as a matter of fact, they were dealing with me in the style of the old gladiatorial combats between Mirmillons and Gauls, wherein the Mirmillon cried: "It is not you I am aiming at, Gaul, it is the fish I am aiming at." So my name was kept out of sight and not mentioned, in order that most serious charges, if it please the gods, might be developed against me, whose name is Zwingli. While we were thus contending together, Mark Röust, President of the Senate, tried by entreaty to persuade the men of Constance to listen, to which entreaty the suffragan replied that he knew with whom he should have to deal if he listened. Huldreich Zwingli was too violent and choleric to make any duly and moderately carried on discussion possible with him. I answered: "What wrong have I ever done you? And what kind of a way of doing is this, to worry so harshly and bitterly a guiltless man who has done his duty by Christianity, and to refuse to hear any explanation? I have always felt myself bound to hope, unless I am mistaken (but perhaps I am mistaken), that if anyone ever came forward to contradict the truth and teachings of the Gospel, it would come to pass that the High Prelate of Constance would rush to its aid before all others and hear the whole case, and this by your help especially, whom he has even now employed as delegates because of your pre-eminent learning. For what would ye do if I wanted to go to him without your knowledge? If I feared to meet you? If I refused to have your opinion in the matter? Now, when I do nothing of the kind, but ask your presence in order to give an account of my faith and teachings, how have you the face to venture to refuse it? It could not have failed to rouse suspicion if I had allowed you to go away, even though you desired it; now when I appeal of my own accord to your judgment and justice, how do you dare to abandon me?" Then said they: "Our Reverend Master did not wish us to enter into a dispute with anyone, so it is impossible for us to hear you. If you wish to take any point of doctrine to the bishop you are free to do so; if you need anything apprise him of it." But I said: "I beg of you if you are not willing from any other consideration to vouchsafe me this favour, yet grant me this wish for the sake of our common faith, our common baptism, and for the sake of Christ the giver of life and salvation, and if you may not listen as delegates, you still may as Christians." When I had thus adjured them the citizens began to murmur in their indignation, so that at last, driven by the urgent request of the president and the unworthiness of their course, they went back to their seats. Thereupon I began to speak in defence of the teachings of Christ to the best of my ability, and made answer to their main heads in about this fashion:

1. My Lord suffragan has stated that certain persons were teaching seditious and obnoxious doctrines, but I cannot be persuaded that he means this to be taken of me, who for nearly four years now have been preaching the gospel of Christ and the teachings of the Apostles with so much energy. And yet it savours somewhat of this, inasmuch as he made the statement before the Senate. For what concern were it of mine if such teachings were preached elsewhere, provided they were not preached at Zurich? Therefore, since it is not likely that the suffragan spoke of the affairs of outsiders, it is clear that his remarks were aimed at me. However much they disguise it, it is evident that here is the David to whom this Nathan imputed the wrong. But as to the gospel, it is no wonder that in one place or another there should be differences between those

who cling doggedly to ἐντάλωατα, that is, human prescriptions, and those who are unfriendly to the same. For Christ prophesied most clearly that this would come to pass, saying: "I came not to send peace on earth, but a sword. For I am come to set a man at variance against his father, and the daughter against her mother, and the daughter-in-law against her mother-in-law, and it shall come to pass that a man's foes shall be they of his own household."[1] Yet there was no need of this answer either. For Zurich more than any other of the Swiss cantons is in peace and quiet, and this all good citizens put down to the credit of the gospel.

2. As to the reproach, in the next place, that it is taught that no human prescriptions nor ceremonials ought to be kept, I will acknowledge frankly that I desire to see a fair portion of the ceremonials and prescriptions done away with, because the things prescribed are in great part such as also Peter in the Acts says can not be endured.[2] Nor am I going to listen to those who say that Peter spoke of the old ceremonials and prescriptions. Be it understood, though, that if I should grant them this it is still clear that Peter was of opinion that Christians ought to be free from burdens and bitterness of the kind. But if Peter deprecated that old yoke so greatly, which was yet much lighter than that which we bear to-day, what think ye he would have done if there had been question of a heavier one? Now that the old yoke would have been more endurable to Christians than ours (to say nothing for the nonce of the decrees of the pontiffs, which are much more numerous and onerous than the commands of Moses) is shown well enough by the excessive observation of fasts, the careful selection of foods, and the enforced leisure of feast days. For how trifling will the fasts of the Jews become which they ordained at times for those in great sorrow, if you compare them with these stated forty days' fasts of ours, institutions fit for serfs, and those that are

[1] Matt. x., 34–36.   [2] Acts xv., 10.

ordained in a sort of unbroken and continuous row in honour of the saints! Furthermore, if you compare the selection of foods, its observation is more onerous among the Christians than among the Jews. They abstain from certain kinds of food, but not at a fixed period, with the exception of the Passover. We abstain from numerous kinds and for long seasons. And in the enforced leisure of feast days we surpass the Jews very greatly. But if Peter did not want the Christians worried by the lighter yoke much less would he approve the heavier. I denied, however, that I was of opinion that no human prescriptions at all ought to be kept or enacted. For who would not joyfully accept what was decided by the concurrent opinion of all Christians? But, on the other hand, the decrees of certain most unholy spirits, who after the manner of the Pharisees would lay unbearable burdens upon the necks of men and not touch them themselves even with the tip of their fingers, were an abomination. And as to his having said, with a view to rouse the Senate to anger, that we should fail to obey the laws of the state, I said this was not the spirit of Christ or of the Apostles. For Christ had said, "Render unto Cæsar the things that are Cæsar's,[1]" etc., and had paid the tribute or tax. Nay, at his birth his parents reported his name according to the proclamation of Cæsar; while the Apostles taught: "Render unto all their dues, tribute to whom tribute is due," etc.,[2] "and obey them who are set in authority over you, and not only the good,"[3] etc. Hence it was evident that he had spoken more vigorously than truly, as would be made still clearer by an illustration. For all the peoples of the whole world had obeyed the laws most rigorously, even before the man Christ was born. Nay, Christianity was the most powerful instrument for the preservation of justice in general, and the faith of Christ could not be done away with even if all ceremonials were done away with altogether. Nay, ceremonials achieved nothing else than the cheating of Christ and his faithful followers and doing

[1] Matt. xxii., 21. [2] Romans xiii., 7. [3] Heb. xiii., 17.

away with the teachings of the Spirit, calling men away from the unseen to the material things of this world, but this could not be described and explained in short compass.

3. Then I showed that the simple-minded people could be led to the recognition of the truth by other means than ceremonials, to wit, by those by which Christ and the Apostles had led them without any ceremonials, as far as I had been able to learn through the sacred writings, and that there was no danger that the people were not capable of receiving the gospel, which he who believes can understand. They can believe, therefore they can also understand. Whatever takes place here is done by the inspiration of God, not by the reasoning of man, as Christ also thanked the Father, saying: "I thank thee, O Father," etc., "because thou hast hid these things from the wise and prudent, and hast revealed them unto babes. Even so, Father, for so it seemed good in thy sight."[1] And Paul (I. Cor. i., 27) says that "God hath chosen the foolish things of the world to confound the wise."

4. I had nowhere taught that Lent ought not to be kept, though I could wish that it were not prescribed so imperiously, but were left free to the individual. But he for whom Lent was not enough might fast for the rest of the year also; there would not be wanting men to advise fasting, and I presaged that they would be likely to effect more than those who thought that at the frown of their power and the threat of excommunication, everything would fall to pieces with a crash as at the frown of Jove.

5. Certain persons, and they by no means bad ones, had ventured to eat flesh, and they were not tainted, but since they had not been forbidden by the divine law to eat flesh, they seemed rather to have eaten it in witness of their faith than to any one's reproach. And this was clear from the fact that presently when told by me that they ought to take into account the possible cause of offence they stopped, so that there was no need of this fine dele-

[1] Matt. xi., 25.

gation, inasmuch as the evil died out of itself, granting that it was an evil. Still I wondered exceedingly that I had been a minister of the gospel in the diocese of Constance for sixteen years and had thus far never known of the men of Constance having sent anywhere so magnificent a delegation to investigate how the affairs of the gospel were going on, but now when they had found a very trifling observance not broken as much as they seemed to wish, they filled everything with their lamentations, and accused the people of Zurich of being the only ones who had the effrontery to meditate withdrawing from the Christian communion. Yet when the suffragan denied that expression, as I have said, and Brendlin supported his denial, though the whole Senate cried out in rebuttal, I allowed their denial in somewhat these terms: Since you deny the expression, show that it escaped you unawares and I will easily pardon it; as far as I am concerned you shall be free to correct any utterances you please. But the republic of Christ has suffered no offence and no disgrace if some few persons have failed to keep human tradition.

6. And I showed that it was an unsound contention that the gospel writings nowhere clearly allowed the eating of flesh. For Mark (ch. vii. [15]) speaks in this fashion: "There is nothing from without a man that entering into him can defile him." Here I showed by the argument from the preceding (in the way they manipulated the sacred writings) that the argument of the following held good in this way: Therefore, whatever is outside of a man cannot by entering into him defile him. Words are signs to me. A general negative is no sign. If he had said "no food," he would have left out the category of drinks; if he had said "no drink," he would have left out that of food. Therefore, it pleased him who is the Truth to say "nothing." Then he added: "cannot even defile." Hear! The Voice of Truth declares it cannot; man, who is a liar, for all men are liars, says it can. Here the man squirms and says these words are not so clear, and must be interpreted in this way,

but the preceding words must be regarded and the words that follow, though this is what follows: "Do ye not perceive that whatsoever thing from without entereth into the man it cannot defile him, because it entereth not into his heart, but into the belly, and goeth out into the draught, purging all meats?" What can be said more clearly, if you please, even though you regard the preceding and the following?

7. They added the words: "contrary to the decrees of the Holy Fathers and the councils." I answered that Engelhard, the ornament of our city, had carefully weighed with me those in which our friends placed greatest confidence, and that no such asseveration could be made from those which they treated as a sacred anchor. For the question was not whether Lent ought to be done away with, but whether it was permissible by the law of Christ to eat meat at that time. While I forbid no man's fasting, I leave it free to him.

8. They had also added: "and contrary to very ancient custom." Here I frankly granted that it was the custom, and not a bad one. But if it were the custom, why was a proclamation added? I promised that I would certainly see to it that the custom should not be wantonly interrupted.

9. And if this custom (he continued) had not been inspired by the Divine Spirit it would not have lasted so long, in accordance with the words of Gamaliel.[1] I answered that this and other things which were not from the mind of God would be done away in their own good time. For "every plant," says Christ in Matthew, "which my heavenly Father hath not planted shall be rooted up."[2] But selection of foods neither Christ nor the Apostles had prescribed. Therefore no one ought to be surprised if unhappy mortals are turning their eyes towards freedom, since Christ in his loving kindness has now illumined the world more brightly with his gospel by a sort of second revelation.

[1] Acts v., 35 ff. [2] Matt. xv., 13.

10. After this the weighty speaker made his turn to the Senate, appealing to them to stay with and in the Church, for outside of it none was saved. This I met thus: "Let not this exhortation move you, most excellent citizens, as if you had ever abandoned the Church of Christ. For I am persuaded of you that you hold in fresh remembrance what is said in the narrative of Matthew, that the foundation of the Church is that rock which gave his name to Peter the faithful confessor. No one lays other foundation than this, nor can do so. Nay, in every nation and place, everyone who confesses the Lord Jesus with his tongue and believes in his heart that God raised him from the dead shall be saved, whether he be among the Indians or the Scythians, and it is fixed beyond controversy that outside of that Church none is saved, within which we all believe ourselves to be the more firmly as we glory the more certainly in the hope of the glory of the sons of God." Here I might have dragged the man forth and laid bare his notion of the Church, but I preferred to spare him, that he might repent at length of having said before the whole Senate that I was too rough spoken to make it possible to discuss with me. When he had thus made his exhortation I began to look to the end of his remarks, but things turned out differently from what I hoped. For he turned back to this other point and said:

11. That rubbish (for thus, if I mistake not, that crowd call the gospel teaching) was taught without foundation in Scripture. Here again I fled to the protection of the words of Mark vii., as a sort of Achilles' shield, and shot forth these shafts: Do you want clearer proofs presented to you? Is not Christ worthy of belief? Or Mark? I have gathered many passages together, but I abstain from giving the rest now in order not to nauseate the Fathers. Here my lord Engelhard opportunely drew a New Testament from his pocket and bade me interpret the passage of Paul's Epistle to Timothy i., 4. I took the book and translated the passage into German, and it is wonderful how they

The Delegation from Constance 127

all breathed a sigh of relief, recognising the passage, most of them, from the exposition of that epistle that I had made the year before. So much difference does it make at what point things are said.

12. Immediately leaving these points he brought the ceremonials out into battle line again, wounded however, and I attempted to rout them completely again thus: His point that it was the duty of the people's priests to set forth the meaning of the ceremonials I upset in this way: The gospel of Christ had been committed to me to preach assiduously; what the ceremonials indicated those would set forth who lived by them. I admit that I purposely, though quietly, meant to touch the man's sore point in this. For what else do those suburban bishops do but stuff their purses with illusions of consecrating things? But if any master of ceremonials ventured to preach other than the truth to the sheep entrusted to me, I declared I would not stand it.

13. Now what he had said about offences I should have approved in general, if all his words had not seemed to point toward keeping those who were weak always weak, though it is the duty of the stronger, as those fellows wish and ought to be regarded, $\pi\rho o\delta\lambda\alpha\mu\beta\acute{a}\nu\epsilon\sigma\theta\alpha\iota$, that is, to take up and comfort and help the weak, that they may also be made strong. Yet this one thing I added: Since he had spoken much of the anxious care of the High Prelate of Constance to avoid or guard against offence to the Church, had he no exhortation to his priests at last after Christ's fashion, bidding them to put their own immunity behind them and bear the general burdens with the rest of the Christian brethren, and to pay tax and tribute? For Christ, in order not to give ground of offence to those who exacted the tribute money, paid it and performed a miracle besides, but it could not be denied that all the people in every nation were complaining because the priests and monks and nuns were supported in idleness, contributing neither labour nor money for the uses of the State. They

complained bitterly after they had left the Senate that this had been brought in outside the subject, as they say, but it seems to me that nothing could have been said more appropriately at this point, when they were talking of the High Prelate of Constance being so anxious about grounds of offence.

14. In the next place, though I was aware that Paul had suffered Timothy to be circumcised, yet I maintained that he could not be persuaded by any means to allow Titus to be circumcised, and I tried to give the reason for both acts, namely, that with Timothy, while Christianity was still in the green blade, he had suffered the Macedonians to be circumcised that no breach of the peace might arise, but after the new doctrine had grown somewhat more vigorous, and Paul had learned by his perception of this that Titus could be saved without any disturbance, he saved him.[1] Here I put forth all my strength to persuade the Senators to abide by the ancient custom until either the bonds of that yoke were loosened for us or the world itself consented together more clearly for the taking up again of freedom.

15. Finally I said that those could rightfully be said to rely on their own notions and ideas who struggled against the accepted Scriptures and put human traditions before the teachings of heaven, not those who protected themselves by no other weapons or defences than the sacred writings, for the former trusted in flesh and blood, the latter in the truth of heaven alone, not one jot of which could ever pass away. Though I was aware that Paul had compared his gospel with the Apostles finally, I also knew that he did not do it for fourteen years.[2] And though I perceived what they were after with that illustration, their side was weakened rather than propped up by it. For I had insisted a little while before so obstinately that they should be present at my explanation for no other reason than that they might see clearly how I handled the sacred writings; nay, that I was

---

[1] Gal. ii., 3. [2] *Ibid.*, 1.

The Delegation from Constance

ready to give an account of the faith that was in me before the dwellers in heaven, or on earth, or in hell. And finally having begged the Senate to take in good part all that I had said, I stopped speaking, except that when the suffragan began to snap out something more and to drive it in vigorously, that it had been decreed by the Holy Fathers and the councils that meat should not be eaten in Lent, I also began to contend more recklessly and to deny that it had been decreed by any councils, at least by any general ones. At last when he had finished his appendix we adjourned the Senate.

These, dear Brother Erasmus, are the wounds I received and inflicted in the assembly of the Ecclesiastics and Senators; these the means with which I ran to the aid of the feeble. It has all been written down off-hand as it was spoken, for the suffragan had brought a prepared speech with him, but I was forced to fight and defend myself as I stood. If I have said anything more briefly or more fully than it occurred, I think this should be attributed to human weakness, which hardly recognises how little power it has in remembering. Yet the main drift of the proceedings in general I have touched upon, whether in the Senate or in the body of Ecclesiastics or in private discussion. For the evening after the morning they had spoken before the body of Ecclesiastics, I stumbled upon them by accident and talked much with them. Thus I learned just where their sore point was.

Good-by, and if you write to my friend [Hans] Oechsli,[1] greet him for me.

---

[1] He was pastor at Burg, just across the Rhine from Erasmus Fabricius.

XI

A Solemn Warning by Huldreich Zwingli, a Simple Preacher of the Gospel of Jesus Christ, Addressed to the Honourable, Wise, Steadfast, Senior Confederates at Schwyz, that they should Beware of, and Free Themselves from, the Control of Foreign Lords

(May 16, 1522)

[Ein göttlich vermanung an die ersamen, wysen, eerenvesten, eltisten Eydgnossen zū Schwytz, das sy sich vor frōmden herren hütind und entladind, Huldrichi Zwinglii, einvaltigen verkünders des euangelii Christi Jhesu.
In Schuler and Schūlthess ed., ii., 2, 287-298. In Egli and Finsler ed., i., 165-188. Translated by Walter Lichtenstein, Ph.D., librarian of North-Western University, Evanston, Illinois.
Egli in his special introduction to this treatise (i, 155-158) attributes to Erasmus's *Querale pacis* the inauguration of that movement against war which is now one of the most civilised agitations of our modern philanthropy. It was the abbot of Kappel, Wolfgang Joner, who incited Leo Jud, the bosom friend of Zwingli, to translate into German the brochure of Erasmus and it was published by Froschauer, the famous printer of Zurich, in 1521. But though Erasmus was the protagonist, Zwingli is entitled to the honour of an independent follower, and what he says about war is worthy of republication by our Peace Societies, and they are entirely at liberty to use this translation.
Zwingli produced a profound though passing impression. Under the influence of his words Schwyz resolved to abstain, for at least twenty-five years, from forming alliances of the kind he condemned, but alas! the power of the French gold was too great and in a couple of months she rescinded her resolution and entered again into the degrading alliance. But the transitory effect of Zwingli's words is no proof of their weakness. He was a faithful witness to the evils of his times in his country and to-day his exposure of the insensate folly and devilish cruelty of war is good reading. It is nigh four hundred years since he wrote. Happily great progress has been made of late in impressing the common man with the wastefulness and fatuity of war. Once war was the amusement of princes, but the common soldier was

Warning against Control of Foreign Lords 131

the sufferer. He was the loser whichever side won. When this fact is universally, as now it is generally, perceived, then wars will cease and lo! peaceful means will be found always much more efficient in producing the desired results.]

I, HULDREICH ZWINGLI, a simple and plain preacher of the gospel of Jesus Christ, send greeting, my obedience, service, and love in Christ our Lord, to the pious, honourable, etc., senior confederates of Schwyz.

Gracious and dear Lords, Amman [Governor], Council, Assembly of Schwyz. Your Honours may wonder how I dare presume to instruct a whole country at once. But this is only done in accordance with the saying of Solomon: "Give instruction to a wise man, and he will be yet wiser" [Prov. ix., 9], and so I was moved to make known to you my views so that by setting before you a model you may take counsel together all the more diligently, for when weighed down by a sad and painful loss[1] (such as has unfortunately come to you; may God comfort you in your sorrow and guard you from the same in the future. Amen) not everyone is able without advice to find the right way himself. Besides, from your very sorrow there might arise serious quarrels and dissensions among you, by which, however, may God have mercy upon you! the damage will not be made good. In order that by means of the Scriptures and the opinion of worthy men you may be rid of all damage, I have been constrained by that great love toward you, which I have cherished since childhood (for I am a native of the county of Toggenburg and hence feel myself somewhat indebted to you), to make known my views. This I do in order that the damage done to such wise men may not result in still greater disaster, and while it is still an easy matter and the disease has not spread we may correct our mistakes. Otherwise it is to be feared that those princes, who have never been able to subdue us

[1] The reference is to the crushing defeat of the French Army by the Imperial troops in the battle of Bicocca in Italy. The Swiss mercenaries constituted part of the French forces and 3000 of them were slain.

with sword and pike, may do so with soft gold, which may God forbid and may he never deprive you of his counsel and wisdom! Therefore I beg of your wisdom to pardon me for having the presumption to write to you, which I did not in order to curry favour with any lord, but on account of fear of God and love for a worthy Confederacy. May God's wisdom shine upon you! I had to have everything completed within three days, the conception, the writing, the printing, for I learned only on Wednesday that the next assembly would be held as early as the coming Sunday. Zürich, May 16, 1522. God be praised!

A divine warning by Huldreich Zwingli, a proclaimer of the gospel of Jesus Christ, addressed to the honourable, wise, steadfast, senior confederates at Schwyz, that they should beware and free themselves of the control of foreign lords.

God created man of earth, as is written in the second chapter of Genesis, for no other reason (as it seems to me) than that he might be made humble by having been created out of matter, and that the common mother of all, namely the earth, might prevent her children from striving to raise themselves one above the other and also from quarrelling with each other. For the children see themselves born of one and the same mother and nourished in one and the same manner. Aye, the reason why the heavenly Father caused all men to be descended from one man, Adam, was also for the sake of peace, otherwise he might have filled the whole world at once with people, or created men from stones thrown backward, as the poets tell of Deucalion and Pyrrha. So God also created man in his own image, [Gen. i., 27], so that just as the three persons, Father, Son, and Holy Ghost are one God, who cannot disagree or quarrel with himself, thus also men's lives might be led in a spirit of concord, peace, and unanimity. This was also a prayer of Christ, for which see the 17th chapter of the Gospel of St. John [John xvii., 11]: "Holy

Warning against Control of Foreign Lords

Father, keep through thine own name those whom thou hast given me, that they may be one, as we are."

From all the above it is clear that in his eternal wisdom God not only represented unity in the creation, but also in the regeneration, which Christ gives us. Thus, that though in our carnal birth and origin we be not joined together in harmony, we become one by the spiritual regeneration and renewal in one spirit, in one faith, in one baptism, in one Saviour Jesus Christ, as St. Paul writes in the 4th chapter of his letter to the Ephesians [Eph. iv., 1–6]: "I therefore, the prisoner of the Lord, beseech you that ye walk worthy of the vocation wherewith ye are called, with all lowliness and meekness, with longsuffering, forbearing one another in love, endeavouring to keep the unity of the Spirit in the bond of peace. There is one body, and one Spirit, even as ye are called in one hope of your calling; one Lord, one faith, one baptism, one God and Father of all, who is above all, and through all, and in you all." Here God admonishes us with great care and pains through the mouth of the captive Paul to unity and peace: for we are one body, of which Christ is the head, and one spirit or soul, for all men are sustained by the one comfort that we all trust in him, by whom we have been called, Jesus Christ, true God and man. We have one Lord, one faith, one baptism, one God, who is our Father and whose spirit dwells in us. About all this much more could be said, but let us get nearer to the subject in hand.

How does it happen that we Christians who are united by such powerful agencies have much greater quarrels than unbelievers? And how does it happen that in a Confederacy in which until now a fraternal love prevailed, for the sake of foreign lords violent quarrel has arisen? Answer: Real piety, by which is meant true worship and prayer to God, has disappeared among us, as St. Paul writes to the Romans [Rom. i., 28–31]: "And even as they did not like to retain God in their knowledge, God gave them over to a reprobate mind, to do those things which are not convenient; being filled with all unrighteousness, fornication, wickedness, covetousness, maliciousness; full of envy, murder, debate, deceit, malignity; whisperers, backbiters, haters of God, despiteful, proud, boasters, inventors of evil things, disobedient to parents, without understanding, covenant-breakers, without natural affection, implacable, unmerciful." From these words of Paul we learn that all these evils which he enumerates arise when we desert God, do not fully recognise Him, do not look up to Him, do not place our whole trust in him, but on the countrary despise Him and regard him somewhat as we would an old sleeping dog. But I shall not now consider the question whose fault it is that we have forgotten him. That matter I shall discuss at the proper time.

Note well, worthy and beloved sirs, that wherever the above mentioned vices appear, God has been previously forsaken. And, *vice versa*, wherever people forsake God and trust in themselves, the vices named above are bound to follow as a punishment and penalty for the desertion from God. But whoever places all his hope in God, ascribes to him all good and worthy deeds, estimates nothing higher than the knowledge and love of God, such a one God does not allow to succumb to the numerous vices mentioned by St. Paul. And even where such a man is allowed to fall, God protects him so that the fall may not injure him. This Christ shows us in chapter xv. of the Gospel according to John [John xv., 9, 7.] "Continue ye in my love." And in the same place: "If ye abide in me and my words abide in you, ye shall ask what ye will, and it shall be done unto you." And Peter says [II. Peter i., 10]: "For if ye do these things, ye shall never fail." The things referred to would take up too much time to mention, but Peter mentions them just before. And I. John iii. [I. John iii., 6]: "Whosoever abideth in him sinneth not: whosoever sinneth, hath not seen him, neither known him." But that a lapse cannot injure a truly devout person is proved by the fall of Peter [Matt. xxvi, 69 *ff*. and parallels]

Warning against Control of Foreign Lords 135

and of David [II. Sam. xi. and xii.], both of whom humbled themselves after their fall and remained more devout than ever before for the rest of their days. Thus St. Paul writes in the eighth chapter of his letter to the Romans [Rom. viii., 28]: "And we know that all things work together for good to them that love God." Therefore Peter after his denial of Christ, and David through his scandalous murder of Uriah and adultery with Bathsheba, were led to repentance and reformation.

The people of our time, who do not recognise the fact that God has deserted us on account of our sins, are almost not to be counted, so numerous are they. They do not notice our many sins, for we are in fact free of none of those enumerated by Paul above, nor do these people realise how our physical strength is being undermined. Our forefathers defeated their enemies and won their independence only by means of the strength derived from God, and they always gratefully and lovingly gave God credit for his aid no less than did the children of Israel after their escape from Pharaoh and passage of the Red Sea, when they sang [Exod. xv., 1, 2]: "I will sing unto the Lord, for he hath triumphed gloriously: the horse and his rider hath he thrown into the sea. The Lord is my strength and song, and he is become my salvation." Furthermore, our ancestors did not kill Christians for pay, but fought only for independence, so that their bodies, lives, wives, and children might not be subjected to the wantonness of an insolent aristocracy. God favours such independence, as he proved when he led the children of Israel out of Egypt because the Egyptian kings and people maltreated them. For this read Exodus. Furthermore, later when the Jews demanded a king he informed them of the power and abuses of kings [I. Sam. viii., 10–27], undoubtedly warning them to beware of such rule. See also St. Paul's letter to the Corinthians [I. Cor. vii., 21]: "But if thou mayest be made free, use (strive for) it rather."

Thus God continuously increased the honour and

property of our ancestors in such bountiful fashion that no prince was ever sufficiently strong to defeat them. There can be no doubt that such was not due to human strength, but only possible by means of divine aid and grace. Thus they were assisted wherever they fought for country and liberty: at Morgarten, at Sempach, at Näfels in Glacis where 350 men attacked a force of 15,000 eleven times and finally routed them completely. At this battle there were also thirty men from Schwyz present. Many other localities, where they attacked, and came back joyfully and with honour, have now for nearly two hundred years remained quiet and unmolested.

But now that we begin to be well satisfied with ourselves and on account of things, which are purely from God, think ourselves most intelligent, which unfortunately is decidedly the lot of all human kind; and since we have fattened and become great in temporal riches and honours, now, I say, we draw away from God and pull in another direction [Deut. xxxii., 15]; also 52d Psalm [Psalm lii., 7]: "Lo, this is the man that made not God his strength; but trusted in the abundance of his riches, and strengthened himself in his wickedness" (vanity), which is his great courage and renown. But he is no more than empty air; for nothing righteous, strong, or good is to be found supporting us. We poor human beings desire to be continuously strutting about, which is very distasteful to God, as we can see by II. Sam. xxiv. [II. Sam. xxiv., 1 *ff*], where David took a census of the children of Israel in order to see how powerful he was, doubtlessly ascribing all credit for the might of the nation to himself. Therefore God became angry and offered David the choice of three plagues [II. Sam. xxiv., 11 *ff*], one of which he must select as punishment for having counted the people. David selected the bubonic plague, so that he himself might be stricken. Note that when David wished to brag and count his force, he showed that he desired to know the extent of that power which was not his, but God's. For this David was severely punished, so that he might remember the words of Moses, as given in the 32d chapter of Deuteronomy [Deut. xxxii., 30]: "How should one chase a thousand, and two put ten thousand to flight, except their Rock had sold them, and the Lord had shut them up?"

Why might not then God also punish us, since we are continuously boasting of our power in some such fashion: we have done this; we shall do so and so; we can act thus; no one can withstand us? Just as if we had made a covenant with death and with hell, therefore as Isaiah says in his 28th chapter [Isaiah xxviii., 15]: "when the overflowing scourge shall pass through, it shall not come unto us: for we have made lies our refuge and under falsehood have we hid ourselves." Just as if we were made of iron and other people were pumpkins. Just as if no one could injure us, like those heroes, who wished to guard themselves against the Deluge by means of the enormous tower of Babel, as you may read in the eleventh chapter of Genesis [Gen. xi., 1–9]. Yea, he will certainly not let our pride go unpunished, and if he has shown much patience, it has been in the hope that we might reform. If we do not better our conduct, it shall happen to us as it did to Sodom and Gomorrah and to those who would not reform until the Deluge came, as Peter writes in his second letter [II. Peter ii., 4 *ff*].

Some time ago there were several among us who were so childish as to forget themselves and God and allowed their greed to mislead them, so that the devil, the enemy of all good men, sent just as he did the serpent to the first man, so sent in our time the pious people, who said to us: Men and heroes, why do you remain in this country and among these hills? Why do you hold on to this rough country? Serve us, we shall pay you well. Your name and possessions will become great in the land, and your might will become known to all men and will be feared by them. Just so the serpent said to Eve [Gen. iii., 5]: "Ye shall be as gods." Solomon warns in Proverbs xi. to beware of such promises [Prov. xi., 9]: "The hypocrite with his mouth destroyeth his [friend] neighbour." And Christ also says [Matt. vii., 16]: "Ye shall know them by their fruits. Do men gather grapes of thorns, or figs of thistles?" By which Christ means to say that these people, mentioned above, attach themselves only to those from whom they expect to continue to derive much profit. Hence they treated a foolish Confederacy in such a fashion, seeking merely their own gain, that without regard to our native country we cared more for maintaining their power and empire than we did for protecting our own homes, women, and children (of this good man beware). And how we have suffered from all this! Within the memory of man we have sustained greater losses at Naples, Novara, and Marignano in the service of these lords than we had since the Confederacy has existed; and while when waging our own wars we have always been victorious, in foreign service we have always been badly defeated.

But it is to be feared that all these evils are counterbalanced in the minds of people to whom selfish aims are more important than the common weal. Nevertheless the commonwealth is suffering more and more, and is increasing daily in direct proportion to the spread of greed, incontinence, wantonness, and disobedience. Our only hope consists in a complete reversal of our behaviour and a realisation of the danger which we are running into.

The greatest danger that we are risking is the divine anger, as expounded in the second chapter of Micah [Micah ii., 2, 8, 9, 3]: "And they covet fields and take them by violence; and houses, and take them away: so they oppress a man and his house, even a man and his heritage." And later: "Ye pull off the robe with the garment from them that pass by securely as men averse from war. The women of my people have ye cast out from their pleasant houses." "Therefore, thus saith the Lord: Behold, against this family (people) do I devise an evil, from which ye shall not remove your necks; neither shall ye go haughtily: for this time

Warning against Control of Foreign Lords 139

is evil." These words of the prophet, which show the ravages of war and the threat of the divine anger, are sufficiently clear. Everyone should think well of what war might mean to him if he were done to as he did to other Christians. Let us suppose that foreign mercenaries invaded the country, devastated your meadows and fields and vineyards, led away your cattle, gathered together your household effects to take away; had previously killed your sons in the act of protecting themselves and you; insulted and outraged your daughters; kicked your good wife, while she was on her knees, begging them to have pity on her beloved ones; and dragged you, pious old man, out of your hiding-place in your own house and killed you in the presence of your wife, regardless of your trembling and honourable age and the lamentations of your wife; and finally reduced your house and home to ashes: if all this happened and the heavens did not open and pour down fire, and the earth were not cleft asunder to swallow such rascals, you would say there is no God. But if you did all these things to another, you would maintain that such is the right of war. But let us see who is regarded a brave soldier, as judged by the deeds of war seen by the Greek poet Euripides who says in *Hecuba*:[1] "In war he is regarded as evil who does no wrong, and who does not consider man the same as a frog." But unfortunately in war many gather great wealth, disregarding the anger of the Lord, which is foreshadowed so terribly in the fifth chapter of Isaiah [Isaiah v., 8, 9]: "Woe unto them that join house to house, that lay field to field, till there be no place, that they may be placed alone in the midst of the earth. In mine ears said the Lord of hosts, Of a truth many houses shall be desolate, even great and fair, without inhabitant." Furthermore, we must not let ourselves be shaken in our belief by the statement that war is a means of divine punishment, and that therefore there must be someone to make war upon someone else. In the Old Testament many wars are described.

[1] Verse 608.

In answer to the first part of the argument let us hear what Christ says according to the 18th chapter of Matthew [Matt. xviii., 7]: "Woe unto the world because of offences! for it must needs be that offences come; but woe to that man by whom the offence cometh!" Thus many deserve to be punished and God inflicts war upon them; but woe unto them who wage the war! God punishes the evil by the hands of the evil, as may be seen by a perusal of the 29th chapter of Ezekiel [Ezek. xxix., 17–21], in which is described how God punished the city of Tyre by the hand of Nebuchadrezzar, and then later punished these same Babylonians, though they had been, in accordance with the divine will, the means of punishing the children of Israel by captivity and imprisonment which is known to this day as the Babylonian captivity. Concerning this all see the 51st chapter of Jeremiah [Jer. li., 1–5]: "Behold, I will raise up against Babylon, and against them that dwell in the midst of them that rise up against me, a destroying wind; and will send unto Babylon fanners, that shall fan her, and shall empty her land: for in the day of trouble they shall be against her round about. Against him that bendeth let the archer bend his bow, and against him that lifteth himself up in his brigandine, and spare ye not her young men; destroy ye utterly all her host. Thus the slain shall fall in the land of the Chaldeans, and they that are thrust through in her streets. For Israel hath not been forsaken, nor Judah of his God." We see that God takes away victory in the same manner that he grants it. The former he does whenever a people wish to gain an advantage by their own unaided strength or seek to abuse their power. No nation has ever become great by war that has not ultimately been cast down by war. This is proved by the history of Israel, Sparta, Athens, Persia, Macedonia, Assyria, Medea, and finally by Rome, whose empire was greater and more powerful than that of any other. But what are they other than the conquered now? All the people they ever conquered could easily turn the tables now.

In answer to the second part of the argument, I say: The

Warning against Control of Foreign Lords 141

children of Israel waged war either against sinful races, who would not permit them to enter the promised land, or, after they had arrived at their goal, against such as would not leave them in peace. These wars of the Jews merely symbolise the spiritual war that we born in Christ and resurrected ought to wage against vice and unbelief, as St. Paul says in the 10th chapter of his first letter to the Corinthians [I. Cor. x., 11]: "Now all these things happened unto them for ensamples; and they are written for our admonition." Or to put it another way: God used them as agents to punish the wicked. But that does not mean that the agents in such cases are good. God can turn evil to good. So I hope that our present misfortunes are sent by him for our improvement. When words no longer avail, the rod must be used; and if this also does not help, the headsman must finally be called in. Where God punishes there is still hope for grace, as Solomon tells us [Prov. iii., 11, 12]. Let us see to it that we learn to fear and know that such boasting, pride, and warfare, as we have been guilty of, do not please him, as is written in the 147th Psalm [Psalm cxlvii., 10, 11]: "He delighteth not in the strength of the horse: he taketh not pleasure in the legs of a man. The Lord taketh pleasure in them that fear him, in those that hope in his mercy." He inveighs against those who believe that everything depends upon their advice and counsel: Isaiah in the eighth chapter [Isaiah viii., 9, 10]: "Associate yourself, O ye people, and ye shall be broken in pieces; and give ear, all ye of far countries: gird yourselves, and ye shall be broken in pieces: Take counsel together, and it shall come to nought; speak the word, and it shall not stand." In short [Prov. xxi., 30]: "There is no wisdom nor understanding nor counsel against the Lord." So much concerning the first danger which is incurred by carrying on war and depending upon one's own counsel, thus sinning against God and making no headway, but calling down divine punishment, accompanied by disgrace and misfortune.

The second danger that threatens us from the princes and warfare in their behalf is that ordinary justice and equity will disappear. Thus an old proverb says [Cicero, *Pro Milone*, cap. iv., §10]: *silent leges inter arma*, which means that where armed forces are in control ordinary law is suspended. The word martial law is merely a euphemism for force. Use it as you will, turn it and twist it as you please, it signifies force. It is said that the disobedient must be brought to reason by force of arms if they will not submit to the law. Answer: Since you raise objections derived from secular matter, I shall reply in human fashion: Yes, if in war one only injured the disobedient, or war were only waged to make one's own people obey proper demands, we could put up with it. But how do you explain the fact that you take money from a foreign lord to aid him wantonly destroy, damage, and ravage countries innocent of all guilt? Aye, help lords who ought not to be waging war at all, such as bishops, popes, abbots and other clergymen—all for the sake of money? But if instead of speaking in human fashion, we spoke as Christians, we would say that in any case it does not become us to wage war. In accordance with Christ's teachings [Matt. v., 39, 44, 45], we should pray for them which despitefully use us, and persecute us, and if someone smites us on one cheek we ought to turn him the other also. Thus we may be children of the heavenly Father. Concerning this no more just now.

Furthermore, these lords do harm, because by their gifts they lead men, however wise they be, from the path of reason and righteousness, just as Moses teaches in the sixteenth chapter of Deuteronomy [Deut. xvi., 19]: "for a gift doth blind the eyes of the wise, and pervert the words of the righteous." Oh! what thoughts may not come to us in this connection! Undoubtedly this thought, that many a good man among us has become blinded, so that he devotes all his energy and eloquence to further the praise and interests of some lord, so that the simple-minded, misled by his sweet but harmful words, might be induced to follow his lead. It is also greatly to be feared, that many of these people support and help each other, be it in court, in the council, or in the parish, in such fashion that many a worthy transaction will be subject to falsification and distortion. Of this we are warned in the fifth chapter of Isaiah [Isaiah v., 20]: "Woe unto them that call evil good, and good evil; that put darkness for light, and light for darkness." If some say that we need some lord for we are a poor people in a bleak country, it must be admitted that such is true for those who are not satisfied with simple fare and raiment, for what they want must of course originate somewhere. But if people did not try to stretch higher than the ceiling allows there would be no call for all these words. Julius Cæsar after he had conquered the Helvetians (from whom we in this Confederacy are to a large extent descended) commanded that they till their land again, because it was fertile[1]. How can that be that this land is no longer fruitful, but was so fifteen hundred and fifty years ago? Yes, our country has more, finer, and braver people than any land on the face of the earth, and there is enough produced to nourish us if we will only be content. No, the trouble with us is that we are so blinded by the money of the princes that we think little of the loss of our own flesh and blood, as long as only the prince is satisfactorily served. We care little also for the government, regardless of the fact that disobedience increases and law and order are disregarded; regardless that in time all protection of the upright and all punishment of the guilty will cease. It will come about as a result of all this that the mercenaries will gain control of the government and abuse it in any way that they may wish. Also they will compel us, though we hold ourselves not to be responsible, to say that we are doing something, and we shall be blinded so that we shall not be able to recognise our com-

[1] The exact command was that the Helvetians should return to their lands, be supplied with grain for food, and rebuild the towns and villages which they had burnt.—Cæsar, *Bell. Gall.*, I, chap. xxviii.

mon interests, and we shall not be allowed to consider and act in accordance with our rights and preferences. Understand me correctly: If a prince engages in negotiations with a council or community, and though it is not proper to offer pay or gifts, the transaction is concluded satisfactorily only by means of secret bribes; if then later on it becomes known that corruption was prevalent and it is realised that there was malfeasance in office and the like, I maintain that in such a case we owe the lord in question nothing, and in fact we are entitled to punish him for such deceit in accordance with human laws. And do not be surprised by this statement, the same is to be found even in canon law, and even if the pope himself acts as described above, nothing is due him. Read the chapters [in the *Corpus Canonici*] entitled "De Fraude," "De Falsariis," "De Proditione," and you will find in the papal writings themselves confirmations of my statements. Your Excellencies will see from this that I spoke the truth, though I was bitterly reproached for having said that I wished a hole were made in the agreement with the pope and the messenger had been given something to carry home on his back. That seemed to everyone a very unjust way to proceed. But I spoke as I did on account of the aforesaid reasons, for I knew that the pope had been secretly bribing and therefore nothing was due him. The same principle should apply in the case of every other lord. If it is found that he has gained his ends fraude egisse, *i.e.*, by fraud, one owes him no more than the Romans did Jugurtha, who by means of bribes sought to have the murder of his own brothers entirely disregarded, of which he boasted openly when leaving Rome, saying: "Oh this venal city! A merchant could attain anything he pleased if he only had enough money"; and in fact Jugurtha could have proved the truth of his own words if the upright Metellus Numidicus had not defeated and overthrown him on several occasions and thus seriously injured his cause; for too long a period had Jugurtha bred treachery in Rome by means of his money.

Warning against Control of Foreign Lords 145

And finally he fell into the hands of the Romans. Thus, in accordance with the proverb, "deceit turns upon its own creator," and it is well thus when someone attempts to commit treachery and does something behind the back of upright people.

The third danger is that evil ways are brought home and perpetuated by foreign money and wars. This we certainly can all notice, for our people have never come home from foreign wars without bringing new clothes for themselves and their women folk; also they have introduced new kinds of food, have become accustomed to larger quantities of drink, and employ new forms of swearing and cursing; in short, whatever sinful our people see, they readily learn, so that it is to be feared that unless we cease following foreign lords even more serious vices will be introduced. Furthermore, the bearing of women is made less modest and satisfactory. A woman is weak by nature and eager to have new and pretty things in the shape of ornaments, dresses, and jewels, as is proved by Dinah, who from mere curiosity went into the land of Shechem and there was defiled, as is told in the 34th chapter of Genesis [Gen. xxxiv., 1, 2]. And does it not seem that if something glittering is offered to a woman she will at least be moved thereby, if not even ruined? It is also to be feared that in time much manly strength may be lost, though this has not been noticed so far. Easy life weakens and makes cowardly, for no one wishes to give up comfort and luxury. Who has a love—one says—does not like to die. Hannibal, the most dangerous enemy of the Romans (except covetousness, which was the worst enemy of the Romans and proved their undoing), could not be conquered until he allowed the soldiers to become effeminate. But after he had been at Capua for a winter[1] and permitted the soldiers to disport themselves in wantonness and lust, in the next spring Hannibal began to be defeated, and it was generally said that Hannibal had led an army of men to Capua and

[1] The winter of 216–215 B.C.

was taking a crowd of women away. What do you suppose finally results from all these golden undervests, rings, and silken clothing? Hector reproached his brother Alexander bitterly that he had always lived so luxuriously, maintaining that it had led to his flight from his enemy Menelaus.[1]

The fourth danger is that the gifts of the great lords will breed hate and deceit among us. For envy is the companion of good fortune, so that wherever great comfort prevails, envy immediately is created. And the envy grows apace, whenever one has much more than another. But when want prevails one honest man is as good as another, and the lowest often fight more bravely for their country than the upper classes. And after envy comes also the discord and disgust of those who say: You go ahead, you do this or that; if you gather more money, you ought to gather more of the blows also. In short, war of pious men and money is a school for all sins and a mother which bears us in old age (provided we attain it at all) only bad consciences.

The last danger is that it is to be feared that we may fall into the power of princes, either of those who are in alliance with us or into the power of those who are our enemies. For what is not all to be feared when pride, lack of energy, envy, and discord prevail everywhere? And if we should reach a stage where we are measured by a standard with which we have measured others, we could not bewail sufficiently our lot, but would say like Jeremiah in the ninth chapter [Jer. ix., 1]: "Oh that my head were waters, and mine eyes a fountain of tears, that I might weep day and night for the slain of the daughter of my people." May God forbid that it should happen to us as to the Israelites, who would heed no warning until finally they were in captivity and stealthily sat by the rivers and bemoaned their fate [Psalm cxxxvii., 1].

Therefore, pious, wise, faithful, beloved men of Schwyz, I call upon you by the suffering and redemption of our

---

[1] *Iliad*, III., 39 *ff.*

Warning against Control of Foreign Lords 147

Saviour Jesus Christ, by the honour shown by the Almighty to our worthy ancestors, by the exertion and hardships that they underwent for the sake of our liberty, beware while there is still time; of the money of these clerical lords, which will destroy us and do not follow those who say: It cannot be done; the Confederacy still stands; the display of temper which has arisen is only such as occurs often in a quarrel between husband and wife or in a quarrel among brothers and is not due to any feeling of enmity. Furthermore, we have as many inhabitants as ever; may God protect them! And everything can be easily adjusted if you go about it in good faith and sensibly. At your side you will have our good people of Zurich, the city as well as the countryside, whom I surely hope that in future no lord will be able to induce to make any of these dangerous and harmful agreements. May God confirm them in their good intentions! Furthermore, you have your worthy dependents whose honesty also causes them to shrink from foreign lords. And if you will only walk again in the footsteps of our God-fearing ancestors, I have no doubt that a united Confederacy will be behind you. For if we do not change our present habits, I fear me that we shall suffer severely; yea, I can say in the words of Christ that as others have perished so shall we also perish. See the 13th chapter of St. Luke, where it was told him of some whom Pilate had slain while they were sacrificing, whereupon Jesus said [Luke xiii., 1–3]: "Suppose ye that those Galileans were sinners above all the Galileans, because they suffered such things? I tell you, Nay: but, except ye repent, ye shall all likewise perish." What shall we think, except that a large part are to blame? since we cannot hope that Christ will say in the same way that he does not refer to us. Therefore we should see to it that we reform. For if Christ cited a foreign people as an example to show the Israelites that they must reform, how much more are we, who are warned by the harm done to our own flesh and blood, in need of reform? otherwise the rest will come true [Luke xiii., 3]: "except ye repent, ye shall all likewise perish." Do not worry about the loss of riches. Those are worthless riches in order to obtain which one must perish. Such wealth is nothing more or less than bait by which people are caught like birds in a trap. Nor must you worry about lack of foreign assistance, but say with St. Paul [Rom. viii., 31]: "If God be for us, who can be against us?" Our forefathers were worse off in this respect than we and still got along. The fortifications at Arth and Näfels are no longer needed, the Rhine is a sufficient defence. All such fortifications are useless, unless God protects his people, which, however, he promises to do, saying [Hosea i., 7]: "But I will have mercy upon the house of Judah (those who recognise God), and will save them by the Lord their God, and will not save them by bow, nor by sword, nor by battle, by horses, nor by horsemen." Bethink yourselves of the beginnings of our Confederacy, how he helped our simple ancestors in exactly the manner related above. Just as he said to the children of Israel [Lev. xxvi., 3 *ff*]: "If ye walk in my statutes, and keep my commandments and do them, . . . I will give peace in the land. And ye shall chase your enemies, and they shall fall before you by the sword. And five of you shall chase an hundred, and an hundred of you shall put ten thousand to flight," etc. [Lev. xxvi., 14 *ff*]: "But if ye will not hearken unto me, and will not do all these commandments; and if ye shall despise my statutes, . . . I will set my face against you, and ye shall be slain before your enemies: they that hate you shall reign over you and ye shall flee when none pursueth you." See you what he promises and what he threatens? He will surely keep his word; he does not lie. If we do not follow him, when he is warning us quietly and gently, the time will come when we shall be ashamed on account of our pride. All God-fearing people should call earnestly upon the Lord that he may answer our prayers and cause us to improve. It does not matter that there are many who resist; God is more powerful

Warning against Control of Foreign Lords

than all of them. Let us not cease imploring him by earnest prayer; he will grant us an upright mind and good understanding, and lead us from evil ways into paths of righteousness. Such are the ways of the Lord. Amen.

Schwyz, beware of foreign lords, they will only cause you disgrace.

XII

PETITION OF CERTAIN PREACHERS OF SWITZERLAND TO THE MOST REVEREND LORD HUGO, BISHOP OF CONSTANCE, THAT HE WILL NOT SUFFER HIMSELF TO BE PERSUADED TO MAKE ANY PROCLAMATION TO THE INJURY OF THE GOSPEL, NOR ENDURE LONGER THE SCANDAL OF HARLOTRY, BUT ALLOW THE PRIESTS TO MARRY WIVES OR AT LEAST WOULD WINK AT THEIR MARRIAGES[1]

(JULY 2, 1522)

TO the Most Reverend Father and Lord in Christ, Hugo of Hohenlandenberg, Bishop of Constance, the undersigned offer obedient greeting.

---

[1] [Suplicatio (*sic*) quorundam apud Helvetios euangelistarum ad R. D. Hugonem episcopum Constantiesem ne se induci patiatur, ut quicquam in preiudicium euangelii promulget neve scortiationis scandalum ultra ferat, sed presbyteris uxores ducere permittat aut saltem ad eorum nuptias conniveat. In Schuler and Schulthess ed., iii., 17–25. In Egli and Finsler ed., i., 197–209. Translated by Mr. Henry Preble.

This and the succeeding treatise are almost identical in contents, but the first was in Latin and addressed to the bishop of Constance, and the second in German and addressed to the Diet. The suppliants were perfectly aware that they would receive no answer. The bishop had no authority to grant any such request and the Diet would surely not presume to mitigate an ecclesiastical ordinance. What they hoped to effect was the creation of a popular sentiment in favour of allowing the preaching of the new views, and especially, for this is what they really most desired, the marriages which they intended to make or had made.

The enforced celibacy of the clergy has always been a ground of complaint by both clergy and laity, and the source of much immorality. But the idea underlying it is noble. An ideal clergy is one wholly devoted to the Church, finding in her the complete satisfaction of their intellectual and spiritual nature and in her service their joy and peace. This devotion is more easily obtained in the celibate state, as the Apostle Paul declares (I

Petition anent the Marriage of Priests

Your Excellency will perhaps wonder, Most Reverend Father, what this unusual action of writing a letter to yourself means, and not without reason. For nature has ordained that the unexpected should create not only wonder, but at times even a feeling of dumfoundedness. Yet we would have you to be entirely free and undisturbed in regard to this matter which we are laying before you. For we do not come to your Excellency in regard to anything very troublesome, but to find help. For we are so sure that you are both a most pious lord and a most loving father that there is nothing we do not promise ourselves from you. And this the fact itself shows, for we should never have ventured to write to your Fatherhood unless we had had thorough confidence in it. We desire, therefore, humbly to beg you to listen kindly to what we are going to disclose a little later, to hear it graciously, and to take it in good part. This is demanded both by the matter itself, which drives us to this appeal, and by the office which you fill as a loving father. The matter itself, to come to it at last, is this: Your Most Reverend Fatherhood knows how for a long time the heavenly teachings which God, the Creator of all things, willed to have made plain unto the poor race of men by one no way inferior to himself, by his Son, in all things his equal, have, not without the utmost loss to the cause of salvation, been lying hidden through the ignorance, not to say evil intentions, of certain persons, and how rudely, when he had determined to recall and renew those teachings in our day by a sort of second revelation, certain persons attack or defend them. For all the efforts of these defenders are aimed at putting an end to the whole conflict by the first onset, and if they fail in this they collapse utterly, but the attacking party are so shamelessly persistent in their contention that though thrown upon their backs by the boss of the shield of Holy Writ and pierced

---

Cor., vii., 32). But the history of those churches whose clergy are obligated to live celibate lives abundantly testifies to the impossibility of getting these clergy to be chaste.]

by the sword of the Spirit, which is the word of God, they will not yield, but would rather contend against Christ than abandon their pretensions, until they be compelled to abandon both Christ and their own pretensions, after the fashion of the Jews of old, who having fought against the living Christ till they had slain him, pursued him even when dead, till they all likewise perished themselves. And though we do not by any means willingly predict this same ill-omened end for the present misguided lot, we cannot help fearing that it may come to pass sometime, and for that we are not without reasons. For as in the old days the Jews cast out in vain from the synagogue those who believed in Christ (for the faith grew more and more each day), so in these days of ours, if any continue to frighten away or even to destroy the real heralds of Christ, they will meet with the same result. Therefore must the words of Gamaliel[1] be pounded into them often, that they may keep their hands off of those who bring us the commands of heaven. For if it be of God it cannot be destroyed, for it were folly for any to try to fight against God; but if it be of men it will perish of itself. Meanwhile most watchful care should be taken lest, as those poor wretches perished miserably in their doomed city, some disaster overwhelm us unawares. For the word of God has never been disregarded with safety. Therefore, Most Reverend Father, we beseech you by our Lord Jesus Christ, not to join those who aim at putting under a bushel, nay, at extinguishing, the light that came into the world to illumine all men, and who call evil good and good evil, turning sweet into bitter and light into darkness,[2] but rather to join those who have this one desire, that the whole concourse of Christians return to their head, which is Christ, and form one body in him, and, having received the Spirit of God, recognise the blessings bestowed upon them by God.[3] And this we see is by no means the case with those who promise themselves

[1] Acts v., 34 ff.
[2] Isa. v., 20.
[3] Col. i., 18; I Cor. xii., 12 ff.; Eph. iv., 16.

Petition anent the Marriage of Priests 153

some sort of peace, if human prescriptions be set before Christ even. In God we ought to be made one, for He Himself is one. In man, who is constantly divided against himself, how is it possible that we be made one? Christ prayed to the Father to make us one in him, and shall man dare to promise us unity in him?[1] In one God, in one faith, in one baptism we shall certainly be made one, for these are one. In some one man, when there are so many laws contradicting each other and such divergent opinions, so far are we from being made one that in no surer way can we be led astray into error and disagreement than in this. Nay, we see one and the same man often at variance with himself in these points.

Those things that we have just set forth and all other things that urge us to unity, whence can they be more clearly and purely got than from their very fountain head? He that draweth from that shall abound in the water that springs forth into everlasting life. But the well is deep, and we have nothing to draw with, unless he who is eager to be drawn brings us rope and bucket and windlass, and after the manner of Moses, graciously opens a well for our feeble souls, at which the thirsty sheep may drink and be led back to the heavenly pastures, which surely are found in no other corner of the universe than in the Gospel.[2] For what other fountain head is there than Christ himself, who invites us to himself freely, saying: "If anyone thirsteth, let him come to me and drink."[3] For he desires that we all receive of his abundance, we who are in need of all things. For we have neither silver nor gold wherewith to satisfy him, but he urges us to hasten to him with joyfulness, to drink freely. Who has ever shown himself so liberal an innkeeper among men as to suffer his wine to be poured out and distributed without charge save Christ alone, who

[1] John xvii., 20 ff.
[2] It would seem that Zwingli here made a slip. He meant Jacob (see John iv., 6), not Moses.
[3] John vii., 37.

bestows his blessings free so plentifully? And if we shall not seize the favour that offers itself to us thus freely, what hope awaits us? What excuse, pray, shall we make? Of what tortures shall we not judge ourselves worthy if we repel from us him who desires to become so near a friend? We are aware that our life differs all too widely from the pattern of the Gospel, but is the Gospel on that account to be abolished and done away with? Ought we not rather to devote ourselves vigorously to correcting our faults according to its standard and to subduing our feebleness, since it is the one thing, could we only believe it, from the inspiration of which salvation will come to us, according to the command of Christ when he sent forth his Apostles to preach the Gospel with these words: "Preach the Gospel (not your own theories or decrees or the regulations which some chance shall happen to dictate) to every creature." And he added: "Whosoever believeth" (the Gospel which has been preached, that is), "and is baptised, shall be saved," and on the other hand, "Whosoever believeth not, shall be damned."[1] Since therefore, as we have said, God, as of old he used to warn Israel time and again by the mouth of his prophets, now deigns in our day to illumine us with his Gospel, in order to renew his covenant which cannot be annulled, we have thought that this opportunity ought by no means to be neglected, nay, that we ought to strive with unremitting effort that as many as possible may share in the glory of this salvation. And inasmuch as meanwhile a report reaches us that by the wickedness of certain persons your heart has been so hardened that you mean shortly to put forth a proclamation warning us to turn aside from the Gospel if in any part it shall prove at variance with human tradition, though the report hardly deserves credence among us, yet we are moved somewhat, not indeed to hesitate in slothful fear, but to pity your lot, if things are as they are commonly reported, that this pestiferous class of men, who confound all things

[1] Mark xvi., 15 *ff*.

to serve their own purposes, have been able to extend their influence even to yourself. But heaven forbid! For we place such high hope in you that we doubt not we shall do a thing acceptable to you if we shall show the utmost faithfulness in the interests of the Gospel. For we cannot in any way be persuaded that you desire to see the duty that belongs peculiarly to your office neglected and abandoned. For Christ sent you not to baptise nor to anoint, but to preach the gospel. May heaven bless our undertaking! We have determined to spread abroad the knowledge of the Gospel with uninterrupted effort, and to do it so seasonably that none shall have a right to complain that we have done him any injury. But if we shall not attain a prosperous issue in this according to the judgment of men, there is no cause to wonder. For it is a rock of offence and a stumbling-block and a sign that is proving false. For he came unto his own, and his own received him not.

For these reasons it is becoming that your Fatherhood should look with favour upon our vigorous efforts, which though perhaps uncommon are by no means unconsidered, and that you should not only permit but help and advance this business, which is Christ's, not ours. That will be above all things honourable and worthy of a bishop. Nay it will belong to you, not to take upon your shoulders some part merely of the work undertaken, but, like Moses, to lead the way and to beat back or destroy the obstacles, so far at least as you can; and you can by encouraging and urging men to this task, or, if that is too much, by approving and favouring it, and removing grounds of offence.

For among the things that threaten most to harm the budding teachings of Christ are grounds of offence. For how, by the everlasting God, will the simple-minded commons believe in him who even while he preaches the Gospel is thought by them to be licentious and a shameless dog? Can anything happen more disastrous to our sacred calling? We beg you, therefore, to show yourself as indulgent towards the second part of our petition as we believe you to be.

We think that your most Reverend Fatherhood is not unaware how unsuccessfully and scantily the prescriptions in regard to chastity that have come down to our times from our predecessors have been kept by the general run of priests, and oh, that they could have vouchsafed us strength to keep their commands as easily as they gave them! Yet God willed not that this be granted to man, that this gift of gods and angels might not be put down to the credit of man, but of God only. For this is plainly shown by the words of Christ (Matthew xix., 10–12) when, after much discussion had taken place between himself and the Pharisees with regard to marriage, and his disciples said that, if the case were such as the discussion showed, it were better not to marry, he answered that not all men were capable of chastity, but only those to whom it had been given, wishing to show that it was a gift of God that was given to some men in such wise that they might recognise that the **divine goodness** and not their own strength was of avail in this thing. And this is evidently indicated by what follows a little later, when, having made particular mention of eunuchs, he leaves it free to every man to keep or not to keep the law of chastity, saying, "He that is able to receive it, let him receive it." He meant, no doubt, that they to whom it was granted from above were bound to keep the law. For otherwise none could hold out under it. We, then, having tried with little enough success alas! to obey the law (for the disease must be boldly disclosed to the physician), have discovered that the gift has been denied unto us, and we have meditated long within ourselves how we might remedy our ill-starred attempts at chastity.[1] And turning the matter over on all sides, we found nothing encouraging or propitious until we began to chew the cuds, as it were, like the cattle, over those words of Christ just quoted. For then a sort of loathing of ourselves began to creep over us from the odour of it until we began to be disgusted that through careless thinking we had made a law unto ourselves of that which

---

[1] *Cf.* letter of Zwingli to Heinrich Utinger, Dec. 5, 1518. (vii., 110 *ff*).

Christ had left free, as if the maintenance of chastity depended upon our own strength. Then presently a blush of shame overspread our faces, just as Adam, when he was going to be like the gods, found first nothing but his own nakedness,[1] then an angry God, and shortly after a whole cart-load of ills. For who would not repent when he had looked upon the pitiable result of his own carelessness? For what else is it, by the everlasting God! than absolute folly, nay even, shamelessness, to arrogate to one's self what belongs to God alone? To think one's self able to do that than which there is nothing one is less able to do? But after that loathing of ourselves through which we recognised at once our rashness and our weakness, the hope of a remedy began to show itself, though from afar. For weighing more carefully Christ's words and the custom of our predecessors in this matter, we found that the whole question was far easier than we had thought. For when he says, "All men cannot receive this saying," and again, "He that is able to receive it, let him receive it," he prescribes no punishment for them that cannot receive it. Nay, either because of the vastness of the thing which he did not wish enjoined upon each and all, or on account of our weakness, which he knows better than we ourselves, he did not want this thing laid up against us, and so left it free. Therefore our souls which had been nigh unto despair were mightily refreshed when we learned those who were unable to receive the saying were threatened with no punishment by him who can send both body and soul into hell.

But the fathers seemed to have cast an anxious eye in this direction too, when they showed themselves unwilling to enjoin chastity upon all without exception, or to require a vow of chastity from others—the priests, at least—and even shielded human weakness with clever words, as was proper, in this way: When the sponsor who was accustomed to make answer for all who were to be confirmed was asked, "Are they righteous, these whom you present?" he was wont to answer:

[1] Gen. iii., 10.

"They are righteous." "Are they well trained?" "They are well trained," etc. When, however, they came to chastity—"Are they chaste?" he answered, "As far as human frailty allows." Thus it appears that neither our predecessors nor the fathers in our own day wanted that bound hard and fast which Christ had suffered to be free, lest they might smear the sweet yoke of the Lord with bitter wormwood.

Having, I say, thus balanced these considerations, to wit, that we are held to the maintenance of chastity by neither divine nor human law, we considered nevertheless that though chastity go free, yet animal passion ought not to roam promiscuously, but to be bounded by rule and constancy, and forced into reasonable limits, like the rest of the course of our life, which though free becomes wildness and confusion, unless it be restrained by moderation, that we sink not to the level of swine. And this we see the Maker of all things willed from the beginning of creation, when he fashioned for Adam from his rib one woman only as a helpmeet and not a group or crowd of women, and joined her presently by so firm a bond that a man leaves father and mother sooner than his wife, for the two unite to form one flesh. Futhermore if we run through the whole of the New Testament we find nowhere anything that favours free concubinage, but everything in approval of marriage. Therefore it appears to us most true and most right that for a Christian no third possibility besides chastity or marriage is left, and that he should live chastely if that is given unto him from above, or marry a wife if he be on fire with passion, and this we shall show more clearly in a little while from the truly sacred writings. Hence we beseech your mercy, wisdom, and learning, illustrious Leader, to show yourself the first to lay hold upon the glory of taking the lead over all the bishops of Germany in right thinking upon Christianity, since you see Christ bestowing especial favour upon this age of ours and revealing himself more clearly than for several ages since, while from the whole great body of bishops scarcely one or two thus far have shown themselves fairly on the side of the revivified Christianity, and while others continue to thrust ill-feigned chastity upon the unfortunate general body of our fellow bishops, do you suffer those who are consumed with passion to marry wives, since this, as has been shown, will be lawful according to Christ and according to the laws of men. From the whole vast crowd we are the first to venture to come forward, relying upon your gentleness and to implore that you grant us this thing, not, as we think, without due consideration. For when on one side we were being crushed by human ordinances, struggling in vain against the weakness of the flesh (for the law stimulates to sin rather than restrains it), and on the other, Scripture was smiling upon us with approval, we thought it no wrong to bring forward the passages on which we rely, that it might be evident to you whether we treated them intelligently or not, and when it appeared, as we hoped, that we had employed the Scriptures righteously, that you would grant what we ask for in all humility.

The first passage of all that makes us free and that we trust to as to a sacred anchor is Matthew xix. For we reason thus from it: If Christ willed that chastity be free to us, good-by to the man who tries to make a law of it. The demonstration of the second is: If at the voice of God Peter feared to call that common which God had purified,[1] we may boldly declare that it is not right for any man to declare that that is not lawful which God has suffered to be lawful. For if in that which is of little account God was unwilling to accept the judgment of Peter, how much less in a matter of much greater moment will he accept the judgment of one inferior to Peter? Our feeling on this point is clear enough from what has gone before, when we add that the words of Christ on the subject we are speaking of are the words of him who is the way and the truth and the life.[2] For he says in another place, "The words which I have spoken are spirit and life."[3] How then were it not lawful and safe to trust to them? Nay we shall believe

[1] Acts x., 15.   [2] John xiv., 6.   [3] John vi., 63.

accursed rather than merely wicked anything that shall have been sought out to contradict the words of God. They are spirit and life, the things that he has said. Therefore what we say is flesh and death. The second passage is Paul to the Corinthians I., ch. vii., 1 and 2: "It is good for a man not to touch a woman. Nevertheless, to avoid fornication, let every man have his own wife, and let every woman have her own husband." Here first we concluded that he would be blest to whom it had been given of God to be able to do without a wife. And while we willingly yield this glory to those who live chastely, we are grieved that it has been denied unto us, though we bear it patiently with God's help. Next as to the point that, to avoid fornication, every man should have his own wife. He who said "every man" made exceptions of none, neither priest nor monk nor layman. Hence it is clear, as we hinted above, that for a Christian there is nothing between chastity and marriage. He must either live chastely or marry a wife. The third passage is in the same chapter, verse 9: "If they cannot contain, let them marry: for it is better to marry than to burn." Therefore if one cannot contain one's self, if one burns, let him marry. We have been so on fire from passion—with shame be it said!—that we have done many things unseemly, yet whether this should not be laid upon those to some extent who have forbidden marriage we refrain from saying now, thinking it enough that the fire of passion alone (and that so frequent and violent as to threaten the mind) is pronounced sufficient reason for marriage. The fourth passage is verse 25 in the same chapter: "Now concerning virgins I have no commandment of the Lord; yet I give my judgment," etc. Paul, the teacher of the nations, the chosen instrument of God, with whom Christ had spoken intimately from heaven more than once, says that he has no commandment of the Lord in regard to virginity, and has an unpurified man such commandment? Then too Paul had said much of the value of virginity and its advantages, and much of the trials and unhappiness of marriage, and he added, verse 35, "And this I speak for your own profit; not that I may cast a snare upon you," wishing, though he had greatly praised the state of virginity, not to seem of opinion that it ought to be commanded. The fifth passage is I. Timothy iii., 1 *ff.*: "This is a true saying, If a man desire the office of a bishop, he desireth a good work. A bishop then must be blameless, the husband of one wife," etc. And a little later he adds, "having his children in subjection with all gravity." Here we noted that though it is a thing of high repute to be a bishop, yet he bids a bishop have a wife, whether one only, or one at a time we will not now discuss. We noted also that the name bishop is the name of an office, not one of arrogant pride, and therefore we had no fear to call ourselves also bishops, that is, watchers, because the other terms which are in common use to-day either seem over-ambitious or are foreign words. With the name of watcher, however, how can anyone be puffed up? Can he think it a state of high dignity and not a position of duty when the only function of a watcher is to watch? The sixth passage is from the same Paul to Titus, i., 5 and 6: "For this cause left I thee in Crete, that thou shouldest set in order the things that are wanting, and ordain elders in every city; if any be blameless, the husband of one wife, having faithful children," etc. And this passage is as like unto the passage above as one pea is like another. The seventh is likewise from I. Timothy, ch. iv., 1–3: "Now the Spirit speaketh expressly, that in the latter times some shall depart from the faith, giving heed to seducing spirits and doctrines of devils, speaking lies in hypocrisy, having their conscience seared with a hot iron, forbidding to marry," etc. Here we would have those prick up their ears who make a fine show of chastity and keep it ill; for what they do secretly is wicked even to think of. The Spirit speaking in Paul says that in the latter days, in which we are no doubt also included, it shall come to pass that some will turn away from the faith unto their own works which are not of God. Also that this shall happen at the instigation of evil spirits who shall speak things good in appearance only, and shall commend them especially by the mouths of those who go about in sheep's clothing raging like wolves, and therefore they have ever been singed in their own eyes and condemned by their own judgment. And they shall forbid marriage. Behold, Most Reverend Father, the origin of their feigned chastity! The eighth passage is Heb., ch. xiii, 4: "Marriage is honourable in all, and the bed undefiled; but whoremongers and adulterers God will judge." This passage seems so clearly to confirm our contention that we think it the duty of bishops (granted that they be watchers) to drive into marriage those whom they have detected in fornication. For fornication must be met, because besides exposing one to judgment it also offends one's neighbour.

Influenced then by these passages we are at length persuaded that it is far more desirable if we marry wives, that Christ's little ones may not be offended, than if with bold brow we continue rioting in fornication. To this your Highness will no doubt agree when you reflect that the sin of him who offends one of the little ones of Christ can scarcely be atoned for, even though a millstone be hung about his neck and he be cast into the depths of the sea. And what, pray, is a stumbling-block of offence, if the shameless fornication of priests is not a stumbling-block of offence? And let your Highness not deign to listen to those who snap out like this: Behold, Most Reverend Fathers, the religion of these men! What else are they after than turning the freedom of Christ into the lust of the flesh, according to the judgment of Paul to the Galatians, v., and of I Peter ii., 16? For to make no mention now of how the cohabitation of marriage is regarded by God, although we do not deny that the act proceeds distinctly from the flesh, yet we know that it is far from harmful, since Paul says (I. Corinthians vii., 28): "And if a virgin marry she hath not sinned," because God no doubt looks without anger upon this thing on account of our weakness, or rather the sin dwelling in us. And the same Paul (Galatians v., 19) reckons it not among the works of the flesh. Yet this answer is not necessary, since it is clearly evident that if we had wished to indulge in this thing for pleasure's sake, we should never have allowed ourselves to be tied up with the halter of wives when thus, besides suffering countless arrogances, we are cut off from the opportunity of making good the unpleasantness and other drawbacks of a long married life. But since most of us fill the office of bishops, in which above all things there should be no room for grounds of offence (for a bishop ought to be blameless, as has been made clear above), we have all tried to see how we could cease from the offence, while in other respects (if we may speak freely without boasting) we are not of such untutored morals as to be in ill repute among the flock entrusted to us for any other failing save this one alone. For the sake of Christ the Lord of all of us, therefore, by the liberty won by his blood, by the fatherly affection which you owe to us, by your pity of our feeble souls, by the wounds of our consciences, by all that is divine and all that is human, we beseech you mercifully to regard our petition and to grant that which was thoughtlessly built up be thoughtfully torn down, lest the pile constructed not in accordance with the will of our heavenly Father fall some time with a far more destructive crash. You see what the world threatens.

Therefore your Fatherhood ought to regard it as wise foresight and not unreasonableness that we come to petition you. For unless wise aid be applied in many places it will be all up with the whole body of ecclesiastics. And please do not refer us to the decrees of the predecessors of your Fatherhood. For you see how they fail to meet the case, and delay in the hope that though we have been first beaten with rods we can then presently endure the sting of scorpions.[1] Our weakness must be indulged, nay, something must be ventured in this matter. O happy the invincible

[1] 1 Kings xii., 11.

race of Hohenlandenberg, if you shall be the first of all the bishops in Germany to apply healing to our wounds and restore us to health! For what historian will ever pass over the achievement unmentioned? What scholar will not trumpet it abroad? What poet will not sing it to coming generations? What embalming will not protect it from decay and destruction? The door of well doing is surely open before you. You have only to take care lest you do not hold your hands firmly clasped and so let the offered opportunity slip through them. For we presage that things are going to put on a new face whether we will or no, and when this happens we shall lament in vain having neglected the opportunity of winning glory. We have on the side of our request that Creator who made the first human beings male and female; we have the practice of the Old Testament, which is much more strict than the New, under which, however, even the highest priests took upon their necks the gentle yoke of matrimony; we have Christ, who makes chastity free, nay, bids us marry, that his little children may not be offended, and our petition meets with loud approval on all sides. Nay, even Paul, speaking with the spirit of God, enjoins marriage. All the company of the pious and judicious are with us. If you disregard all this we know not how you can embrace your race with affection, for you will surpass their brave deeds, and win more than their laurels and statues, if you only grant us this favour. If, however, you cannot possibly be persuaded to grant it, we beseech you at least not to forbid it, according to the suggestion of another than ourselves. For we think you are brave enough to do right without fear of those who can even slay the body. And in fact you will have to refrain at least from interfering. For there is a report that most of the ecclesiastics have already chosen wives, not only among our Swiss, but among all peoples everywhere, and to put this down will certainly be not only beyond your strength but beyond that of one far more mighty, if you will pardon our saying so. Accordingly, scorn us not as of little ac-

Petition anent the Marriage of Priests

count; even a rustic often speaks very much to the point. And though we be but little children, we are yet Christ's, and, far from scorning us, you may confidently trust that salvation will be yours if you receive us. As to ourselves, we shall never cease to sing your praises if you but show yourself a father to us, and shall render you willing and glad obedience. Grant a gift to your children, who are so obedient that they come to you before all things, and so trusting that in this matter, however difficult it is thought to be, they have ventured to appeal to you only. The Most High God long preserve your Excellency in prosperity and in the knowledge of God! We pray with all humility that you will take all we have said in a spirit of justice and kindness.

Einsiedeln, Switzerland, July 2d, 1522.

Your Most Reverend Fatherhood's most obedient servants,

BALTHASAR TRACHSEL,
GEORG STÄHELIN (Calybeus),
WERNER STEINER,
LEO JUD,
ERASMUS FABRICIUS,
SIMON STUMPF,
JODOC KILCHMEYER,
HULDREICH PISTORIS (Pfister),
CASPAR MEGANDER (Grossmann),
JOHN FABER (Hans Schmid).
HULDREICH ZWINGLI.[1]

---

[1] These were all prominent clergymen. It is incredible that they were the only priests who were unchaste or had made clerical marriages. Trachsel of Arth was dean of the Chapter of the Four Cantons; Calybeus (Stähelin), of Galgenen, later pastor of Freienbach, canton Schwyz; Steiner, priest of Zug; Jud, the well-known friend of Zwingli, then people's priest at Einsiedeln; Fabricius, priest of Stein on the Rhine, the one to whom Zwingli sent his account of the visit of the delegation from the Bishop of Constance; Stumpf, priest at Höngg, canton Zurich; Kilchmeyer, a canon of Lucern; Pistoris (Pfister), pastor of Uster, canton Zurich; Megander (Grossmann), chaplain of the hospital attached to the Dominican monastery; Faber (Schmid), a canon of the Great Minster, Zurich.

XIII

A Friendly Request and Exhortation of Some Priests of the Confederates that the Preaching of the Holy Gospel be not Hindered, and also that no Offence be Taken if to Avoid Scandal the Preachers were Given Permission to Marry

(July 13, 1522)

[Ein früntlich bitt und ermanung etlicher priesteren der Eidgnoschafft, das man das heylig euangelium predigen nit abschlahe, noch unwillen darab empfach, ob die predgenden ergernus zu vermiden sich eelich vermächlind. Translated by Lawrence A. McLouth, Professor of German, New York University. In Schuler and Schulthess ed., i., 32–51; in Egli and Finsler ed., i., 210–248.

Of all the documents which have come down to us from the Reformation this and its predecessor will strike a modern Protestant minister as two of the most extraordinary. It is a pity that Zwingli confounds in these two petitions two words which should be kept separate—chastity and celibacy. What priests and monks and nuns take is not a vow of chastity, but of celibacy. That is they engage not to marry.]

TO the pious, provident, honourable, wise, members of the cantons, lands, and neighbouring districts, our gracious favourable and dear lords, we, some of the priests and heralds of the Gospel of Jesus, offer our obedient, willing service and submission in the Lord Jesus Christ our Saviour.

Pious, provident, etc., hearers, our first humble request is, that your Wisdom will not at once take offence on account of the petition, which we bring before you as before our fathers, although it may appear at first strange or unfair.

We hope, that, when you thoroughly understand the matter according to our explanation, you will act in the case, having put aside all astonishment or displeasure, just as happened to St. Paul, Acts xvii., 17. When at Athens he began to preach of our Lord Jesus Christ and the resurrection of the dead, they laughed at him first; but, after they thoroughly understood the matter, many of them were converted to the Christian belief, especially one of the highest magistrates called Dionysius and a noble lady, Damaris. And so we also hope that when the subject is heard to the end, all of your reasonable hearts will become favourable. And it is a fact —in order that the matter may not longer be delayed—that we have heard that some of our lords of the Assembly have viewed it as wrong that one should preach the holy Gospel, which now goes forth through all Christendom, as though it were something new and unheard of; the blame of which action is perhaps that of those who have not been able to apply such divine doctrine most to the purpose, or have perhaps mixed with it something that does not belong to it. Otherwise we well know, that there is in the praiseworthy Assembly no one who would venture to oppose God's Word. Wherefore we have undertaken in this paper to inform everyone briefly of the contents of the Gospel lest anyone take serious offence thereat; this is done for the good of the common Assembly and for the consolation of all tender consciences.

Now the Gospel is, as Paul writes to the Romans, I., 16, nothing but the power of God for the good or welfare of each who believes, be he Jew or heathen, although from the beginning of the world it was first revealed to the Jews. He says it is the power of God. This is to be understood in this way: if one desires the good and happy life, which is revealed as coming after this life (for the philosophers also concede that, and each feels in himself that he has much anxiety and worry as to how it will be with him in the hereafter, but can find neither Him who gives happiness nor can teach the way to Him), then one always feels the need of help from one greater, stronger, wiser, and more certain than he himself is. This need and want Almighty God from the beginning of the world has known and provided for, in this, that He everywhere revealed Himself, made Himself known to us in all goodness, that we might not come in error or despair in our wondering desire for the life to come after this life. And everywhere to those who have found Him, accepted Him, and put their trust in Him, He has shown His power and presence so clearly that one can never sufficiently wonder at His mercy.

Adam He treated graciously according to the character of the matter, Abel the righteous He avenged, Enoch He translated, Noah He warned of the flood and protected, Abraham, Isaac, Jacob, Moses, David, and others innumerable He so plainly led and loved, that their names and memory even to this day show that it is all nothing but a gracious manifestation of Himself for the good of us poor human beings, and that which is called the Gospel is the same as "Good news" in German. For what better can be offered to the poor human race, if it wanders in ignorance of God and blessedness, than that which makes God known to it, guides and blesses it? Is that not the power of God and not of man? Is it not this power which brings us blessedness, and not man himself? Therefore He first revealed Himself in kindness to men, that they might learn to know Him as a father by His kindness. Therefore also Christ taught us to call Him father first of all, before we asked anything of Him, speaking thus: "Our Father," by which word we are assured that we can safely put in Him all our trust and confidence, because all comes from His power.

Since now in the Old Testament Almighty God has by His power often revealed Himself to men by conversations, miracles, and other things, so that men might at all times know God's power and grace; and since they by their wantonness and hardness of heart have alienated themselves from Him, He finally desired to arrange with the human race through

His only Son [Hebrews i., 1], who also with miracles as Nicodemus speaks, [John iii., 3], and with truth of the doctrine certainly showed that He was a son of God, in order that His abundant mercy might be more richly revealed to men. For, as He was formerly inclined in love to the Jews, so He desired through His Son to draw to Himself by kindness all the human race. This will be clearer to us, if we relate the leading works of Christ. Is it not a great and effective means of teaching humility, that the Son of God, otherwise like His Father, condescended to accept the weakness of men [Philippians, ii., 6], that we might all give up pride and come to God? That He was born poor in a manger, then brought up in the midst of hard labour, does not that teach contempt of riches, the gaining of one's bread not by violence or usury but by the work of the hands? [Ephesians iv., 28]. That He healed the sick everywhere, if they put their trust in Him, does that not teach that we should put all our trust in Him and help one another? [Galatians vi., 10]. That He suffered for us the most disgraceful death, in order that He might save us from the power of death, the control of the devil and sin, did that not surpass all human kindness? That one should perhaps die for a righteous man, as Paul writes [Romans v., 7], would be commendable, whereas He, who is righteous, suffered death for us sinners and unrighteous, does that not teach us not to depend upon our own righteousness, but alone upon His making us righteous, His saving, and His having mercy, though we are all sinners? That He on the cross in the midst of all pain and suffering called to His heavenly Father on behalf of His murderers saying: "Forgive them, for they know not what they do,"[1] does that not teach us to be without desire for revenge, without hatred, without demur? And very many other examples are heard daily from the Gospel.

Now we will hear some portions of His doctrine. Does He not teach us that we can do nothing of ourselves and are nothing, even in things which affect the body, without

[1] Luke xxiii., 34.

Him, when He says [Matthew vi., 27], "no one can add a cubit to his stature"? And we should of course understand, that if we cannot add anything to the body, over which we think we have the most power, we must in all things depend only on Him. Does He not teach us not to take thought for nourishing the body and for collecting riches, by means of the lovely figure of the flowers of the field and the birds of the air, which He clothes in beauty and feeds? All things which are necessary to our soul and bodies, does He not well teach us to ask of Him briefly with "Our Father in heaven"? Does he not teach us that the true worship of God is of all things the pleasantest to Him? [John iv., 23]: "The true worshippers shall worship the Father in spirit and in truth." Does He not teach us truly that in all worry, trouble, grief, we should come to Him? [Matthew xi., 29]: "All ye that are weary and heavy laden, come to me and I will give you rest."[1] Does He not teach us the way of justice and truth, when he says [Matthew v., 37]: "But let your communication be Yea, yea; and Nay, nay; for whatever is more than that cometh of evil"? Does He not teach us verily the way of truth, when He says, "I am the way, the truth, and the life" [John xvi., 6], and that "whoever enters through Him shall find pasture" [John x., 9]? Does He not teach us how surely to gain everlasting life when He says [John vi., 40], "Verily, verily, I say unto you, whoever believes in me, hath eternal life"? Does He not teach us how great faith we may put in His word, when He says, not a jot or a tittle shall be taken from His Word or the law, until all things therein contained be fulfilled [v., 18, and xxiv., 35]? Are not all these and many more not certain examples of good news, when the power of God is opened to human weakness?

As before stated, the mercy of God was never more richly revealed than through the Lord Jesus Christ our Saviour, and for this reason, that we all receive of His fulness together [John i., 16], which is so great that it makes

[1] The motto of many of Zwingli's printed writings.

all men, which ever have been, are, or shall be, rich in God, innocent, and blessed. [Hebrews x.]. For no other name is there under the sun, in which we can be blessed [Acts iv., 12], than in the name of Jesus Christ. Here one is to understand not only the syllables or letters of the word "Jesus," but the being blessed in His power, in His mercy, and from His suffering, so that in the name Jesus one will understand all His being and deeds, in which we, trusting and believing, are blessed. For He came upon the earth to make sinners blessed and whole, whom He also so kindly visited, that people spoke evil of Him on that account. These he answered thus: "The well need not a physician, but the sick,"[1] showing that the pity of God is ready to bless sinners at all times, and that He came into the world to announce this and certainly to keep it. Is it good or bad news, that God has offered us His grace so mercifully, without any merit on our part, indeed when we were naturally children of wrath [Ephesians ii., 3]? Although we are all men, He has revealed to us the riches of His mercy and love, and although we were dead in sin, He has made us alive through the death of Christ, again awakened from the dead, and given heaven as a possession in Christ Jesus, so that He revealed to future men the overflowing riches of His mercy which He has so gently poured out for us through Christ Jesus. Mercifully and freely are we made whole and kept whole through faith and belief (which God has mercifully wrought in us), and that too not from us: It is a gift of God, not from our works, so that no one could boast. For we are His creatures in Jesus Christ created for good works, to which God has ordained us, that we walk therein.[2] Notice here the beautiful meaning in St. Paul, comprehending all the work of God upon us poor sinners, accomplished through His own Son, Our Lord and Saviour Jesus Christ. All that is nothing else but the Gospel, that is, the good news and the announcement of the mercy of God, which we all need. And, although He remarks: "The whole need not a physi-

[1] Luke v., 31.   [2] Eph. ii., 10.

cian," and "I am not come to call the righteous, but sinners to repentance,"[1] still it is not the meaning that anyone is righteous, but that some probably think themselves righteous. These same, as Augustine says,[2] were from the first unrighteous, and, when there was nothing else that made them unrighteous, the assumption of their own righteousness was a sufficiently great sin, as the Pharisee well shows, who boasted loudly in the temple of what he had done [Luke xviii., 11]. Therefore these above mentioned words of Paul should be carefully explained to the people by those who boast that they preach the Gospel, so that all the right can understand its power and contents.

These things briefly stated give us a little view of the Gospel, which is more clearly and more perfectly discovered in springs than in pools and puddles. The springs are the words and acts of Christ Jesus described by the Apostles Matthew, John, Luke, and Mark as much as is necessary for the blessedness of each man. For, as St. John shows, it would be impossible to describe all the words and works which Christ said and did [John xxi., 25]. Accordingly the springs are the preaching and practice of the holy Apostles, the predictions of the Prophets, and the belief of the Patriarchs. With those, however, who in these times teach the Gospel or teach by means of the Scriptures there is a great difference; for some drink from the springs themselves, and give also to others; but others cannot come to the springs, but go to the brooks, which flow from them, but always contain something mixed and dirtier than the springs themselves; and accordingly they are inclined to preach against that which is least of all, and which, although true, is still little to be considered, so that it seriously offends the young and weak in Christ. Wherefore it behooves them carefully to consider what is the most necessary to the welfare of souls and the quiet of our poor human beings. And, if they cannot attain the same by themselves, they should get advice from those who are certain of the springs,

---

[1] Luke v., 32.   [2] Explanatio libri psalmorum. Ps. xxxi., 1, 2.

not from those taught in error among experimenters and quibblers, who lead people only into greater error, but rather from those who are well informed of the right springs of the Gospel. If that had been the case from the beginning, it is well to suppose that no one, or at most very few, would have felt any displeasure.

But who they are which draw from the proper fountains, not every one can understand or know. Hence it is necessary to describe them in a figure of speech, that the simple may begin to understand. Whatever preachers exert all effort to reveal and make known the will, doctrine, meaning, and honour of God, to bring sinners to repentance, and to ease troubled consciences, disregarding their own honour, advantage, and dignity, and do this by means of the before-mentioned fountains, are, as is easy to see, of the same intent and opinion as Christ was, who sought not His own advantage but our salvation. But those who do nothing but judge their flocks, preaching only of their bringing in sacrifices, interest, and tithes, finding each day a new saint to whom sacrifices should be made, boastfully offering for sale many indulgences, filling their preaching with their own power and dignity, and telling how great therein is the power of the pope, they are, as is easy to see, more concerned about temporal good than about God's honour or the piety of the conscience. Not that one should not support a respectable dependent priesthood with offerings, tithes, and other things, but that dwelling upon this alone will show avarice.

Therefore, honourable, wise, etc., gracious and dear Lords, though some who cannot allow nourishment to be withdrawn from their arrogance, undertake to harden and vex you to the point that you should forbid the Gospel to be preached, or preached so that it injure us, or discover sad blasphemy, listen not to them, else ye certainly fall into the disfavour of God. For it is a very bad and arrogant thing when an assuming man will not be instructed by another. How much more injurious it is, when man will not harken to God, so that he proves he is not of God! What arrogance and unrighteousness the holy prophet Isaiah shows to us, xxx., 9–13. "They are a people that only arouse me to anger (he speaks in the person of God). They speak to those who are seers, See not; and to the prophets, Prophesy not unto us right things, speak unto us pleasing things; prophesy unto us error, get out of the way, and from the footpath. The holy God of Israel cease to be preached unto us! O how much evil was thereby done, as we can well see from the prophet, when he says later on: Because ye have despised the word (undoubtedly God's word) and have turned your trust into lies and disorder; therefore this iniquity shall be to you as a breach in a wall, which shall cause its sudden and unexpected fall." Surely the word of God is never disregarded without great punishment, and it has always been useful, wherever it was heard and followed, which Christ Himself very truly shows [Luke vi., 11]: "Into whatever city ye shall come, if they take you not in (the holy apostles and those preaching the Gospel are meant), go again into the street and say: The dust which has clung to us here with you, we shake off over you. But know that it will go lighter with Sodom than with that city: that is, the city which would not accept you who preached me." Also St. Peter says, II Peter ii., 20: "If one has escaped the pollutions of the world through the knowledge of the Lord Jesus Christ, and is again entangled therein and overcome, it is worse after than before." Doubtless nothing is worse for a man's soul than not to want to hear of that by which he is saved, Christ Jesus.

We should also find instructive the treatment which was accorded the disciples at the beginning of their preaching, when the Jews forbade them to preach anything of Christ. But they answered: "One must obey God rather than man" [Act. v., 29]; and they preached about it again and again, until the magistrates were angry with them. Then a wise, pious man arose, named Gamaliel, who commanded the apostles, that is, messengers, to stand apart, and said:

"Heed and consider well what ye do with these men. In the past Theudas and Judas drew to themselves a following, which however broke up with all those who held to them. Therefore depart from the people and leave them, for it is ordered of God, and so ye cannot forbid it or otherwise order it. For ye cannot overcome God; but if it is a human invertion, it will come to destruction." Thus ye should remember, gracious Lords, if one sees clearly, that Almighty God, by showing His countenance through His teaching, that is, the holy Gospels, punishes the world so wicked and desires to call it to improvement—should remember that it becomes us not to resist. For if it is of God, we cannot avert it, while if only a human invention, it will pass away of itself. Paul was stoned in Lystra so that he was left for dead; but when he came to himself again, he entered again into the city, and the city was afterward converted to Christ [Acts xiv., 19]. Likewise was he also in Corinth persecuted, but he ceased not till he had converted the city to Christ, and what he was unable to do in person he did by letters. For God spake to him at night, strengthening him [Acts xviii., 9]: "Thou shalt not fear, but speak, and be not silent, for I am with thee." Thus it was also in Ephesus.[1] There was an uprising in the whole city, so that they seized Paul's companions, Gaius and Aristarchus, and held them in the midst of the furious people, who complained that the honour of the great goddess Diana was about to pass away. And Paul was protected, so that he came not among the people, although he desired to go among them. Still finally the honour of the idol Diana and other idols was put down and that of the true God set up. For the whole city was soon after converted; and the holy Apostle and Evangelist John was buried there with great honours. This instance we exhibit to your wisdom that it may thereby learn that according to the words of Gamaliel no one can hinder the progress of the Gospel, if it is of God; and for that reason not hastened by

---

[1] Acts xix., 23 *sqq.*

anyone. For if it is not of God, it will pass away of itself.

Now, ye wise and pious men, it is our purpose truthfully to preach the holy Gospel as unadulterated as possible for the good of the common Confederation. For as things now stand, we feel the necessity of Almighty God's leading us by His teaching to a better and more pious life; for it is otherwise to be feared that should we remain continually in this condition, God would not endure it. And though we and others should be forbidden to preach the Gospel, it would not for that reason impede his progress; for we can say, as the apostles spoke, when forbidden to preach Jesus at Jerusalem [Acts v., 32]: "One must obey God rather than man." We see that certain great princes and lords, bishops and prelates, although they, as they wish to appear, do not oppose the Gospel, still make the matter vexatious and suspected, by giving to all that preach the Gospel hateful names, saying they are Lutherans, Hussites, or heretics; when there are everywhere enough learned men who, drawing from the true fountains, preach to us the divine doctrine, so that there is no need of any Hussites or Lutherans. If Luther has drunk where we have drunk, then he has in common with us the evangelical doctrine. And people see that forbidding does no good. The force of the Gospel doctrine groweth more and more. Thus we show your Wisdoms that we have nothing in common either with Luther or with anything else that could harm Christian doctrine, even nothing at all in common. As far as we are able, we drink the Gospel doctrine out of the true fountains, without which no one can be blessed, in order that among the people of the pious Confederation we may with all decency and fidelity speak for the same to hungry souls, that their despairing consciences may be set at rest and made steadfast. For no one can set at rest consciences as well as the word of God, as David shows in Psalms lxxvii., 3, 4: "My soul could not be comforted; then I thought of God, and found joy." Also Christ himself

[Matthew iv., 4]: "Man lives by every word that issues from the mouth of God." And therefore rejecting God's word would be nothing less than rejecting the comfort of one's soul: but that is not your intent, as we well know. But when any one is less skilled than he should be in preaching the Gospel, it is well to remember that it is not wrong to enjoin silence upon him. But this we do not wish to do at all (if God wills), but for the benefit of believers preach truly and faithfully the Gospel, which nothing can harm more (in not following) than lewdness or sin, or above all sins unchastity. Therefore we wish now to speak to your Wisdom of this same thing for the second part.

Your honoured Wisdom has seen up to this time the dishonourable shameful life which alas! we have led till now with women (we would speak of ourselves alone), so that we have vexed and angered many, although the fault is partly youthful blood, which no one can entirely control, partly those, who have never wished to command false hypocritical chastity to cease, even though they have seen that chastity was not kept even as God well shows. And the same ones could have disregarded the command, for it is only a human law, not a divine command; yes, they should have disregarded it, because they saw that it was nowhere kept and that much disgrace and vexation to the holy Gospel arose from it. But that this never happened, is to be considered as coming from the fact that it brought some of them much profit. For when one must give 2, 3, or 4 gulden for absolution, how large a sum of money do you think would come in in a year[1]? There arises then here a very great suspicion concerning hypocritical chastity, that it is considered more on account of money than on account of God's will. For among the old Christians no one was made priest till he was over thirty years, and it was proper for them to live in matri-

---

[1] Not only was this tax on priest's concubines exacted yearly, but four or five gulden was exacted for each child born of these unions. About 1500 children were thus paid for in a single year, so general was priestly concubinage. See the note of the Swiss editors, i., 225.

mony like any one else. But later they decreased the age, made it twenty-four, and at the same time forbid wives.[1] May each one see how those circumstances hang together, or how wise it appears, that the age is decreased, and that in the midst of all carnal attacks that are the worst at the twenty-fourth year wives were not allowed, without any grounding in Holy Writ, which nowhere forbids priests to marry but in some places recommends it, as we will shortly show your Wisdom, so that you may see in what our principle is grounded concerning the marriage which we desire to contract, but without injury and vexation to you.[2]

First Christ Jesus our Saviour speaks of chastity [Matthew xix., 10], saying that not every one is fit to use this word, save those to whom it is given by God. Here any one sees that it is not for us but for God to preserve chastity. How now can men command that which is only for God? Just as though one would live from the purse of another, whether he would or not. Thus God desired to keep the heavenly virtue of chastity in His own power, so that man might not proudly assume it or boast of it, but should view it as God's alone. For nothing is more unpleasant to God than a proud spirit, which easily seduces those who keep chastity into pleasing themselves by boasting as follows, saying to themselves: How blest thou art! that thou art not like those who cannot live without doing such things! How much purer and better art thou than they! But with all that no one can know how pure the heart within is. For as long as we wear this most faulty body it is certain that it will attack us in many ways; yes, even by those whom one considers quite chaste, much greater wickedness is alas! committed, than where marriage had occurred. We do not wish to appear as attacking those pious souls, pure from God's gift, recognising that in them with gratitude;

---

[1] For the discussion of the Church's position on the marriage of the clergy, see Emil Friedrich, *Lehrbuch des katholischen und evangelischen Kirchenrechts*. 5th ed., Leipzig, 1903, pp. 158 *ff*.

[2] Almost all the signatories to this petition were married within a year after signing it or were married at the time.

but we complain about the trouble, that, since God has not given us to live chaste lives, men act so hard toward us, in that they trouble us in our weakness which we have in common with them, with the dishonouring statement that that is not proper for us which is proper for all.

Secondly Christ speaks again in the same place [Matt. xix., 12]: "whoever can keep chastity, let him keep it." Here he makes it free, since he says: whoever can keep it, let him keep it. Thus, if he can keep it, let him keep it; if he cannot keep it, then let him marry. But now the keeping of it depends not upon our ability, but upon God; else why does He say: He who can keep it, let him keep it? Not that we should understand "ability," as if it came from ourselves, but as given by God, the meaning is: To whom God has given the power to keep it, let him keep it; to whom ability is not given, he is not bound to keep it. How then have men ventured to forbid it, since God did not wish to forbid it on account of its difficulty? But He gave it to whom He would. And those to whom He gave it became bound to keep it. He to whom it is given, feels it very well, needs no such subtle question as How can I know whither it is given to me or not? Now the sum of this article or words of Christ is: To whom is given by God the ability to keep it, let him keep it; and those to whom it is not given are not bound by any divine law to keep it.

Thirdly, Christ says in the same chapter, verse 4, to the Pharisees: "Have ye not read that He who made the human race at the beginning created man and woman, and said, For this cause a man shall leave father and mother, and cleave to his wife, and the two should become one flesh, so that after that there should be not two but one flesh or body? What God has now united, let man not put asunder." Now hear you first, that marriage is so highly esteemed by God, that the natural law yields to it, when He says: A spouse shall leave father and mother and cleave to his wedded mate. If now one can then leave father and mother, which natural and divine law allow not, but only in this case; much less then can any human law forbid the consummation of marriage or if consummated, break it up. For how could this be reconciled, that divine law yielded to marriage, whereas human law did not? For to that He says: What God hath joined let not man put asunder. Now if a priest marries it is a divine union in marriage. For according to divine law he may marry. Thus no man shall or can put asunder such a union.

Fourthly, Paul says [I. Cor. vii., 2]: "On account of unchastity shall each man take a wife for himself, and each woman a husband." From these words the following conclusion is drawn: Each man, without exception (for whoever says "each" excepts none), if he feels he cannot get along without sexual intercourse, shall have a spouse of his own and be satisfied with his own. This ought to teach us fairly, that each father should say to his sons: "Dear sons, live pure lives. And if you ever feel that desire is overcoming you, tell me, and I will give you wives of your own." This same should each mother say to her daughters. In that case there would be many less prostitutes, many less bastards; and if one married, much less adultery. Besides it often happens that our children choose their own mates; and if they are not married according to their choice, their feelings and thoughts as to their spouses appear to them as the heads upon a Kaiserskreuzer.[1] But in case the above mentioned regulation should be followed, they could not contradict or quarrel; for they would have been so reared from childhood that they might tell their needs. Now if the priest is troubled with desires, Paul tells him to take a wife; for he has excepted no one.

Fifthly, Paul says in the same chapter, verse 8: "I say to the unmarried and to widows: It is properly quiet and good for them, if they abide even as I; but if they cannot control themselves, let them marry; for it is not well for men or women to burn." From Paul's words we can see that not to marry but to live a continent life is a quiet and

[1] An imperial coin.

proper thing. We attack these virtues in none; but those who can remain thus [continent], we consider worthier than ourselves. But this we desire: since we have learned alas! that we cannot remain continent, since God has not granted us that,—we desire that marriage be not forbidden us. For Paul gives no other reason why one should assume sexual relations, except passion. This we alas! confess we have, since we have fallen into disgrace on account of it. Passion one is to understand (as occurring) when man is so excited by the desires of the flesh that he strives for the enjoyments of the flesh. Therefore it is better that he marry, that the feelings be freer, and not rage in such thoughts.

Sixthly, again in the same place [I. Cor. vii., 25]: "Concerning virginity I have no command of the Lord." Notice here that St. Paul clearly admits that he cannot enjoin upon any one virginity, for God has given no command about it. O would that they had also done thus, who have never become like St. Paul in knowledge or virtue, so that where God has not forbidden a thing, they had not made a command of their own! For Paul's meaning is, since God has not commanded chastity, he himself had no power to command it. And when he was asked by the Corinthians, to whom he wrote these words, whether it was proper to remain chaste,[1] or whether one should be forced to remain chaste,[1] his answer through the whole chapter was: Chastity is, to be sure, pleasing to God and also becoming; for in marriage there is much responsibility—that is, care of the wife or husband, or children, or of affairs touching the family. Therefore he advised that he to whom God had granted chastity[1] should preserve it. But no command could he make about it. For God himself had made no command and therefore he says twice in the same chapter, that one is not to take his advice as a command, and that he does not

[1] To suppose the Apostle Paul asked whether chastity was to be preserved is absurd. What this passage plainly says is that under certain conditions celibacy should be preserved; but Zwingli confounds chastity and celibacy.

advise this, in order to get them into trouble. In the words of Paul one also notes that he interprets the words of Christ in the two first passages as we understood them.

Seventh, he writes [I. Tim. iii., 12 *sqq.*]: "This is certain, whatever preacher desires a congregation or parish, desires an honourable office. Therefore a bishop (that is, an overseer or priest, pastor, or lay preacher, all of which are in Greek Episcopos, that is, bishop or overseer) must be blameless, the husband of one wife," etc. Here we see that all preachers are bishops. Also of this opinion is St. Jerome.[1] Also that his office is watching, and that a bishop's office is not of high dignity as they now put on airs, but an office that must be performed without any let up. For if a watch on a station or tower considered himself a great lord and did not carefully watch, he would not be approved, because there is no need of him save to watch. There is also no need of bishops as lords but as unceasing watchmen, although they may have become blind [Isaiah lvi., 10]. So we see that he is to be of a pious decent life, so that one could not easily accuse him of a disgraceful method of living. Accordingly he is to have not many wives, but only one wife; since Paul commands the overseer to have a wife. Let each reasonable man consider what a bad thing an unmarried priest is, even a dangerous thing—of which we do not wish here to say more, in the hope that Almighty God will enlighten His people, that they insist on the honour of their own bishops, when they hear St. Paul commanding priests to have each one wife, but only one.

Eighthly [I. Tim. iii., 12], in the same place where the former announcement is made: "Deacons (says Paul), that is, servants of the bishops, shall be the husbands each of one wife, ruling their children and their servants well." Deacons are all those who help the bishops in the service of spiritual

---

[1] His comment on Titus i., 5; also Epistola 69 ad Occanum, cap. iii., and Epistola 146 ad Evangelum, cap. i. These letters are in *The Nicene and Post-Nicene Fathers*, 2d series, vi.: 143, 288.

things, whom they now call assistants. Those Paul also commands to take wives, so that greater sinning, adultery, seduction of virgins, and whoring be avoided. A very dangerous animal is a young priest who on account of his office has access to young people, women or maidens. Keep straw from the fire! If now he is given a wife he would be like other decent men concerned with the care of his family, wife, children, and other things, so that the ardour of wicked temptation would be removed.

Ninthly, Paul predicts [I. Timothy, iv., 1]: "The Spirit speaketh expressly that in the latter times some shall depart from the faith, giving heed to seducing spirits and the doctrines of devils, speaking lies in hypocrisy, having their consciences seared with a hot iron, forbidding to marry," etc. Here one sees clearly that Paul estimated the great injury to the soul before it came, and wanted to provide against its coming. One also sees that such injury is inspired by the devil in order to seduce souls by a fair appearance; for it has such an appearance, when one says: "Is not purity a beautiful thing? Yes, but where is it? Where is it kept?" Thus the devil desired to dazzle men with such an appearance, so that they would attempt purity and accordingly fall into such shame as would injure not alone themselves but also those with whom they transgress. Yes, to be sure, the devil has here as in all his attacks made use of cunning. For we are so foolish, when a pretty mirror or other thing for exhibition is put before us, that we think it is good and want to be able to keep it without restraint. And the devil well knew that it would well please the common man, if one said: "Yes, of course, priests, who extol and regard God, should lead pure lives." He knew also at the same time that they remained nevertheless human beings, flesh and blood, wanting in all virtues, and that the flesh would for that reason not give up its treachery, but would bring them into greater disgrace.

Finally, the prohibition to the clergy of marriage comes from the devil not from God; this one hears in the words of Paul. Besides Christ says [Matt. xv., 13]: "Every plant, which my heavenly Father hath not planted, shall be rooted up." Now the command of chastity[1] is neither given nor enjoined by God, and God and the devil are not more than two plants. If it is not from God, then it must be from the devil. We speak here only of it as a command: purity is doubtless a very wise gift and virtue. To whom it is given, we greatly congratulate; but we complain, that men arrogantly force us into dishonour, when they have no witness or right from the divine Scriptures. Indeed, what was formerly looked upon with wise consideration in the Councils, have they done away with; and also of this we desire to speak here.

The old fathers in the Synod of Gangra[2] considered the wives of the clergy, and the words of their decision stand to-day in the papal laws Di. xxviii, C. Si quis.[3] If any one teaches that a priest should do away with his wife because he is a priest, be he cursed! Likewise again: C. Si quis discernit. Ibid.[4] If any one consider sinful or vex

[1] *I. e.*, celibacy. God commands every one to be chaste.

[2] Gangra was the capital of Paphlagonia, the district of Asia Minor which bordered on the Black Sea, between Pontus on the east and Bithynia on the west. There in or about 340 was held a council called to take action respecting the ascetic views and practices of Eustathius, bishop of Sebaste. It passed twenty canons severely condemning these views and practices. They will be found in English translation in Hefele's *History of the Church Councils, A.D. 226 to 429*, pp. 325–339. Those of particular value for Zwingli at this time were these:

Canon 1. "If any one despises wedlock, abhorring and blaming the woman who sleeps with her husband, even if she is a believer and devout, as if she could not enter the Kingdom of God, let him be anathema."

Canon 4. "If any one maintains that when a married priest offers the sacrifice, no one should take part in the service, let him be excommunicated."

Canon 9. "If any one lives unmarried or in continence, avoids marriage from contempt, and not because of the beauty and holiness of virginity, let him be anathema."

Canon 10. "If any one of those who for the Lord's sake remain single, in pride exalts himself above those who are married, let him be anathema."

Canon 14. "If a woman leaves her husband and separates herself, from an abhorrence of the married state, let her be anathema."

[3] *I. e.*, Corpus juris can., c. 14, Dist. xxviii.

[4] *I. e.*, Corpus juris can., c. 15, Dist. xxviii.

a married priest, as though he should not hold mass because he had a wife, and for that reason avoid him, be he cursed! Here we fight with their weapons. If the Synod of Gangra assembled in the Holy Spirit—as it did; for it treated the Gospel and the apostolic doctrine alike—why then have those coming later not left the same, instead of doing away with it without the support of Holy Writ? Further, if it is inspired by the devil that one forbid marriage according to the above words of Paul, and if those succeeding have forbidden it without authority of Scripture, then they have done it as inspired by the devil, and the command of the devil has driven out divine freedom. Well-taught church father, well-fed and satisfied, expound the syllogism or the foul crowd will succumb to it.[1] Further, "one should not believe every spirit, but carefully consider whether it be from God" [I. John iv., 1], and whether the rules of the Synod of Gangra are everywhere like the laws left by Christ and Paul, as is mentioned above and here: then they are of the true spirit of God. Further, if it was proper for them to exchange the divine for the human, why would it not become each Christian to cleave to the divine, since the human is so clearly contrary to the divine? For that chastity[2] is left of free choice by God, and that it is forbidden by men, are entirely in discord and out of harmony. Also the excuse is of no avail, when they say that it is mentioned in the next "Distinction"[3] that the ordinances of the Synod of Gangra were done away with honest purpose; for one can make answer: Who has given anyone power, so that that which is left free of God should be enjoined by men?

[1] This sentence is in doggerel:
>Wol geleerter vatter,
>Vol und satter,
>Tund der sylogismum uff
>Oder aber der ful huff
>Wirt aber darnider ligen.

[2] *I. e.*, celibacy. God left it to man's choice if he should marry or not, but will punish unchastity.

[3] Corpus jur. can., Dist. xxix.

And what a whole Council has considered right, should this or that pope abolish? or if two Councils judge contrary to each other do they do it not the less in the Holy Spirit? Or is this Spirit so inconsistent with itself and forgetful that it inspires one thing to-day and to-morrow something else? Since now that cannot be, one must always say that such happens from the shortcomings of the Council; but these things we should try according to the line of the Scripture, as is said above. If one thus tries the Synod of Gangra may it endure the trial! For that it has constituted itself in conformity to divine permission; wherefore it shall fairly stand; and what is not in conformity with the divine will shall not stand. Besides the clergy have long lived according to the mode of life approved by the Synod of Gangra, and not according to the ordinances of those who wanted to force chastity[1] on the clergy. St. Hilary [born at Poitiers, France, became bishop of that city about 355; died there 367], in his time a bright light in Christianity, had wedded wife and children, while he was bishop of Poitiers. Until up to seven hundred years after the birth of Christ some priest's sons became popes, as is stated in Di. 56[2]: "Hosius [bishop of Cordova, Spain, born about 257, became bishop about 295; died about 357] was the son of a sub-deacon, and was a pope.[3] Pope Bonifacius I [418-422] was the son of a priest called Jucundus; Pope Agapetus I [535-536] was the son of a priest named Gordianus; Pope Theodorus I [642-649] was the son of Theodorus, bishop of Jerusalem; Pope Silverius I [536-567] was the son of Pope Hormisdas I[4] [514-523]; Pope Deusdedit I [615-618] was the son of Jucundus, a priest; Pope Felix III [483-492] was a born Roman, the son of a priest; Pope Gelasius I [492-496] was

---

[1] He means celibacy.

[2] Corpus jur. can., c. 2, Dist. lvi. What immediately follows is Zwingli's translation from the Latin, with chronological matter supplied and errors corrected.

[3] This is a mistake. Roman Catholics claim that he represented the pope in the Council of Nice, 325. But he never was pope himself.

[4] Zwingli says that he was the son of a Roman bishop, Silverius.

Priests to Preach and to Marry 187

an African,[1] and the son of Bishop Valerius; Agapetus, born at Rome, son of Gordianus, a priest[2]: all popes of Rome. Although the canonists wish to say that these were born out of wedlock, they do so that they may establish this licentious chastity[3]; and those undoubtedly born in wedlock they insult after their death. For all these popes lived in old times when piety and honour had much greater results than in our times, so that people would hardly have allowed those to come to such prominence who were born in dishonour. Wherefore it is well to remember that they were not so ill-born."

For in those times the marriage of the clergy was an unsettled question. For Nicholas, the first of that name, who was pope [from 858 to 867][4], had ordered that priests be allowed to marry. The Bulgarians (Bulgaria borders on Hungary) asked him what they should do with their priests who had taken wives, being of the opinion that they should be driven out. And he answered them, Di. xxviii, Consolendum [Corpus jur. can., c. Dist. xxviii]: Although the priests had acted culpably and wantonly, still they should endure it after the example of Jesus Christ, who suffered the bad among the good. Augustinus, the holy teacher, if one reads aright, Confessionum, libro sexto, cap. xv, complains that he so loved his first love whom he allowed to return again into Africa, by whom he had a son, that he took no wife but hoped, all the time of her absence, that she would come back to him, and therefore would take none in marriage, but rather satisfied the impatience of love with another woman, wherefore he complained of himself before God, and thought he had done wrong. For it would have been better to have married, as he himself shows in the preceding chapter xii, in which he overcame and persuaded Alipius, so that he said he wanted to marry but had never ventured to do so, but now would, because Augustinus had approved

[1] Another error. He was born a Roman.
[2] This is a repetition of what is said above.
[3] He means celibacy.   [4] Zwingli gives merely one date, 859.

marriage so highly. From which we may truly conclude, that at the time of Augustinus, who lived 433 A.D.,[1] no opposition was made against the marriage of the clergy, and that Augustinus had two wives, one after the other, instead of wedded wives according to the decision of the Council of Toledo,[2] Di. xxxiv, Is qui: Whoever has no wedded wife but instead a concubine, him shall people not turn away from the altar or partaking of the sacrament; indeed when he is satisfied with one wife, let her be called wedded wife or concubine.[3] Then Augustinus complains of his weakness, that he was not able to wait till she returned from Africa (though she never came), but was satisfied with one other. A great number of proofs of this kind could be brought together. For to speak finally of the subject: Let one command as much as one will, nature is not so easily controlled: it is the power of God to keep chastity, not our ability. How then do they venture to set up a command, which man cannot obey with his own strength? Indeed it is only a piece of hypocrisy, though no reference is here made to those who have such grace from God. Then it was true also of the pious old fathers that they did not keep chastity[4]; they were also men. Although in our times chastity is falsely assumed for a time under fair appearances by some, but soon the truth comes out. They have begotten children by concubines, committed adultery, seduced maidens, from which deeds very great misery has sprung, murders and other evils. Finally: Naturam expellas furca, tamen usque recurret—that is: Though you drive nature out with a stick, it will return again.[5] Unavoidable errors one must not desire to overcome, but should see how they are most properly to be endured.

Tenthly, Paul writes again to Titus (i., 5–7): "For this cause left I thee in Crete (an island now called Candia, whence they get Malvasia wine), that thou shouldst set

---

[1] Augustinus was born 354, died 430.　　[2] In Spain, 400 A.D.
[3] Corpus jur. can., c. 4, Dist. xxxiv.　　[4] He means celibacy.
[5] The quotation is from Horace, *Epist.*, I: epist. 10, verse 24.

in order the things that are wanting, and ordain honourable elders in every city, as I had recommended thee. If any be blameless, and has only one wife, true and faithful children, of whom one cannot say that they live riotously or are unruly. For a bishop shall be one of whom one cannot complain." These words of Paul are still clearer than those above in Article VII, although the meaning is the same. But there are good things to be noticed in them: first, that old honourable men shall be made bishops in each city—that is, priests or lay-pastors. They must not be sent from Rome, from which they bring us no divine teaching, but how good Corsican wine is and what pretty prostitutes there are on the Campo Floro. Second, that these words "only one wife" shall be so understood that he shall have not more than one wedded wife at one time, and not according to Jewish or heathen customs that he should venture to have more than one wedded wife. Third, that the bishops shall see to it that their children are brought up more correctly than commonly the custom is. Fourth, that you may hear that a bishop is nothing more than a priest; and that you do not worry that he says "in each city," which word he understands as meaning each church community. For in Ephesus there were in one "city" many bishops, Acts xx., 17—that is, preachers. Otherwise should one understand "bishop" after the kind of the present bishops, one would need ten Ephesuses. Fifth, that bishops should be of pure life above other men. But how can he be of pure life, if it is not proper for him to take a wife and if he cannot be chaste? How many priests are pious, well-taught bishops or overseers, on whom one can lay no blame for anything except that they say, he does not live a chaste life, or he is a whorish priest. See, that single sin takes from them all faith in the eyes of men; let him love God as he will, let him teach as faithfully as he will, everything is spoiled, as soon as one hears that he does not live piously as far as chastity is concerned. How great injury that causes, any reasonable man can estimate. Ah, how blind men are, that they do not remove this disgrace, although God and reason favour!

Eleventhly, Paul writes to the Hebrews (xiii., 4): "Marriage is a highly desirable thing, and an undefiled bed, but the impure and adulterous God will judge." These words of Paul those of the Greek Church have always brought up against the Roman defenders of pretended chastity; marriage is desirable, an honourable thing. According to the former it is established not by a fool but by God; consequently it is a medicine for sin that is innate in us and from whose attacks none is free, as long as he lives. And it has its foundation in a law of God: Love thy neighbour as thyself. For Almighty God, knowing and pitying our shortcomings, that He may aid them, has united marriage with faith and belief, in that whoever keeps faith and truth in marriage, finds no injury in marital relations. For God considers faith kept with one's fellow-man as faith kept with Him. Therefore Paul says: "and an undefiled bed." For what one does to his neighbour, one does to God. Indeed God does not consider Himself loved, unless one's neighbour be also loved. Therefore He commands the offering, which is to be made, be left upon the altar till one has become reconciled with one's neighbour, and judges His honour according to the good of one's fellow-men. It also has its foundation in natural law: What you would not have done to you, that do not unto others. If you would have your spouse remain true to you, leave another's untouched, thus to speak of other persons, daughters and serving-maids. And for this reason the Greeks would not be forced into pretended chastity, and are as good Christians to-day as we are; yes, better, in this that they are satisfied with single spouses. And we are licentious, as it pleases us, and the high bishops suffer it, as is to be noticed. That is of use, not considering that it causes offence in one's fellow-men, which they should avoid of all things according to the opinion of Christ [Matt. xviii., 7]: "Woe unto him by whom offence cometh!" Now the present offence comes from none but the high bishops. For chastity[1] is enjoined not by God or by the holy apostles, but by the bishops. Nor can one say that while priests live impure lives now, in times past they were chaste. We say no. For if one reads the decree (that is a papal law) he will find that the deacons and hypodeacons have always opposed this prohibition, as well as the priests. For St. Hilary, in his times a light among all Christians, had wedded wife and children. Another evil happens, because God is displeased with the wicked impurity of the clergy, namely, that the children born therefrom are commonly considered wicked, dishonourable outcasts. Whence comes this? From this, that the men—that is, high bishops—have prevented their being born in wedlock; and those who were rightly created by God, are disgraced before men by the prohibition of men, which thing Christ earnestly forbade. [Matthew xviii., 10, 6]: "Take heed that ye disgrace not any of these little ones who believe in me. For whoever shall offend or disgrace one of these little ones (for thus in this place St. Chrysostom understands the word *scandalon*),[2] it were better for him that a millstone were hanged about his neck and that he were sunk in the depths of the sea." Indeed the disgrace brought upon the poor children of men is the cause of very much evil. If it is a daughter and if her birth is not soon made honourable in the sight of men, she soon despairs and takes up a loose life, remaining all her days a courtesan, to be offence to all men. But we do not wish to be understood as touching the honour of those who live in piety, although they are children of the clergy, of which there are, if God will, many, but hope we have showed that this disgracing is the cause of much sin, nothing of which the children caused, that this injury is done them not by God but by men, who have disgraced God's creatures on account of their own avarice. For these children whom they have themselves disgraced

---

[1] That is celibacy.

[2] See his commentary on Matthew. Homily 69. In *The Nicene and Post-Nicene Fathers*, 1st series, x., 420 *ff*.

they should care, so that the disgrace be removed from them before God and man. If it is a man child, in some places he is allowed to take up in secret no honest calling,[1] so that he is forced to become nothing but a good-for-nothing fool. Often such despair brings with it a carelessness in the father and mother, who think: Thou canst not bring honour, etc. The conclusion is that marriage is an excellent and honourable thing, which is also not forbidden the clergy in the Old Testament, which is much stricter than the New. But though the wise bishops, who wanted to be wiser than even God, who could probably have forbidden it, had He thought it useful and honourable, have brought about so praiseworthy a state of chastity,[2] still we will let them answer for it to God, and it will doubtlessly go hard with them. For Christ says [Matthew xv., 9]: "For in vain do they worship me, since they teach the doctrines and commands of men."

These and many other reasons from the Scriptures have influenced us, honourable, wise, and respectable Sirs, to win your Wisdom in the matter of the marriage which we desire to contract, indeed some of us to publish marriages already entered into, which your Wisdom will not especially oppose, in view of the great dishonour which we have shamelessly allowed to be put upon us, in view of the great offence thereby offered all men, and in view of our sore consciences with which we have daily performed the divine service of God's word and other sacraments, but always realising our unchanging weakness and having no peace. Therefore I urge your Wisdom, as our fathers (for we are all born of one praiseworthy Federation and are yours and of yours) by God our Creator who made us all of one clod of earth, that we recognise each other as brothers, by the blood of Jesus Christ, shed for us all, that no one ask more for himself than for another, by the Spirit of God, who is God, who in all His enlightening and inspiring never for-

---

[1] An illegitimate son could not get into any guild, in many places.
[2] It should be celibacy.

bade the clergy marriage, indeed even commanded it: pity us your true and willing servants, some of whom have just reported themselves as willing to marry and some of whom as desirous of making their marriage public, grant us this, so that that which is no sin before God, may not be disgraceful before men. And since we have most faithfully busied ourselves all our days at home and abroad in the interest of your honour, grant us that we be freed from this disgrace of impurity and may live in honour among you. For it would ever be unfriendly, if those, whose honour we have increased, wished at all times to forbid us honour before not only kin and neighbours but also strangers. It is we also who have suffered good and evil with you in trouble, be it pest or war, and have always acted as decent honest folk. And so it is not from lasciviousness but from love of the honours of pious marital purity, that we appeal to your wisdom. For if it came from lasciviousness, we could serve that end much better if we had no wives. We know well what trouble, care, and labour comes with marriage; we know also how easily every day we could desert the women, whom we have, alas! known in the past. Therefore it is not from lasciviousness, but from modesty and love of the souls committed to our care, not to make them wicked forever. We have most of us outgrown our youthful ways and are generally nearer forty than thirty. You will also not hear those who will cry out with many a remonstrance: Will dare you take wives? You have sworn chastity.[1] Here listen, gracious sirs. No one has sworn chastity with other words than are demanded here. When the bishop who ordains the priests asks if they are pure, then the speaker answers: "As far as human weakness can suffer or endure." See, gracious Sirs, in this affair we have sworn this way and no other. This we will prove by the lord bishops themselves, though there is no need of it: no one denies that, as we hope. Since now we are sufficiently aware, alas! that we have fallen often from

---

[1] He means celibacy.

weakness, and that therefore neither oath nor command binds us, also that St. Paul says: It is better that a man marry, as is mentioned above, Art. V, let yourselves be influenced to recognise publicly that which we do before you, and if there had not been so great a desire for honour we would truly never have covered up our disgrace. Also do not consent to hear those who will cry out: Who would rear their children, they would commit adultery, we would have to consider their wives as beggars, they would rule us with their children,—and make other complaints. We will in this and other things according to the admonition, as is finally contained in the herein articles. Listen also not to others who say: Is it not a disgraceful thing to sleep with a woman and next morning hold mass? Answer: Can one not also do that if he has stayed with a harlot? If we had not conscience otherwise than that we so far forgetting God and ourselves should be inclined to such wickedness, we would not need to direct this admonition to your Wisdom. It happens that our consciences are clear, that we can live in marital relations without offending anyone: the oversight of the conscience does not allow one to commit such a sin. And so we admonish you as our fathers: Allow us to live in honour with our pious fellow-citizens; and although there is no ground anywhere in the Scriptures for it, still if we have erred, overlook or forgive us our marriages. For each father must overlook or forgive his son something. For we are still yours, of your blood and soil, of your faith and heart, and no one of us is defiled with anything dishonourable save before the world. And if we may speak of doctrine without vainglory, we would wish still to commend ourselves more; but be this enough for us, though that we are all so taught and made eloquent by the mercy of God, that we can with fair propriety speak the healing doctrine of our Lord Jesus Christ.

But in case this does not help, dear, gracious Sirs, as we hope, still we beg you most humbly to protect us from the violence of the pope of Rome and all clergy. Thus we shall protect ourselves by the consolation and protection of the Scriptures; so that, if we did not protect ourselves by the authority of Scripture, we would be willing to stand the consequences as is fair. And if anyone wishes to discuss the subject publicly or later into a written discussion about this, we will with God's help overcome all adversaries by means of Scripture. Let no one fear because there are many adversaries; the Word of God, freedom, and the favour of His mercy are on our side. Not to speak with arrogance, we think too that you owe us that protection; we are yours, and our ancestors from earliest times have always rendered assistance to those threatened by injustice, whence a high reputation has grown up in all lands for the Confederation. How much more should you not refuse protection to us against those who would use force with us; since we have looked to you with entirely confident hearts, especially when in many places of the Confederation it has been customary from times past, in case a priest was wanted, to lay upon him the condition that he have a wife of his own, and leave theirs untouched (undefiled), which was often considered foolish by many. But they really acted wisely, if they had only added to the requirements, that the priests should wed these wives; as it is, they have not treated them in an entirely friendly way, by leaving them thus in a state of dishonour. God put such into your minds! For truly and by the loving God we swear, by the welfare of our souls, that it will be divine and honourable in you, and honourable and wholesome for us. We shall also with faithful industry be of service to your Wisdom at all times, so that your Wisdom shall of necessity clearly see that no evil has come about. God be with you! Amen.

These are the requests which we express in the interest of peace and quiet, which we wish steadfastly to preserve with God's help:

That neither our wives nor our children should be deprived of the right and justice of your Wisdom, but, as is the custom with the laity, should enjoy rights, as the family of any honest man usually does.

That where one of us is with justice found to have committed adultery, we wish to be understood as giving up and submitting, so that we would without opposition yield, if we were dismissed from the living or parish.

That we would no more assume that we might give to our children the livings which we hold, and in no way claim to possess what belonged to the living or the church.

That if any one considered himself injured or likely to be injured in other things by our marriage, we would submit to the reasonable judgment of the authorities, so that the marriage be not injurious or disadvantageous to anyone.

That we do not wish to be understood as encroaching upon the rights of anyone, but (as recommending) that each priest who desired to marry should lay before his lords articles to which they could have easy access.

Wise and honourable Sirs, we have wished to sign our names, but have not done so for several reasons which we shall at the proper time make known and bring forth, for in the little book (pamphlet) there is much that will require the names. No more now than this: God's will be done on earth as in heaven!

Given the 13th day of July, 1522.

XIV.

DEFENCE CALLED ARCHETELES, IN WHICH ANSWER IS MADE TO AN ADMONITION THAT THE MOST REVEREND LORD BISHOP OF CONSTANCE (BEING PERSUADED THERETO BY THE BEHAVIOUR OF CERTAIN WANTONLY FACTIOUS PERSONS) SENT TO THE COUNCIL OF THE GREAT MINSTER AT ZURICH CALLED THE CHAPTER.

(August 22–3, 1522)

[Apologeticus Archeteles adpellatus, quo respondetur paraenesi a reverendissimo domino Constantiensi (quorundam procaci factione ad id persuaso) ad senatum prepositure Tigurine, quem "capitulum" vocant, misse. In Schuler and Schulthess ed., iii., 27–76. In Egli and Finsler ed., i., 256–327. Translated by Mr. Henry Preble, New York City.

This is Zwingli's reply to the admonition which the Bishop of Constance, the diocesan of the city of Zurich, addressed to the chapter of the Great Minster on May 24, 1522. Zwingli was not mentioned in it but rightly regarding himself as the chief agent in bringing in the new ideas which were condemned by the Bishop, he made this reply. His delay in doing so was probably due to his absorbing occupations in other directions. The treatise was written hastily, he informed Myconius, in sending him a copy (August 26, 1522).

There are numerous allusions to the treatise in the Zwingli correspondence. Thus Zwingli in writing to his bosom friend, Myconius, on August 23, 1522 (*Werke*, n. e. vii., 567), promises him a copy, and this promise he redeemed on the 26th (*ibid.*, 569); on April 11, 1524, he alludes to it when writing to Konrad Hofmann (viii., 169), and lastly to Konrad Sam in Ulm on February 12, 1527 (Schuler and Schulthess ed., viii., 28), he imparted information regarding it as Sam was somehow unacquainted with it. In letters to Zwingli from Michael Hummelberg on August 26, 1522 (*Werke*, n. e. vii., 574), the same on September 4 (p. 578); Melchior Macrinus, on September 30 (p. 588, he calls it α καλω); Sebastian Meyer, on November 11 (p. 612); Johannes Zwick, on November 27 (p. 820); and Hedio on February 10, 1523 (viii., 22), mention is made of it. But the gem of the collection is this delicious effusion from Erasmus, written from Basel, September 8, 1522 (p. 582), on receipt of Zwingli's present of a copy:

"I have read some pages of your apology [*Archeteles*]. I beseech you for the sake of the glory of the Gospel, which I know you would favour and which we all who bear the name of Christ ought to favour, if you should issue anything hereafter, treat so serious a matter seriously, and bear in mind evangelical modesty and patience. Consult your learned friends before you issue anything. I fear that that apology will cause you great peril and will injure the Gospel. Even in the few pages that I have read there are many things I wanted to warn you about. I do not doubt that your prudence will take this in good part, for I have written late at night with a mind that is most solicitous for you. Farewell."

The Rev. Dr. B. J. Kidd, in his valuable collection of *Documents of the Continental Reformation* (Oxford: Clarendon Press, 1911), characterises the *Archeteles* as "rather truculent" (p. 389). It was this quality probably which offended Erasmus.]

In this treatise square brackets are used to indicate either the translation of the Greek term or terms which Zwingli used or references which are more exactly given than these are by Zwingli.

TO the Most Reverend Father and Lord in Christ, Hugo von Hohenlandenberg, Bishop of Constance, Greeting, Huldreich Zwingli, preacher of the church of Zurich at the Great Minster.

That I again trouble your Highness with a letter, most noble Bishop, overwhelmed as you are by such a mass of duties, I do not think will be laid up against me, for I know that I am speaking to one whose highest pleasure it is that the name of Christ be spread abroad as widely as possible; and His business, as it is not of men, so it can in nowise be undone by men. But now that for about six years I have laboured to the best of my ability with the talent entrusted to my keeping, that when the Lord came and demanded His gain, I might not slothfully bring forward with fear and shame the one idle talent wrapped in a napkin, lo! I am denounced before your Highness as a destroyer of the Lord's fold, not its guardian or shepherd. And this thing, as was fitting, caused you to send to us at Zurich that unnecessarily magnificent delegation of three scholars,[1] and I rendered such account to them before the Council of my teaching, which is not mine but God's, that every one might have been content with it, if only he weighed the case in accordance with his judgment and not his feelings. And

[1] See his letter to Erasmus Fabricius, p. 113 of this volume.

when I thought the matter had been settled in entire peacefulness, as has been the constant and only object of my effort, certain impatient fellows began to gnash their teeth, not so much because they had found anything wrong as because they had not conquered and slain their adversary and levelled everything with the ground; and they began to look for an opportunity to make a disturbance, until, having thought out a scheme for harassing me secretly and underhandedly, they made you the patron of their design, and soothed their jealousy at the risk of your good name, forgetting that a counsellor was regarded, even among the ancients, as a sacred thing, and one not to be abused of any man. For, by their continual outcries and insinuations they finally dragged you into sending to the Council of our canons, which we call the Chapter, a document of admonition that is as far removed from any learning as from any moderation. For, this I divine rather than definitely assert, led by the following reasons particularly: first that you are not capable of anything of the sort yourself, and this you may take to mean that you could not accomplish anything even if you could do this kind of thing, nay, that you could have accomplished more, if you had given utterance to your thoughts in the German language[1]; secondly, that you meditate nothing but what is peaceful, while this admonition is so full of violence and threats, so pregnant with them that it might bring forth if necessary, nay, has already brought forth, this pamphlet which you see dedicated to your Highness. It is called "Archeteles" on this account, because it is masculine and is going to put an end, I hope, to all controversy between those gentlemen and myself, so that after this first engagement, with a continuous document at least, they will themselves make an end of strife and contention, and it may truly be the beginning and end of the entire quarrel, for I call God to witness I have none with them, so much so that I wonder at nothing more than what reason could have driven them

---

[1] The Bishop of Constance was a notoriously poor latinist.

to send to a place where there was no disturbance a thing which they expected would serve as an apple (ἔριδος) of discord, to arouse disagreement and strife. For I will say freely what I think. In their whole harangue they thunder forth the word peace, like those prophets whom Jeremiah denounces for continuing to cry, when there was no need, "Peace, peace; when there is no peace" [Jer. vi., 14]. For at Zurich, as far as the teachings of Christ are concerned, everything is as quiet as anywhere in the world, even the laymen in general are so well versed in the Gospel that they will not listen to any other teachings. And this you will see more clearly from this example. While hitherto reckless mendicant friars had spouted forth in the pulpit whatever came into their heads, the Council has forbidden them to preach anything which they had not drawn from the fountain head of the two Testaments of Holy Writ.[1] Wherefore it appears that these gentlemen see discord where, in the words of Paul, the name of God is glorified with one mind and one mouth [Rom. xv., 6]. And yet they have been disappointed in their hope, for, having heard the admonitory document, I only blushed with shame that men of this kidney should be turning their eyes greedily upon me in the session of the Chapter, and rejoicing at the attack upon me, but I by no means grudged them this as long as the weapons with which I was attacked were not stronger than they were. For, all that has been patched together here is so poverty-stricken in its barrenness and awkwardness that I do not know but it would have been wiser to pass it all by with contempt than to refute it, if the injury they are doing by it to the Sacred Writings had not challenged me to come to the aid of these. For, with one or two exceptions, whenever they take the Sacred Books in their hands they twist them so that they cannot hide their pain in silence; whenever they declaim they are so clumsy that you would think they had purposely aimed at raising a laugh. I say nothing of their solecisms and

[1] This was in 1520.

barbarisms, for to these our ecclesiastical ears have become hardened.

Therefore, most kindly Bishop, if you see them handled here a little freely, there is no reason to wonder; for they have deserved it by their recklessness and ignorance. And the same is demanded by the office that I fill. I must contradict and refute them, and, like faithful Abraham, who when he heard that Lot had been captured by the enemy even slew kings to set him free, I must rescue the Sacred Writings so wickedly tortured, and I feel sure that by that achievement I shall restore the spoils of highest honour to our great Melchizedek [Gen. xiv., 13 *ff.*]. For, although this whole performance seem on the face of it to be in accordance with your orders, I am not at all willing to understand it in that sense. For I want your good name to be intact and inviolate at all points, because I am pretty strongly convinced that where there is any talk of the doctrines of Christ, you hold the soundest views, and that you bid those of your Council to settle in the most suitable way the disputes that may happen to arise at this time between the heralds of God's word. Let them see to it how well they do it. There is a report, however, that some of them do not act in all things as you would have them, but as their own diseased minds dictate. And in this admonitory document this is clear to everybody, for mention of my name is there avoided simply for the purpose of cutting off an opportunity for an answer on my part, though meanwhile I am attacked on all sides with the most damaging suspicions and am almost buried under them. How much more fitting it would have been—I appeal to your sense of justice—if I had taught anything impious, as these gentlemen will have it, to engage with me openly and to show definitely by the authority of Scripture, where and in what I had done wrong! As it is, by filling everything with their frightful lamentations, what else are they calling into doubt and suspicion than the whole teachings of Christ which I have preached so strenuously? But they shall get no satisfaction; for if they had ever been minded to listen to those teachings they would not have hidden themselves, like cuttle-fish, in their own inky blackness, though by the help of him whose business is at stake I have so strained and purified and cleared this blackness that their purposes are evident to all and only their names are missing. These too, if they go on, as they have begun, attacking me from under cover, I shall be obliged to make known. I would rather they should suffer me quietly to lay the food of heaven before the sheep entrusted to my charge, to fill them with it and burn them with the fire of love, than that by their tricks and insinuations they should call me away from the sweet repose of letters to defend myself. I shall not, if they like to delight their spirits with quarrels, grudge them their contending constantly if they please with whomever shall be seasonable, so that they do not assail me, at least in a spirit of altercation. The opportunity to admonish or discuss shall be theirs at all times, so that they grant that the Sacred Writings are a sacred anchor, not to put trust in which is most faithless and wicked, and so that they come squarely to try conclusions with me. Otherwise, I too shall claim the right πρὸς κρῆτα κρητίζειν [to fight the devil with his own weapons].[1] If anybody shall call this arrogant, most excellent Bishop, I beg him to think over the things that I thought over until the divine spirit made stable that which it wrought in me, to wit: When we see[2] the race of man worried and troubled, through the course of life, as to the attainment of happiness hereafter, and this not so much from natural vigilance as from the desire for life, the breath of which God, the Creator, breathed into our nostrils from the beginning of creation. Yet no way shows itself anywhere by which that happiness can be found. For if one turns to the philosophers, there is among them so much divergence of opinion about happi-

---

[1] Plutarch, *Vitæ Aemil.*, c. 23; *Lysandri*, c. 20.
[2] The *dudum* of Schuler and Schulthess seems smoother than the *quum* of Egli and Finsler.—H. P.

ness that one is filled with disgust at them; but if to the Christians, one finds much more confusion and vagueness among some of them than among the heathen, some of them aiming to reach happiness through human tradition and the material things of this world, relying, that is, upon their own human notions, while others rely only upon the mercy and promises of God, and both struggle with tooth and nail, as the saying is, to get their own opinion accepted. Placed thus at the parting of the ways, whither shall I turn? To men? If you say, "Yes, to men," I continue: "To those who in the old days when Christianity was still a new thing were held to be wise, or to those who just before our day showed forth folly rather than wisdom?" Here the opponent will struggle and become dumb, like the chief men of the Jews when asked by Christ, "The baptism of John, whence was it?" [Matt. xxi., 25 *ff*.]. And if you press him very hard he will admit that one must turn to the men of old, as worthy of more authority both for their antiquity and for the holiness of their lives. And when you add: "Even among these one can find things at variance or inconsistent with the writings of the Evangelists and the Apostles. To which, therefore, do you think one ought to accede?" he will answer, unless he be a blockhead or a dumb brute, "To the things that were uttered under the inspiration of the Spirit of God." For the things which are of human wisdom, however magnificently coloured and decked out, can deceive, but not the things that are of God. Here one needs the sinews of faith, which if any man lack, he will totter and faint and fall.

As I turned these things zealously over in my mind, I say, most excellent Bishop, and prayed to God to point out the right way to my hesitating soul, He said, "Thou fool, reflect on this: The truth of the Lord abideth forever; cling to that truth" [Ps. cxix., 90]; and "'Heaven and earth shall pass away, but my words shall not pass away' [Matt. xxiv., 35]; the things of man shall be done away, but the things of God are unchangeable"; and "'In vain they worship me, teaching the doctrines and commandments of men'" [Matt. xv., 9], as if God ought to follow our suggestions, or as if, when we had contrived something which at first sight seemed beautiful and good and even holy, it were straightway going to please Him. Rather ought we to strive always to depend upon Him with our whole heart, and not upon our own desires and contrivances, like sluggish slaves who will suffer many stripes if they neglect the will of their master and do their own. Therefore, putting all else aside, I came at length to have trust in nothing and in no words so much as in those which proceeded out of the mouth of the Lord. And when miserable mortals, forgetting both themselves and God, tried to palm off their own works as His, I began to look to see whether any means could be found by which one could detect whether the works of man or of God were the better, especially as I saw not a few straining every nerve to make the simple-minded accept their own utterances as divine, even though they were at variance with, or in direct opposition to, the words of God. And as I sought, it occurred to me that all things are made clear in that light which saith, "I am the light of the world" [John viii., 12], which lighteth every man that cometh into this world; and again [I. John iv., 1], "Believe not every spirit, but try the spirits, whether they are of God." And seeking for a touchstone, I find none other than the stone of offence and the rock of scandal, [I. Pet. ii., 7], upon which are broken all who, after the manner of the Pharisees, make the word of God of none effect through their tradition. Having, therefore, put these things together in this way, I began to try every doctrine by this touchstone, and if I saw that the stone reflected the same colour or rather that the doctrine could bear the brilliancy of the stone, I accepted it; if not, I rejected it. And finally it came to pass that at the very beginning of the test I began to discover whether there were anything added to the real doctrine or inserted into it, and then I could not be driven by any force or any threats to put in

Archeteles: Reply to Bishop's Admonition

the human things, however they puffed themselves out and tried to appear fine, the same trust as in the divine. Nay, if any set of men taught their own notions that were not consistent, or rather were quite inconsistent, with the divine, I flung this saying of the Apostle at them, "We ought to obey God rather than men" [Acts v., 29], until those who have such an exalted opinion of their own utterances and little or none of those of Christ, got the worst possible opinion of me, and this I regard as the surest sign that the procedure is most acceptable to God and beneficial to me. For "Woe unto you," he says, "when all men shall speak well of you!" [Luke vi., 26], and "Blessed are ye when men shall hate you . . . and shall reproach you and cast out your name as evil, for the Son of Man's sake," and "Your names are written in heaven" [Luke vi., 22, and x., 20].

Therefore, if envious persons ever denounce me to your Highness as disregarding or scorning human traditions, know that this comes from my having found them to be at variance with, and in opposition to, the divine teachings, and that I cannot be made to fear what man can do to me. For, though he cast out my name, I am sure that it will have honour with God; for the name of God will never be more surely glorified than if my name is held in the worst repute among men, and if he slay my body, he will establish my soul in everlasting life. To this treasure, namely, the certainty of God's word, must our hearts be guided. For this neither time nor moths can reduce to naught, but they can titles and priesthoods and statues and gold and fine raiment and feasts and coaches and mules. Do you see what has driven me to refuting their bloodless document of admonition? This, verily, because I see that by their very speech, which, as Christ witnesseth, is the surest messenger of the heart, their feelings with regard to divine and human things stand forth clearer than light. And since they cannot rest and will not suffer the budding knowledge of Christ to grow, I would have their words known far and wide, that they may be the better guarded against. It is not I who condemn them, but the Lord speaking by the mouth of Ezekiel, and saying [Ezek. xiii., 3 *ff.*]: "Woe unto the foolish prophets, that follow their own spirit, and have seen nothing! O Israel, thy prophets are like the foxes in the deserts! Ye have not gone up into the gaps, neither made up the hedge for the house of Israel to stand in the battle in the day of the Lord. They have seen vanity and lying divination, saying, The Lord saith: and the Lord hath not sent them: and they have made others to hope that they would confirm the word. Have ye not seen a vain vision, and have ye not spoken a lying divination, whereas ye say, The Lord saith it; albeit I have not spoken?" and the rest of the things that are written in chapter xiii. Who does not see that by these words that class of men is hit who say with their tongue, "Lord, Lord" and "the temple of the Lord, the temple of the Lord" [Jer. vii., 4], but in their heart look to this: "Whosoever shall swear by the temple, it is nothing; but whosoever shall swear by the gold of the temple" [Matt. xxiii., 16], and this: "Whosoever shall swear by the altar it is nothing, but whosoever sweareth by the gift that is upon it is guilty "[Matt. xxiii, 18]. And yet they would have themselves appear the while as champions of the divine law and name and of the Gospel. Therefore your Highness should avoid both their advice and their conversation, unless you desire to expose yourself to the greatest derision. I will not say here how roughly they handled a few days ago certain pious men and true heralds[1] of Christ, though you had not ordered such harshnes. But this is not generally known, and the belief is current that everything is done by your authority and command, which may sometime cast a great stain upon you, even without your knowing it. For this matter should not be carried on upon a basis of power, but upon that of the sanction of the Sacred Writings. For the more authoritatively

---

[1] Allusion to the treatment accorded to George Brunner and Sebastian Hofmeister. See Finsler's note *ad loco*.

you exercise your power, the more will you render yourself odious to all men. For we ought to take the Holy Scriptures as our guide and master; if any one uses them aright he should be unharmed, even though our little doctors be ever so much displeased. Otherwise calamity will fall upon us sometime, for the knowledge of the Sacred Writings is to-day upon the lips not only of the ecclesiastics but of almost the entire community. Therefore nothing ought to be done which savours of authority rather than of reason and the divine purpose; for nothing more would be accomplished than Paul accomplished by kicking against the pricks. For the study of the Gospel (to say nothing meanwhile of the majesty of God) is too vast a thing to be put to sleep or to death by the persecution of one or two individuals, and if it were kept under for a time by the wickedness of certain men, it would yet burst forth into a fiercer flame. You should therefore be wary and wise, and pray the Lord to guide your path, and, to make an end finally, you should take it in good part if something be taken from you to be added to Christ. For thus you will make the house of Hohenlandenberg most illustrious and your own soul most acceptable to God. The Most High God grant this! Amen. I beg you for the sake of Christ to examine from top to bottom this whole matter which is under discussion here. For it could not longer be hidden, and ought not to be, that certain persons were arming with your power their own hostility to Christ and his teachings. I have watched for a long time to see if some one from all the diocese would not challenge them into the arena and put a stop to their walking with heads thus high in air, and now that no one has appeared, I have come forward myself. May it be $εὐκαιρῶς$, to victory, and to the glory of Christ, and may He preserve your Highness long in prosperity! For I, too, wish you well. Zurich, August 22nd, in the year 1522.

Yours devotedly,

HULDREICH ZWINGLI,

preacher at the Great Minster of the Church of Zurich.

Admonition Sent to the Chapter of the Great Minster by the Most Reverend Lord Bishop of Constance.

Hugo, by the grace of God and of the Apostolic See, Bishop of Constance, to our sincerely beloved in Christ, the venerable and honourable Provost and Chapter of the Collegiate Church of the Great Minster of Saints Felix and Regula at Zurich in our diocese, greeting and sincere affection in the Lord.

I. We have for some time, dearly beloved, heard reports that there are, almost all through Germany, people who cry out day and night that the people of Christ have been wrongfully oppressed until now by the heads of the Church with hard and burdensome regulations, observances, and ceremonials, in consequence of which such persons are trying with all their might to cast off and do away with ceremonials, and

II. in this golden age (for that is what they call it) in which the Gospel is at last beginning to shed its light upon mankind, to lead back the mass of the people to

III. the freedom of the Gospel. But when they strive to pull up out of the field of the Lord what human ordinances they

IV. call tares and cockles, we see, alas, the wheat also being rooted up before our eyes. For have not hateful contentions arisen from this, and is not the whole business carried on with recriminations, after the pattern of silly women? Is not every one saying:

V. I am of Paul, I of Cephas, and I of Apollos? Is not, in short, that happening which is apt to happen among sheep when in the darkness of night

VI. a raider, a wolf, has broken into the fold? They flee, and some run unawares into the wolf's jaws, some plunge against a wall in front of them, and some wander about in panic-stricken uncertainty. So the body of the Church is affected in these days by a sort of spirit of dizziness, and some go feeling their way in the dark, as it were, not knowing what direction to take, others move about in a circle,

Archeteles: Reply to Bishop's Admonition

some stand still waiting for the sure light of truth to shine forth out of the darkness, others know not any course to take, but yet deride and judge those who take part on either side. Others are led astray and driven to doing this by various passions, those worst of counsellors, anger,

VII. hatred, jealousy, ambition, and the like, so that, in their zeal to follow after individuals, the real love of peace and calm devotion to truth are abandoned or made war upon, than which wickedness what can be imagined more execrable? You can in fact see some people cling with so much

VIII. animosity to their own undertakings or decisions that they cannot be turned about by any reasoning or pious persuasion. They would rather have everything rush to ruin and destruction with them, than turn their feet back from the path they have entered, even though it be no path. Such people are in short filled with wrath and undying hatred against all whom they see or hear of not only as in opposition to themselves but even as not agreeing with full voice and mind to their opinions. And how much damage and destruction this brings upon the Republic of Christ, any Christian can tell. For how can it be that in so many opposing and

IX. diverging opinions harmony can be restored? Peace was never sought nor found through strife.

X. To what opinion meanwhile is the simple-minded people to attach itself? What shall it embrace? What approve? What shall it do? Whither turn? For

XI. it sees learned and simple, scorning all gospel-taught gentleness and love, and charging upon each other so fiercely and wounding each other so pitiably that every man seems trying to seize his neighbour who does not happen to agree with him in this matter and

XII. to cast him out of the ship of the Church as a sinner and a heretic, while

XIII. he hears on the other side tones full of injury and insult and reviling quite contrary to any Christian piety.

As each side thus attacks and pursues the other, every man finally follows the course that his inclinations lead or his passions drive him to adopt.

XIV. When a faithful minister, who has the misfortune to be a steward of the Lord at such an ill-fated time and amid such a mass of evils, sees the one and only bride of Christ smitten not in one place only but on all sides within and without, and wounded with a mortal wound, with what pain is he not wrung, with what anxieties torn, knowing not, meanwhile, what he ought to do? For if he speaks as love of the bride and the bitterness of a mother's pain suggest, he has to fear wranglings and strife, nay the savage bites of hatred and contumely, and to expose himself to these not from one or the other party, but from both.

XV. But if he prefer to follow the advice of the prophet Amos who saith, "Therefore the prudent shall keep silence in that time; for it is an evil time" [Amos v., 13], and, as the vision of Ezekiel has it, to mourn and groan over all the abominations that are done; or, with the royal prophet,[1] to keep quiet in the wilderness while there is contention in the city[2];

XVI. the truth of the Gospel stands in his way: "The good shepherd giveth his life for the sheep. But he that is an hireling, and not the shepherd, whose own the sheep are not, seeth the wolf coming, . . . and fleeth" [John x, 11, 12]. Since, therefore, we are of those ministers whose lot has fallen upon

XVII. these dangerous times, and we see the evils constantly increasing, and the peace disturbed, and

XVIII. offences multiplied in the fold of the Lord,

XIX. with the introduction of new errors not less dangerous than the earlier ones, and meanwhile the peace, that we have long been waiting for with great longings, cometh not, but confusion,

XX. we are forced to act by "the zeal of the house of God" [Ps. lxix., 9; John ii., 17], in one part of which at least

---

[1] David. [2] Ps. lv., 9.

there is a watchful guardian. Led by zeal for the faith which at baptism we swore to defend, by zeal against the present schism under which our holy Mother Church is suffering so severely, we have determined to shut our eyes and delay no longer, but to toil in season and out of season, to preserve as far as possible the unity handed down by the Lord through his Apostles to us their successors, and to gather into the Church the wandering and erring sheep which, by factious perversity and heretical tampering with the faith, certain persons are separating from our mother.

XXI. Therefore we exhort you, brethren, and according to the mastery of the Lord and his Gospel we entreat you: Watch against the snares of the devil, and, both for your own salvation and for that of the Lord's whole flock, keep guard more energetically against this deadly heresy.

XXII. For they are renewing the old-time attack upon the unity of the Church, and are bringing into play again their sacrilegious machinations with their customary wiles. Is not the party of the old-time heretics visible here? Does not the accursed plant which the Heavenly Father hath not planted show this? These are the same nostrums with which in old days they turned the simple-minded away from the real cure of their trouble, the same sophistical tricks and exhortations, that, forsooth, they might not live in harmony with their own bishops and priests, nor hold fast to the discipline of the Church in peace and faith according to the commands of the Lord, nor keep inviolate and unstained in their walk the glory of the Christian profession, which is founded upon obedience and harmony. The same policy, the same overturning of things, is now again in process of introduction at the hands of certain persons to the downfall of salvation, that God be no more prayed to, and that he who has denied Christ appeal no more to Him he has denied, that after the wrongdoing repentance of the sin be also taken away. They will not that satisfaction be made unto the Lord through bishops and priests, but, leaving the ministers of the Lord, they would

XXIII. raise up a new and sacrilegious custom contrary to the directions of the Gospel.

XXIV. And in order to include all the machinations of the devil for the destruction of the simple-minded, they cut off the prayers and orisons through which, if anything especially foul and monstrous has appeared in the Church, the Lord ought to be appeased in long and uninterrupted penitence, and, under a lying pretence of an insidious peace, call upon the sick and wounded

XXV. to take to heroic measures, a recklessness, to wit, that leads to destruction. Alas that this is so plainly shown by these times of ours in which there is no place for obedience and peace and quiet, and the bitterness of rebellion and strife and persecution seems to have spread over all things. Hence we warn you again, dearly beloved, not to trust wantonly to these destructive utterances, nor feed the fever of fallacy with acceptance of fallacy, nor take poison for a healing draught or death for salvation.

XXVI. Be not deceived by the authority of these people nor by the learning with which they proclaim everywhere that they have the spirit of the Lord.

XXVII. For with adulterous teaching they seek to break down the chastity of the Church and to violate the truth of the Gospel.

XXVIII. The Lord cries and says: Hearken not unto the sayings of false prophets, for the visions of their hearts deceive them. They say, but not out of the mouth of the Lord, Ye shall have peace. [See Jer. xxiii., 16, 17.]

XXIX. Peace they bring, who themselves have no peace. They promise freedom, when they are the slaves of corruption.[1] They, who have withdrawn from the Church, offer to raise up and bring back to the Church those who have fallen laden with many burdens. They who walk in the darkness of error would restore you to the light, and

XXX. undertake to furnish the food of the Gospel to all, when they are themselves tortured by the pangs of a

---

[1] II. Peter ii., 19.

Archeteles : Reply to Bishop's Admonition

fatal hunger. Let no man cause you to wander from the way of the Lord which you have learned from the cradle. Let no man drag you Christians away from the Gospel, from the teachings of the Church, and

XXXI. from the pious traditions of the ancients.

XXXII. Let no man take from the Church you who are the sons of the Church. Let those perish by themselves who wish to perish. Let those alone remain outside the Church who have withdrawn from the Church. Let those alone be without their bishops who have revolted against their bishops.

XXXIII. Accept our advice, who are compelled and are ready to make an accounting to the Lord for you, and withdraw not from the Church you have thus far believed, nor from its priests, for it is written [cf. Deut. xvii., 12]:

XXXIV. "The man who shall have puffed himself up in his pride so as not to listen to his priest or judge, whoever he shall be in those days, that man shall die."

XXXV. We desire, nevertheless, nay urge, that the Gospel be preached and known and kept, only let it not remove any man from the fold and unity of the Church, without which

XXXVI. there can be no Gospel; Christ is one, and the Church is one, and

XXXVII. there is one apostolic seat placed upon a rock by the voice of the Lord. Another altar besides the one altar cannot be set up, nor a new priesthood besides the one priesthood be established.

XXXVIII. "Whoso gathereth not with me, scattereth."[1]

XXXIX. False and impious and sacrilegious is whatever is set up by the favour of man to the injury of the order of the Church.

XL. Reason does not dictate nor does the natural reverence we ought to feel for our forefathers counsel this sudden casting off with hostile violence of the traditions, observ-

---

[1] Luke xi., 23.

ances, and ceremonials of the fathers. For I do not admit that those people should here be listened to, who

XLI. resist the ceremonials and ordinances of the fathers simply on the ground that they are, as they say, the inventions of man, and not from the Spirit of God, but things laid upon the Christian multitude as a burden and an oppression by dreamers and perverted spirits;

XLII. as if the same notion could not be got up in regard to the traditions of the Apostles and

XLIII. of the general councils. Let injurious clamour of this sort cease, therefore, and let unholy suspicion, such as the least of these gentry would regret in his own case, be not showered upon the good fathers who

XLIV. are commended to us as much by their lives as by their teaching . . . Let the general good also invite us to retain the observance of the ceremonials of the Church at least

XLV. for the time being. For all political order would

XLVI. fall to the ground, if the things which had been

XLVII. agreed upon by general consent, or

XLVIII. at least acceded to, could be found fault with, or

XLIX. called to the test of a new standard at every man's own sweet will. For where has there ever been an opinion so unanimously accepted that no objection could be made to it by people influenced by devotion or ignorance or mere contrary-mindedness and the itching to get up something new? It is, therefore, fair, and has been sanctioned by law and custom, that every decision affecting a body of people should rest

L. upon the voice of the majority in matters at least which are not

LI. at variance with the divine law, as in the present case. If, on the other hand, it were free to any and everybody to obstruct the course of things, nothing more would be accomplished than if

LII. there should be kept up between the masters of

a ship a bitter and continuous quarrel, one wishing to make sail, another to shorten sail, one striving to tack to port, the other to starboard. For when the decision of the majority has been reached, is it not wiser to help carry it out or at least not persistently to oppose it, and so

LIII. to reach some sort of a harbour, than, in the uncertain hope of a better harbour, to throw everything into confusion and evident mutiny? Finally, what is more likely, that

LIV. one person should be deceived, or the whole community? What is more probable, that the consciences of a few should be at fault, or of all? Granted that their counsels seem to them, or even perhaps

LV. are, sounder

LVI. counsels; yet of what advantage to the general body, of which they are but a small part, is this obstinate

LVII. attempt to drag it elsewhere, when it is moving in the opposite course without risk of losing its soul? To what does it give birth but strife and offences and confusion? Granted even that the whole body was wrong in establishing or accepting a ceremonial system thus far maintained, and that, as is the portion of human ignorance and frailty, some things have become mixed with the Christian religion which are not altogether in harmony with the Gospel and Holy Scripture, yet the Christian piety which we ought to show in all our dealings with all men demands that, with a view to their instruction, we

LVIII. make some allowance for those who err with good intentions, at least if their error be not excessive, rather than expose everything to such manifest uproar and rebellion. It was no doubt in this sense that the dictum was made:

LIX. A universal error has the force of right. As, therefore, our beatified Pope of blessed memory, Leo X, and his most serene majesty, Charles V, Emperor of the Romans, recently

LX. condemned new doctrines of this kind, and promulgated their condemnation in official documents,[1] on the ground that such doctrines were contrary to the order of the Church and contrary to the law of the Gospel and to the unity of Gospel ordinance, we appeal to you whom the Holy Spirit has appointed

LXI. to rule with us the Church, which he won

LXII. by his blood—we appeal to you by that pity which all Christians feel at the thought of vile schism in the Church, his spotless bride, to see that these doctrines are put off, put aside for the time, not preached or discussed or taught, openly or in secret, also that nothing be

LXIII. altered, changed, or made different in the ceremonial of the Church, until

LXIV. those whom it concerns come together for the business of the Church, and conferring together render a decision regulated by regard for discipline and mercy, and

LXV compare the Scriptures together, so that we may all walk in the house of the Lord in one mind and one step and one path, until we win the true peace in him who hath made the two one in Jesus Christ, our Lord. Finally we beg you, yourselves and through those entrusted to you, diligently to offer prayers meanwhile to the Lord, that he may

LXVI. be appeased by the restitution that is due him, and may wash away the sin of the wrongs we have done to merit these things. Pray for the things that make for the peace of Jerusalem, that the Lord may "do good in [his] good pleasure unto Zion; build . . . the walls of Jerusalem [Ps. li., 18]. This, Venerable and Honourable Brethren, beloved to us in Christ, is what, led

LXVII. by our fatherly affection for you, we determine to write to you at this time of confusion, begging you by the bowels of compassion of our Lord, Jesus Christ, to abide in the unity of

---

[1] The Pope's Bull against Luther, June 15, 1520, and the Emperor's edict at Worms, May 26, 1521, against the same. These, slightly condensed, are given in the original Latin in B. J. Kidd's *Documents of the Continental Reformation* (Oxford, 1911), pp. 75–79, and 87–89, respectively. There is a full translation of the Bull by H. E. Jacobs, in his Life of Luther (N. Y., *Heroes of the Reformation*), pp. 413–435.

LXVIII. Holy Mother Church and in obedience to those set over you, and not to cast away thus hastily the ceremonies of the Church introduced by our forefathers, and this we strongly hope and confidently promise ourselves from you. The Most High God deign to keep

LXIX. His Church in peace and you in safety! Amen. Given at Constance the twenty-fourth day of May in the year of our Lord one thousand five hundred and twenty-two.

HULDREICH ZWINGLI'S REPLY.

To you I must now address my words, who two months or so ago put forth a certain document. Your names I willingly and gladly omit to mention, that they may not be in ill repute among good men, and that I may not provoke you unduly, for I have a hope that you will finally leave the asses and come over to the oxen, abandon the goats for the sheep. Not that I do not know your names or could not set them out as a laughing stock to the crowd, but I think it more profitable, for the advancement of Christ's teaching, not to do so. Although it may give rise to suspicion of others than yourselves as authors of the document, yet I have preferred to spare your names rather than to answer the viciously wanton suspicions of certain persons. For I am going to treat you as you would by no means treat me if I treated the cause of the Gospel in your style and defended myself with weapons like yours. And I pray to God to enlighten and guide my mind so that I shall say nothing unworthy of him, and yours so that you shall take everything that I say in good part, that casting aside all strife we may come together into one body in Christ and think in harmony in the Lord Jesus. Amen.

I. In the first place, therefore, what was the need of accusing me, a Swiss professing Christ among the Swiss, of raising this disturbance, since you say that it is taking place only in Germany, and the Swiss are not reckoned among the Germans? Yet, meanwhile, though I have been watching almost a whole month, I have been unable to discover that you have sent a like admonition to anybody anywhere in Germany. Why do ye not apply your remedy to the diseased part? Know ye not that Christ said: "They that are whole need not a physician, but they that are sick"? [Luke v., 31]. It becomes apparent, therefore, that it is I to whom ye are singing your little song; for I fancy you have more sense than to be applying a remedy to a limb that you do not consider diseased. But in this matter I owe a certain amount of gratitude to you, because it has pleased you to give me a sort of general hint, unless perhaps you did it to cut me off from an opportunity to answer. This I rather think, however, you are offering me, in order not to be forever using the same subterfuge and exposing yourselves to ridicule. And as to the matter itself, it is not thought to be such a very unworthy deed if one complains that Christ's poor sheep are being crushed under burdensome ordinances and observances. For that holy man Moses did the like [Exod. ii., 11] when he slew the Egyptian and freed the Israelite and finally led all the people out of captivity. But why do I bring up such ancient matters? Christ himself was moved to compassion when he saw the multitude neglected like loose and outcast sheep that had no shepherd, so that presently he said unto his disciples, "The harvest truly is plenteous, but the labourers are few," and bade them pray the Lord of the harvest that he would straightway send harvesters [Matt. ix., 36–38]. And so Paul, who was ready to become accursed for the sake of the Israelite brethren, that they might at length loathe their burden of laws and ceremonials [Romans ix., 3]. It cannot be denied, I think, that the hodgepodge of human ordinances is so tremendous that hundreds of those Cyprian oxen were not enough to eat them up; and no wonder, since every one thinks himself at liberty to make new ones to his heart's content, and no one objects or resists, so that now they have all but accepted this bit of tyranny, "whatever the prelate will he may," though Christ gives warning to the contrary, saying [Matt. xv., 9]: "In vain do they worship me, teaching for doctrines the commandments of men." If, therefore, these things profit us nothing before God, yet meanwhile weigh upon the poor sheep to such a degree that God, pitying them, promised by the mouth of his prophet that he would take away the shepherds who fed themselves, and would visit and free the scattered sheep [Ezek. xxxiv., 10], (Here I beg of you to read the whole chapter, that you may be taught how offensive to God are those shepherds such as you would like to make him, who yet on account of the goodness of his heart cannot be made such,) what harm is there, pray, if one complains that the people of Christ are unduly kept in constant oppression? He does nothing else, surely, than what God himself hath done, and Christ, and Paul, and Moses.

II. What harm, pray, is going to happen to us if the whole rubbish-heap of ceremonials be cleared away, since God declares that he is worshipped in vain by these things? The sayings of the Lord are pure sayings, silver tried by fire and cleansed from earth, aye seven times cleansed. Are we, therefore, to mix dross with the silver again? Are we to change to dross those who have become the true metal of Israel? "The house of Israel is to me become dross" [Ezek. xxii., 18]. You should consider, therefore, whether this age of ours be not rightly called golden by them who look to setting the words of God in all their purity before hungry souls, and allowing none of the vanities of human recklessness to be mixed therewith. But they would make it an iron age who cannot suffer this, saying: Depart from us. We want not the knowledge of thy ways. We have no use for thee. Hence they cry out: Seize him, bind him, cast him into prison, lay on the cords of torture, bring on κύφωνας, the pillory, drown, hang, burn, that verily the words of Christ may be fulfilled [John xvi., 2]: "The time cometh, that whosoever killeth you will think that he doeth God service." To such, therefore, the age is not golden, but it is to those who by the fire of that trial are proved to be pure gold and bright silver and gems, and to those whose consciences, pitifully torn by the slayers of souls, are now at last brought into the quiet haven of true piety, whom the Lord feeds upon the mountains of Israel by the rivers, and in all the inhabited places of the country, in fat pastures [Ezek. xxxiv., (13 and) 14], whom the Lord feeds and they shall want for nothing, whom the Lord hath led out into broad pastures and has saved because he willed it.

III. They do rightly who call us to the freedom of the Gospel, for by that alone are we saved. Hear Christ in the last chapter of Mark: "Preach the Gospel to every creature. He that believeth" (after the Gospel has been preached, to wit) "and is baptised, shall be saved."[1] The truth hath made us free; therefore are we truly free; the Son hath made us free [John viii., 32]. How shall a slave reduce us again to slavery? We owe nothing to any man save mutual love (though the Apostle means this to be understood without derogation of the authority of kings and potentates). How do certain men, then, venture to require of us more than the talent that was entrusted to them?

IV. Here, to begin with, I wonder at the flowery and poetical elegance of your diction, when you say: "What human ordinances they call tares and cockles they strive to pull up." You were imitating the great comedy writer, I suppose, when he said, what plays he had written he hoped might please the people, or "What you think such is not a real marriage." For the whole phraseology otherwise is so lifeless and without grace that I have seldom seen so long an effusion so devoid of all charm, and were it not for this floweret which sprang up here so opportunely, no one could read the thing without nausea. But I return to the subject. Tares and cockles they call human ordinances, yea, and dross and rubbish and sawdust, everything that is foreign to the thought of Christ, and that came forth from hypocrisy, greed, and $\varphi\iota\lambda\alpha\upsilon\tau\iota\alpha$, or self-love. Here again

---

[1] Mark xvi., 15 *ff*.

gratitude is due you because you allow that the Gospel teaching is the wheat. But when, alas! you see the wheat also being rooted up before your eyes, you show plainly that the parable which Christ sets forth in Matt. xiii., 37–39, and explains there, has not been very thoroughly studied by you. For you would otherwise have seen that Christ is speaking there not of different kinds of teachings but of different kinds of men, of whom some have not so cast off all shame as not to shrink from sinning openly, yet do not abstain from sinning, albeit their wrongdoing is not of a heinous character, but such as human life can scarcely be gone through without. This is an offence nevertheless to some of the weaker brethren. He bids us bear with these, "for in many things we offend all" [James iii., 2], and the mote must first be cast out of one's own eye, that one may properly draw out the beam from one's brother's eye [Matt. vii., 5]. Hence Christ here bids us to look with indulgence upon certain usual and commonplace shortcomings, but he holds a different view of greater sins, as when he bids us pluck out the eye—that is, the seeing or watching thing, the teacher or bishop, if it offend, and cast it from us, and so with the hand and the foot [Matt. v., 29, and xviii., 9]. You will never find Christ or the Apostles speaking in such a way as to show a wish that we should suffer any pernicious teaching inconsistent with God's word to spring up among us. For Christ himself bitterly hits the scribes and Pharisees for putting God's commands in the background and teaching their own traditions [Matt. xv, 3]. He also cries out that they sin, saying, "Ye sin, knowing not the Scriptures," though they knew their own traditions. And he calls them to the study of the Scriptures, saying, "Search the Scriptures" [John v., 39], and meaning evidently to turn them away from their own devices and fabrications. Paul also reminds Titus, that a bishop ought to be one "holding fast the faithful word as he hath been taught, that he may be able . . . to convince the gainsayers" [Tit. i., 9]. John bids us [I. John iv., 1] "try the spirits, whether they are of

God." There are hundreds of passages that bid us to look out that human teachings be not accepted in the place of the teachings of God. And if it be said: "These people of yours have called human teachings tares and cockles. What of it, if one just turns things a little and changes the sequence somewhat, but does not vitiate the real meaning?" It fits exactly that human wisdom, tradition, knowledge, be called tares and cockles, because an enemy hath sown them among the harvest of God, while the bishops were asleep, or rather abetting. So far there is no flaw in the parallel, but there will be one if you go on to the following—"Let both grow together," and the rest. But, to finish this section, if you see the wheat torn up with the tares, it were yours to see to it that the wheat be not destroyed, not the tares. You ought to help those in your neighbour's ship who are hauling in a net full of large fish, and not those who are building with wood and hay and stubble. And this especially now that ye see so large a number of the most learned men straining every nerve in this direction, so that from this consideration, if from no other, we can recognise the work as of God, because now that the light of learning and of tongues has come into the world, exceeding few abuse it for mercenary purposes. Our Lord Hugo ought to have been urged to embrace more ardently the cause of Christ towards which he was pointing in the beginning of this drama (for I hear that utterances of his were noticed to this effect, "I desire, even at the utmost personal loss, that the teaching of the Gospel be advanced"), he ought to have been urged to sow the good seed more industriously and guard it more strenuously. This was a case for spurring on the runner if he had determined to make Christ's glory the grander, not for throwing an evil spell upon him as he was making a good race.

V. "But if any man seem to be contentious, we have no such custom, neither the churches of God" [I. Corinth. xi., 16]. But whence arose the contentions? Was it not from the carnal [I. Corinth. iii., 3], who say, "I am of Scotus,

I of Thomas, I of the Bishop of Rome"? Yet Paul [Galat. ii., 5] would not give place to them even for an hour, although the case at hand was that of circumcision only, not of sure salvation, nor of Christ, nor of judgment. Therefore terrible punishments await us, if after the light has come into the world we love the darkness rather than the light. To which, if you please, do you think we ought to give place, to those who have built their house upon the rock of Christ or to those who have built upon the sand? If on the side of one or the other we must fall, on whose side must we stand? On the side of those who stand even though they fall, and so stand, and shall stand, that no blow of evil can ever befall them, or of those who while declaring themselves fixed upon the surest foundation have already fallen, for whom the blackness of darkness is waiting, "and their damnation slumbereth not"? [II. Pet. ii., 3]. I beg of you by all the gods and goddesses, since the matter in dispute is whether as much ought to be attributed to the traditions of men as to the word of God, has it never occurred to you, that all men are liars, and, on the contrary, that God is true [John iii., 33; Rom. iii., 4], or these sayings: "I am the way, the truth, and the life" [John xiv., 6], or "He that followeth me, shall not walk in darkness" [John viii., 12], and hundreds of others? And in occurring to you, does it not give rise to the feeling, If thou shalt embrace this truth thou canst not be deluded, but if thou embracest the truth of men, however much it disguises itself, thou canst? What reason is there, then, why thou shouldst not follow the sure and unquestionable rather than the doubtful, aye, fallacious? We must contend, no doubt, if we wish to convince the gainsayers, only let it not be done in a spirit of contention, but with the purpose of vindicating the words of God, and not with the tricks of the philosophers but with the strong arms of Scripture. Thus did Stephen upbraid the Jews, quoting from the early Scriptures, and when they resisted though they ought to have been convinced, he cried at last, "Ye stiffnecked and uncircumcised in heart and ears, ye do always resist the Holy

Ghost" [Acts vii., 51]. And thus did Paul often speak, especially to the Romans[1] in the last chapter of Acts, where, after having tried for nearly a whole day by passages from Scripture to make them believe in Christ, he finally brought out this shaft from Isaiah [vi., 9], and hurled it at them: "Go unto this people, and say, Hearing ye shall hear, and shall not understand; and seeing ye shall see, and not perceive: For the heart of this people is waxed gross, and their ears are dull of hearing, and their eyes have they closed; lest they should see with their eyes, and hear with their ears, and understand with their heart, and should be converted, and I should heal them." But if any fault is ever to be found on account of contention, surely it ought to be found with those who have made it their effort to show forth unto the world how much they can do by contending and relying only upon the hair-splitting of the sophists and not upon those two swords, the Old and the New Testaments, except so far as their shameful ignorance compelled them, driving them, whether they would or no, to take into their hands weapons strange to them from any quarter. Yet these two swords are those which Christ bade his disciples to give their cloaks, nay sell their shirts, to acquire. These people may be called contentious, as far as I am concerned, as also those who, after the fashion, or, as you say, pattern, of silly women, spit out reproaches upon others as it were, a fine lot of $αἰχμηταὶ\ καὶ\ πρόμαχοι$ [warriors and champions, of the truth], to be sure.

VI. Not to confuse the declaimers here, I will show in short compass who are the wolves and raiders and the rest of the characters named in such tragedy style. Christ is the shepherd [John x., 11]. His sheep are they who know his voice and follow him as he goeth before them. But they are thieves and robbers and not merely raiders, who by some other way than by the door, which is Christ, climb up into the fold of the sheep. Wolves are they that put on the aspect of sheep, but in their hearts think of nothing

[1] To the Jews in Rome.

else than how they can seize and tear in pieces the tender sheep. Wolves, I say, are they of whom the Benjamin of the Apostles spoke when he foretold [Acts xx., 29], that after his departing would come those who would grievously afflict the flock and not spare it. Now let us see to whom those tragic ἐπιφωνήματα [appellatives], in the very beginning of the effusion can rightly be applied. When the simple-minded Christians, not perceiving that false prophets had sunken to wolves, but judging them from their aspect as sheep, put up with them, these, changing all the devotion of shepherds into the madness of wolves, began to seize upon, scatter, and destroy everything, in order to fill up the vast maw of their lusts, not satisfied to stuff their belly with the milk and wool and flesh even of the sheep which they had seized, but breaking their bones also and leaving no bit of cruelty untried. Then I confess that a good part of the sheep, marvelling when they saw themselves butchered by those in whom they had placed their refuge, fled away from such certain destruction. But this did the poor creatures no good. For those mighty Nimrods hunted and pursued them and swallowed them like so much bread. But after he who promised to remain with his own even to the fulness of time could not longer bear this ruin of his own, he called certain men after his custom, men not wise according to the flesh (for God hath made the wisdom of this world foolishness [I. Cor. iii., 19], but lowly men, to bring his name unto the kings and potentates of the earth, just as in the days of old those had done who from fishers were made Apostles. And as soon as this was heard among the people, it is wonderful how they all began to breathe freely and to give thanks, and stop their flight, feeling that a leader was come and enrolling themselves under him, abandoning meanwhile those who besides the empty name had nothing worthy of a shepherd and turning to the shepherd and bishop of their souls, they who a little while before had been as like as possible to lost sheep, according to the saying of Peter [I. Pet. ii., 25], and who now walked in that light which lighteth every man who cometh into this world, and thus could not stray or go wrong any more. Hence it is clear that all this brew of ceremonials is of no concern to those who have already come back to wisdom, but only to those who still stumble about in the darkness of human devices, disregarding Christ and his teaching. It can not be said that these mock at their shepherds, for they worship them as gods and are as like unto them as possible. But if you fancy that those who have gone over to the side of the Gospel mock at their leaders, they are not on fire with such hatred as you complain of a little later. There is none who is so derisive of his neighbour as he who cannot possibly be persuaded to accept the divine sayings instead of those of men. They say: "What have I to do with Christ or with the Apostles? Customs have changed and demand an altogether different system of life. Poor clown, do you assert that our bishops with all their splendour can come down to this humble plane? They are not only wiser but have given us precepts far preferable to those of Paul or Peter or even Christ himself." These are they, doubtless, who in their madness make a laughing stock of the simple heralds of Christ and hold them in reproach [Wisdom of Solomon (in the Apocrypha) v., 3], but God also will laugh at their own calamity [Prov. i., 26].

VII. Here I will first comment upon your style, when you say, "Others are led astray and driven to doing this," etc. What proposition, pray, do you oppose to this as a co-ordinate, or join to it? You will say, no doubt, the one that follows, "You can, in fact, see some people," etc. But animosity (to use your word) is a passion. Therefore it is included in the previous proposition. Then it must be noted that your word *consiliatrices* is put for *consultrices*, counsellors. For *consiliare* means to them what the Romans meant by *consulere* or *consilium dare*, give counsel. Hence *consiliator* for *consultor*, counsellor, which they sometimes put for senator, by the same process by which they say *fornix*, ein Ofen,[1]

---

[1] There is evidently a blunder here. Could an original "fornax" and

an arch, *fornicator*, ein Ofner, an arch-frequenter, a fornicator. As to the matter itself, it is not commendable for one to do anything with bubbling over wrath or ambition, though Paul rejoices for the Gospel even if it be preached "of strife or envy" [Phil. i., 18]. And this you also ought to have done, provided the necessity of the situation demanded it and you had examined that passage, for there is scarcely any one who is not roused to indignation sometimes at wrong doings. Whether these feelings can be called wrath I will not now discuss, especially as even the Holy Scriptures attribute such to God [I. Kings, xi., 9]—"The Lord was angry with Solomon," and [Isaiah lxi., 8] "For I the Lord love judgment, I hate robbery for burnt offering." Therefore I am led rather to rejoice for the Gospel with Paul, whether it be preached in season or out of season. If any seem to be jealous of those who make the uproar, it does not seem to me to be so much jealousy as reasonable grief because they are not willing in any way to come back to sense. But hitherto the heralds of Christ have been thought to strive for none of the objects of ambition, the champions of human devices for all such, praise, glory, honours, wealth, office, kingdoms, and everything that is esteemed best worth while, and this in the time when modesty, that last blessing in evil days, was not yet obsolete. Now nobody strives to satisfy his ambitions thus, but every one seizes with tooth and nail everything he can lay hold of, so that Isaiah [i., 23] says truly, "Thy princes are companions of thieves." Now as to the ambition with which you can reproach our party also, that they covet glory and praise, if not bishoprics and priesthoods, you say nothing to the point, for this defect can be hidden by denial and you cannot prove that afterwards. Hence it is clear that you said this in a cavilling spirit, and yet it does not apply to these, who do not "gather grapes of thorns, or figs of thistles" [Matt. vii., 16]. Of those it can, however,

---

"fornacator" have been changed by somebody into the more piquant "fornix," "fornicator"?—H. P.

truly be said, "which creep into (rich men's) houses and lead captive silly women laden with sins"[1] [II. Tim. iii., 6].

VIII. Those who through the knowledge of our Lord Jesus Christ have escaped the pollutions of this world, according to the words of Peter [II. Peter ii., 20], and are not willing to become again entangled therein, ought not to be reckoned as obstinate but as firm in their faith, being unwilling to withdraw from the sacred commands that have been given unto them. For having tasted that the Lord is sweet and that he shall be blest who puts his hope in him [cf. Ps. xxxiv., 9], they have begun to cease to fear what man can do to them, and neither present things nor future things can separate them from the love of Christ, just as the companions of Ulysses, having eaten λωτου τὸν μελιηδέα καρπόν [the honey-sweet fruit of the lotus], would not return to their people [cf. Odyssey ix., 93 ff.]. For "No man, having put his hand to the plough, and looking back, is fit for the Kingdom of God" [Luke ix., 62]. Even God himself by the mouth of his servant Jeremiah encourages them not to yield, saying [ch. xv., 19], "If thou take forth the precious from the vile, thou shalt be as my mouth: let them return unto thee; but return not thou unto them. And I will make thee unto this people a fenced brasen wall: and they shall fight against thee, but they shall not prevail against thee: for I am with thee to save thee and to deliver thee." From this I think it is sufficiently clear that they are not only guilty of no sin who cannot be turned away from the truth of the Gospel, but do well and wisely and steadfastly, if they struggle continually for it with all their might and ever keep before their eyes the watchword "Endure to the end." Let those mad men have done, therefore, who think that the divine should yield to the human.

IX. Peace Christ prayed for for his own when he had risen from the dead, the same peace which before his death he had given and left to the Apostles [cf. John xiv., 27], but not

---

[1] The Latin seems somewhat truncated here, but I think I have expressed its meaning.—H. P.

the peace of the world, which belongeth to sinners, forsooth, to those who "have made a covenant with death, and with hell are at agreement" [Isaiah xxviii., 15], and who believe that the soul of man is destroyed with the body like the beasts, as all their life beareth witness. For they build like the Milesians as if they were to live forever, and enjoy their pleasures as if they were to die to-morrow, humming to themselves these words of Paul [I. Corinth. xv., 32] or of Sardanapalus (from whom I mistrust Paul borrowed it to characterise their devotion to their bellies): "Let us eat and drink, for to-morrow we die." These, I say, fear every breath of air lest the quiet of their enjoyments be disturbed in some part; they cry "Peace, peace," when "there is no peace unto the wicked" [Isaiah xlviii., 22]. But if they fancy that they have a perfectly calm mind, they are ἄθεοι [atheists]; if they are not ἄθεοι [atheists], they are to be pitied. For believing that God hath given unto us τὸ Εὐαγγέλιον [the Gospel], as the doctrine of salvation, if they yet do not yield or defer to it, it is evident that they are beyond hope, and that they have forsaken Christ, as Demas forsook Paul [II. Timothy iv., 10], "having loved this present world." But if they weighed more carefully the words of Christ, in which he declares that he came not to send peace upon the earth but a sword, with which fathers should be set at variance with their children, etc. [*cf.* Matt. x., 34], and that passage of John [xvi., 33]: "These things I have spoken unto you, that in me ye might have peace. In the world ye shall have tribulation; but be of good cheer; I have overcome the world"; and the passage of Isaiah [xlviii., 18], "O that thou hadst hearkened to my commandments! then had thy peace been as a river, and thy righteousness as the waves of the sea,"—if, I say, they had looked carefully at these things, they would be doing nothing else than trying how peace might be established between God and us, and how human things might yield to the divine, and by yielding become divine. For this is the true peace, which is had in God and not in one's passions which boil in constant turmoil like the waters of the Channel.[1] That peace, nevertheless, has friendship with all men as far as in it lies, according to the teaching of Paul; this other with none who oppose our desires. Therefore, most excellent gentlemen, whoever you are, you enter upon your task in vain. For there will never be peace between those who are of Christ and those who are of the flesh. For the first, like their master, will never cease to fight, and the second will never yield, unless the illuminating spirit shall sometime enlighten them and draw them to itself. Yet meanwhile it is given to those followers of the Lord to live in gladness and the enjoyment of peace in Christ even if they suffer persecution. For they rejoice with the Apostles that they suffer shame for the name of Christ [Acts v., 41]. The others, as shown above from Isaiah, have no peace and no rest. I pray the Most High God to deign to look upon them with graciousness as He looked upon Peter when he denied him, that they may be turned back to him in wisdom and give glory unto God. Amen.

X. The common people, endowed with the harmlessness of the dove, will yield to the Gospel alone, and the less vitiated with the dregs of human traditions, the more capable they are of receiving the heavenly teachings, to which they flee for refuge in confidence as to a sacred anchor.

XI. When they see the learned at swords' points with each other, they judge more clearly than the little scholars themselves which side is right according to Christ. For "he that is spiritual judgeth all things" [I. Cor. ii., 15], and they are the really spiritual, for they depend wholly upon the spirit—that is, the mind of God.

XII. I hear no men more arrogantly reproach with the name of heretic for the slightest possible cause everybody who already has or is beginning to have sound views than men of a class to which I sincerely trust you do not belong.

XIII. There is a class of men so shameless that though

---

[1] The channel between Bœotia and Bœotia—because of its ebb and flow, the classical simile of instability.

they are a constant stumbling block to the unhappy people through their unblushing sins, they will not listen to any sort of warning, far less to any correction or improvement. I wish, indeed, that they would strive to be other than they are reputed to be—nay, I exhort them for Christ's sake to strive. And when this takes place, justly grounded criticisms will cease, or if they do not cease, they will no longer disturb them. For they will learn, meanwhile, that they shall be blest of whom evil is said, and they will try to show that the slanders poured out upon them are poured out upon men most undeserving of it. But what wickedness is this, despitefully to entreat him who is appointed to be an example unto the rest, and to refuse to listen to any warning? I admit, as far as I am concerned, that I have often said that a fair proportion of the bishops of our time are not real but counterfeit bishops, and I do not think I ought to be blamed for it either, since Isaiah calls such "dumb dogs" [Isa. lvi., 10], and Christ calls them "thieves and robbers" [John x., 1]. I am speaking of those who have not entered into the sheepfold by the door. For you will find few who fill the office of bishop to the best of their ability, and do not rather conduct themselves as rulers and satraps and kings. I would that all who have spoken in these days unrestrainedly had spoken passionately rather than truly. It is the duty of all and especially of the heads of the Church to see whether their ill repute is deserved or undeserved. For Paul teaches that an elder convicted of sin is to be rebuked publicly [cf. I. Tim. v., 20].

XIV. Up to this point you have been telling what has happened, I think, but now you wish to make it appear dangerous for a bishop to open his mouth, and you count up the dangers to which he would be exposed—namely, that he would be spoken ill of, and would get into strife. What would you have said if he had even run the risk of stripes? Christ sent out his disciples as sheep in the midst of wolves [Matt. x., 16, and Luke x., 3], and yet he says that the shepherd goeth before his sheep [John x., 4]; and again, that the good shepherd layeth down his life for the sheep, but not so the hireling. For when the wolf cometh, he leaveth the sheep, and fleeth [John x., 11 and 12].

If, therefore, the bride of Christ was so wounded within and without as you desire to make it appear, what need of this and delay? Why do you coddle the bishop in his delay, or rather why do you delay him when inclined to act quickly? There was need of haste. The bishop ought to have been roused as quickly as possible, with "Ho there, see how your flock is perishing! Why do you tarry? You ought to be the first to run into danger." Then if he had been inclined to delay, saying, "My good name will suffer, I shall be reviled, I shall have to wrangle," you should have said "Oh, coward! dost thou not remember what Christ said?—'Ye shall be hated of all men for my name's sake'" [Mark xiii., 13, and Luke xxi., 17]. As it is, since the bishop is minded to believe that there is nowhere surer or readier salvation than where Christ is preached, and ye are trying to hinder him, is not that equivalent to saying that you have so worked upon and stirred up our most kindly bishop as to make him accuse me of an abominable deed, to wit, the ravaging of the sheep-fold of Christ? Now you will have it that the one and only bride of Christ is wounded. I admit that she is wounded, not with a mortal wound, but in love. That is an easy and pleasant wound, nay one so acceptable that she bears with calmness that the priest and the Levite should pass by upon the other side and not look back [Luke x., 31, etc.]. For she knows that the good Samaritan is at hand who will cleanse with wine what is foul and soothe the sore places with oil, and take her upon his beast to the shelter of the heavenly mansions. But they who do not recognise the physician shall suffer pitiable torture, not only from the pain of their wounds but from despair of a physician. For they spend all their substance upon physicians who apply the poultice of human traditions to the wound and so draw a false skin over it, but heal it not in itself nor perceive any cure. What need of more? "Woe unto [you] that call evil good, and good evil; that put darkness for light, and light for darkness; that put bitter for sweet, and sweet for bitter!" [Isaiah v., 20].

XV. I could wish that you had better understood the utterances of the prophets. For what you quote from Amos is diametrically opposed to your case. For Amos [ch. v., 5] is upbraiding the children of Israel because they had abandoned the Lord and made [sacrifices] unto calves and idols in Bethel and Gilgal and Beersheba, leaving off righteousness and turning judgment to wormwood, and because they feared not Him who ruleth the whole universe, whose name is the Lord. For He shall overthrow the strong and lay low the mighty, because they hate him that rebuketh, and abhor him that speaketh uprightly. Therefore, though they raised up lofty dwellings of quarried stone, yet should they never live in them, because they had robbed the poor. So also should they never gather the vintage of their cunningly planted vineyards, for He knew their sins, to wit, that being reverenced as parents by the simple-minded people, they yet showed themselves like the cruelest enemies, receiving money from the rich and crushing down the poor. Yea, and things should become so bad that the wise man would not dare to open his mouth on account of the viciousness of that time. See, I pray you, whether time has turned backward to show us this picture of evils, now that some persons practise so unblushingly all that savours of tyranny that from fear of injuries and excommunications and dreadful things no sagacious man ventures to utter a murmur. See, I say, how unfortunately you dip into hidden writings, when you use those which cry out against your own side. I do not now recall where your quotation from Ezekiel is found, but wherever it comes from, I think you have quoted it with the same judgment and appropriateness as the passage from Amos.

XVI. For what is written in Ezekiel v., 11, whence it seems that your quotation was gathered, is as thoroughly against you as anything could be. So also the passage from the fifty-fourth Psalm.[1] For the prophet is there calling down the curse of discord upon the Israelites for their faithlessness, and this also fell upon them for having crucified Christ. And there was as much contention in the city of Jerusalem as there ever was in Troy or Carthage or Athens. In short, οὐδὲν πρὸς ἔπος βάλλ' οὕτως [this talk of yours is not a bit to the point].

XVII. I wonder that the times now first seem dangerous to you, when the evils, in consequence of which Paul [II. Tim. iii., 2] reckons the times as dangerous, began to show themselves long ago and have run riot so down to our time that a large number of the most learned men have been unable to hold their peace longer after the example of the prudent man whom you cited a little while ago from Amos so inappropriately, if you will pardon my saying so. Indeed they are ready to undergo any danger rather than keep silence before such foul abominations. Who would call these present times dangerous when the sheep of the Lord are sought out and set free and fed? They *are* dangerous if death is an evil, but not to those to whom you would make it appear, but to those, forsooth, who are taught that the soul cannot be destroyed by these people who can destroy the body. But about these I do not think you are so very anxious. Therefore from this fear of yours I free you by these presents. I want to warn you here, since you keep indulging in the same complaints and the same words, so that when an answer has been made to what you had said before, you are constantly running back to the same point, I want to warn you to look out lest δὶς κράμβη θάνατος [you prove a back number].[2]

XVIII. Offences have been multiplying for about a thousand years, especially at the hands of those who do not care a snap for the little ones of Christ, whom he wished not to have made of little account, when he said [Matt. xviii.,

---

[1] Fifty-fifth in the King James version.—H. P.
[2] Basil the Great, *Epistola*, 187. (Trans. in *Nicene and Post-Nicene Fathers*, 2d series, vol. viii., 223; "twice cabbage is death.")

Archeteles: Reply to Bishop's Admonition 235

10], "Take heed that ye despise not one of these little ones" who believe in me. But these men, disregarding the words of God, teach the little ones their own sayings, and turn to themselves the hope of those (I mean the little ones) whose only hope ought to be in Christ, stamping the grace of God as obsolete while marking with approval their own penances. They mercilessly frighten and drive to despair the feeble voice of conscience, selling that which ought to be freely given away and requiring chastity,[1] which Christ left free, while they abuse their power of the keys as they call it, and at the same time teach that all their fulminations must be accepted whether rightly or wrongly hurled forth. They defend their own luxury when compared with the Gospel simplicity and condemned from time to time, and think it right to regulate even the clearly divine ordinances according to their own sweet will. The day would fail me if I tried to count up all their offences, though these ye regard not as offences, but if a vinedresser or a shepherd or a husbandman eats meat in Lent, as the sacred city of Rome ventures to do without harm, that ye call an offence.

XIX. Here you commit two sins, one against those who proclaim the Gospel to-day, in saying that they are spreading new errors; the other against yourselves, in calling those earlier things you mention dangerous errors, under whatever head you class them, unless by earlier you mean the errors with which Christians were deluged in old days, when according to Sabellius there were three Gods, according to Arius one God and one ὑπόστασις [substance], while Manichæus held that Christ pretended to have taken upon himself the nature of a man, and Marcion taught that there were two Gods, one the creator of the good, the other of the evil. Worse errors than these, I say, are sown abroad to-day now that that country bumpkin Zwingli is preaching the Gospel with such energy and risk of harm. But your words when carefully weighed do not seem to be meant to apply

[1] Meaning celibacy.

to these earlier errors, but to those into the place of which the Gospel errors are stepping.

XX. Βάλλ' οὕτως πάλιν [you are throwing out the same stuff again] if you mean that schism, by which certain persons have separated from Christ and turned to men and created things, and by "mother" her who is our mother, the heavenly Jerusalem, the bride of Christ without spot or blemish, and by "wandering sheep" those who have strayed from Christ the true light and are wandering in the darkness of human traditions,—if you mean the "factious perversity" by which the human is contumaciously accepted as divine and Christ is abandoned for sordid gain, and that "heretical tampering with the faith" by which certain persons wantonly twist the meaning of the sacred writings to the winning of their own advantage. For he is the real heretic who interprets the sacred writings not by the light of Christ but by his own. If, I say, this is the way you understand these terms, οὕτως βάλλετε [you are at it again]. I do not use the singular for fear our most Reverend Lord of Constance should fancy that my words were directed to him, when, as a matter of fact, I desire that his authority be intact at all points.

XXI. "According to the mastery of the Lord and his Gospel" you entreat (you say "according to" for "by" the mastery of the Gospel). What you are trying to indicate, I do not understand, for Christ forbids his disciples [Matt. xxiii., 10] to let themselves be called Masters. And in Luke [ch. xxii.] he commanded, saying, "He that is greatest among you, let him be as the younger; and he that is chief, as he that doth serve." But why do I follow up these things again as if there were a grain of sense in the whole effusion? As to your bidding me watch against the snares of the devil, I will do so sedulously. For I know well enough that, in the words of Peter [I. Pet. v., 8], "as a roaring lion, [he] walketh about, seeking whom he may devour." I know, too, with what weapons he should be resisted, to wit, strength and steadfastness of faith, and trusting to these, I shudder not at the gates of hell nor at the tortures which the good are made to suffer in this world.

XXII. What do I hear? Am I playing such a damnable game? Bringing into play again sacrilegious machinations and old-time heresies? Who could refrain from upbraiding under such circumstances? Through many lines you rage and rave and riot so that for the violence of your raging you have no clear idea yourself of what you are saying. You wish to seem to be urging the unity of the Church, when your words breathe nothing but rebellion, uproar, war, destruction and whatever belongs thereto. What will happen under such circumstances if I proceed to strike back with revilings at those whom I know to be the instigators of this barbarous accusation? Will not that happen which the divine Paul predicts? [Gal. v., 15]—"But if ye bite and devour one another, take heed that ye be not consumed one of another." And ye cannot make denial, saying that those things were said with general application, for you have not sent a like threatening admonition to any others, nor are there in our whole chapter more than one or two who do not share your sentiments. Hence it is absolutely clear that you were aiming at me alone. And if you maintain with the utmost vigour that these things were written simply as an admonition to myself, what was the need of embittering so harshly a matter which really does not apply to me? You say, that I might be the more carefully on my guard. Do ye think me so stupid and senseless that I have not any perception at all? But let that pass. I appeal to your intelligence,—is not this whole thing, by whatever name ye call it, brandished at me? I wish, therefore, not to return like for like, but to return your own utterances in about the same brevity that you use in this section, but corrected first and renovated by the gauge of the Gospel teaching, and you can then regard them as my declaration of principles. I shall not cease to try to renew the old-time unity of the Church of Christ, setting snares for no man but often turning them to good when set, as I will prove through yourselves as witnesses, and never intending to lend myself to any faction, much less to one of heretics. For I have never planted any other plant than that which Christ planted at the direction of his Father, which cannot be rooted up. For three years ago now (to give you an account of the preaching I have done at Zurich), I preached the entire Gospel according to Matthew, and at that time I had not even heard the name of those persons to whose faction you accuse me of belonging. I added the Acts of the Apostles to the Gospel immediately, that the Church of Zurich might see in what way and with what sponsors the Gospel was carried forth and spread abroad. Presently came the First Epistle of Paul to Timothy, which seemed to be admirably adapted to my excellent flock. For there are contained in it certain canons, as it were, of the character worthy of a Christian. Here, inasmuch as certain smatterers showed perverted opinions of the faith, I postponed the Second Epistle to Timothy until I should have expounded that to the Galatians. Then I added the other. But the before-mentioned smatterers now went to such a pitch of mad impiety that they well-nigh made the name of Paul a disgrace, throwing out these pious ejaculations, which, of course, do not offend anybody: "Who was Paul, pray? Was he not a man? He was an Apostle, to be sure, but a sort of outside one only, not one of the twelve. He never talked with Christ. He did not put together any portion of the faith. I believe as much in Thomas or Scotus[1] or whom you will as in Paul." So I also expounded both the Epistles of Peter, the standard-bearer of the Apostles, that they might see clearly whether both men spoke under the inspiration of the same spirit, and when I had finished these, I began the Epistle to the Hebrews, that they might recognise more plainly the goodness and glory of Christ. From this they will learn that Christ is

---

[1] Thomas Aquinas, doctor angelicus, born 1227 or 1225, died 1274; Johannes Duns Scotus, doctor subtilis, born c. 1265; died 1308. The first was a Dominican, the second a Franciscan.

the great High Priest, and they have in fact nearly learned it already. Nor is there any ground for your accusing me in regard to certain writings. For before these came into my hands I had begun the business, nay had promised to do so about a year before. They will learn also that Christ, having been made a sacrifice once for all, has accomplished their salvation forever. This is the seed I have sown. Matthew, Luke, Paul, and Peter have watered it, and God has given it splendid increase, but this I will not trumpet forth, lest I seem to be canvassing my own glory and not Christ's. Go now and say that this plant (to come back to your point) is not of the Father in Heaven. I have not, I say, used any false nostrums or tricks or exhortations, but in simple words and terms native to the Swiss I have drawn them to the recognition of their trouble, having learned this from Christ himself, who began his own preaching with it. I have never drawn away any one from harmony with his bishop, if he was a bishop and not a thief or robber such as Christ characterised in John x., 12. From what sources I have drawn the discipline of the Church I mentioned a little while ago. I have vigorously urged my flock to hold fast to the glory of our profession, saying, "Seeing then that we have a great $ἀρχιερεά$ [high priest] that is passed into the heavens, Jesus, the Son of God" [Hebr. iv., 14], hold fast to that confession, and seek not honour from one another, as Christ bade the Jews not to do because it interfered with their believing in him [John, v., 44], saying, "How can ye believe, which receive honour one of another, and seek not the honour which cometh from God only?" Mark these things carefully, I beg of you. I call my flock absolutely away, as far as I can, from hope in any created being to the one true God and Jesus His only begotten Son, our Lord, he that trusteth in whom shall never die. I try with all my might to make them ask forgiveness of him who desires to be freely asked even though we are sinners, saying [Matt. xi., 28], "Come unto me, all ye that labour and are heavy laden, and I $ἀναπαύσω$" [will give you rest].

This I believe so firmly that if occasion should arise I do not think I have need of any bishop or priest to make satisfaction for me. For Christ did that once, when he delivered up his body as a sacrifice for us, and washed us with the blessed bath of his blood. The whole body of the presbyters I reverence as I do the angels of God. Though I abominate them that are given up to their bellies, yet I forbear and suffer the weeds to grow up with the grain. I enjoin upon my flock to pray without ceasing but in soul and spirit, and to worship the Father in spirit and in truth, according to the saying of Christ. Nay, I bid them knock even to importunity, as the parable of the widow in Luke teaches [Luke xviii., 1, etc.].

XXIII. He that gathereth not with Christ, scattereth abroad, and he that is not with the same is against him [Matt. xii., 30 and Luke xi., 23]. How can the Gospel itself now be at variance with the Gospel teaching? Do ye think that God's state is worse than Satan's? If he were divided against himself, his kingdom could not stand, [Matt. xii., 25], and think ye that God's kingdom can stand if He be at variance with Himself? He would be divided against Himself and at variance with Himself, if His Gospel were opposed to the Gospel teachings. I might proceed to hit the nail on the head here, and show just what Gospel teaching ye are fighting for so valiantly, but I prefer to show myself more modest where I rather think ye have no modesty at all.

XXIV. Do I not teach long and great penitence, when I am continually crying: "μετανοεῖτε [repent], go and sell all that thou hast and give to the poor" [Matt. xix., 21], and "Give alms, and all things shall be pure unto you"? [cf. Luke vi., 38]. Meanwhile I forbid—I do not deny it—giving to those who own so much gold that they even load their mules with it, by the which neither mule nor rider is the better off, however. For so it would come to pass that even the swine should be forced to wear gold in their snouts, and the poor would die of hunger. Yet Christ said

Archeteles: Reply to Bishop's Admonition   241

that these should be like as the most faithful supporters among his followers.

XXV. What ye mean by heroic measures, I do not understand, but I know this, that Christ vigorously urges his disciples to boldness when going to meet the monsters of this world, saying [John, xiv., 1], "Let not your heart be troubled," neither be afraid. In the same passage you call insidious the peace that I desire us to enter into with God, whether it be insidious or simple and sincere. What follows presently is of the same stamp with your shrieks of lamentation in sections 23 and 24, where I promised not to set forth what sort of a Gospel you would like to champion if you might.

XXVI. I never boasted that I had the spirit of God, but I confidently hope meanwhile that He will not be absent from His own work, He whom I have so often found prospering the things He was accomplishing through me. I wish, therefore, that you would make true charges against me, and not such as some violent emotion suggests. Yet am I well aware that there is a sort of holy boasting, from which neither Christ nor Paul shrank. For Christ said, "I am the good shepherd [John x., 11], and "all that ever came before me are thieves and robbers; but the sheep did not hear them" [John x., 8]. "I am come that they might have life, and that they might have it more abundantly" [John x., 10]. "I am the light of the world" [John viii., 12], "I and my Father are one" [John x., 30], and hundreds of other such things. Paul said, "For I suppose I was not a whit behind the very chiefest apostles" [II. Cor. xi., 5],[1] and "Though I would desire to glory, I shall not be a fool" [II. Cor. xii., 6], and "In nothing am I $\upsilon\pi\grave{\epsilon}\rho$ $\lambda\acute{\iota}\alpha\nu$ [behind the very chiefest] apostles" [II. Cor. xii., 11],[1] and "I laboured more abundantly than they all" [I. Cor. xv., 10]. Therefore it might be that I have taken some credit to myself in regard to the sacred writings, but if I have ever done so, I know that I did it

---

[1] The Douay version keeps more literally to the slightly different Latin in these two cases.—H. P.

sparingly. But as I turn the whole business over carefully in my memory, I recall that it was once imputed to me as wrong that I had said that God spake by my mouth when I was setting forth His word. But that I did, that the crowd might not think that I spoke of myself and give me the credit that belonged to Christ. I even gave distinct warning that no one must make a mistake about that point.

XXVII. Adulterous teachings I think are those which, made up by men given over to their own desires, are sold as divine, and I hate them worse than a serpent. Nay, this bit of a difference which I now have with you sprang from nothing else than my diligent effort to sift out the dross from the gold. I speak the truth, but refrain, I beg of you.

XXVIII. It will first be worth while here to define false prophets[1] according to Christ's understanding of them, that it may be more evident to what sort of people these words of Jeremiah properly apply [*cf.* Jer. xxiii., 16]. Christ says [Matt. xxiv., 24, and Mark xiii., 22]: "For there shall arise false Christs, and false prophets, and shall shew great signs and wonders; insomuch that, if it were possible, they shall deceive the very elect." But with these words he did not bring out the full force of the term, so that what goes just before must be added here. "Then," he says, "if any man shall say unto you, Lo, here is Christ, or there; believe it not" [Matt. xxiv., 23, and Mark xiii., 21]. Now we are not talking here of false Christs, but of false prophets. These, Christ says, will support their false doctrine by showing signs and this shall trouble even the elect. These same men will say (for this word "for" that follows ["for there shall arise"] shows that both apply to the false prophets)—"Lo, here is Christ, or lo, there." I show no signs, nor believe them easily when shown, even if the decision of certain blind persons had served as an introduction to them. I do not hold that Christ is "here" or "there," but wherever two or three have been gathered together in his name, there I know he is in the midst of them [Matt. xviii., 20]. In

---

[1] He so calls the monks.

short, false prophets are they who with signs and wonders, not to say jugglers' tricks, cast a spell even upon the elect, and exhibit Christ where they will. Enough has been said for you, I know; you do not need to have me drive everything home. We must hasten to the words of the prophet who, as representative of God, thus threatens the false prophets: "Behold I will feed them with wormwood, and make them drink the water of gall" [Jer. xxiii., 15]. This is only too true, for they breathe forth not only wormwood and gall, but poison and death, some of them. There follows: "For from the prophets of Jerusalem is profaneness gone forth into all the land." There are no prophets in Jerusalem in these days, from whom we can suffer pollution, but from whatever quarter the world is polluted, there Jerusalem seems to be beyond a doubt. From whomsoever proceed the murder of souls and the contempt of God and men, know that such are false prophets. There follows: "Thus saith the Lord of hosts, Hearken not unto the words of the prophets that prophesy unto you: they make you vain: they speak a vision of their own heart, and not out of the mouth of the Lord" [Jer. xxiii., 16]. Therefore, those who speak out of the mouth of the Lord are not false prophets. Again, those who speak the vision—that is, the purpose, opinion, thought, of their own heart are false prophets. Now see how many of those who are on your side (for they would all venture to declare that these things which have been got up by certain hypocrites are worthy of as much belief and trust as those that have been handed down in the writings of the Gospel and the Apostles), how many, I say, are going to be left and not pass over to the number of the false prophets. How few of these do not teach that a sort of visions should be accepted in place of the Gospel! How few, if any point comes into discussion, do not settle it according to the opinions of men, without any search of the Holy Scripture! See now the wallet hanging from your back, and you will discover how much justice there is in your accusation of those as false prophets who teach, relying solely upon the divinely inspired books, and how greatly you will profit the Christian world, if ye conquer in your defence of hypocrites and preachers of visions. But what need of much speaking? Every time you take the sacred books into your hands, it turns out unfortunately for you. For they almost always are at variance with you, as the next following remarks will show even more clearly.

XXIX. For the words of Peter, which you quote from, II. Pet. ii., 1 *ff*., apply especially to those who with vain arrogance say, "I am the Christ, I have power to bind and to loose, I have power to loose and to kill thee," yet live meanwhile so impurely in the desires and lusts of the flesh, that they entice those who had truly escaped, and promise freedom to those in the bonds of error, when they have themselves fallen into slavery to their very corruption. That is to say, so far are they who arrogate to themselves the powers of God from being able to free others, that they corrupt them the more and lead them astray, being themselves altogether corrupt. I know what you will say to this, but the authority of him whom you are going to oppose to me will not crush me so much as the whole ὑπόθεσις [argument] of this chapter supports me. I will run through it briefly, that what I mean may be made more clear. In that second chapter Peter is putting on their guard those to whom he is writing —that is, all Christians, of course,—foretelling that among us also there will be lying teachers, just as in the old days false prophets crept in, and they will lead the people astray after them, that they may indulge their lusts the more freely, though they will do this quite without being aware of it. And this he shows by many examples, illustrating that the majesty of God when scorned has always mightily afflicted the scorners, and especially those who give free rein to all the lust and uncleanness of the flesh, and κυριότητος καταφρονοῦσι [despise government]—that is, the highest government, namely, that of God. "Presumptuous are they and self-willed," so that they fear not "to speak evil of dignities"—that is, putting behind them, nay, scorn-

Archeteles: Reply to Bishop's Admonition 245

ing, the "dignity" or glory of Him to whom alone glory belongs and in whom alone it is lawful to glory, they would claim for themselves that which belongs to God alone. And what greater insult to God can be done? Now "glorias" in the plural number it is not unusual for Peter to use for the dignity or glory of God. For in I. Pet. i., 11, we read "when it testified beforehand the sufferings of Christ, and the glory [gloria] that should follow." For how could it be that Peter, forgetting himself, should now mean by "dignities" those arrogant elders whom he had chided in the earlier epistle? But the words following show the same thing, nay, the whole body of this chapter shows it, as I have said. For Peter is aiming at nothing else than preventing men from arrogating the divine to themselves and selling human wares for divine. How much that helps your side, ye may look to, yourselves.

XXX. It is of little consequence if those who are devoted to the Gospel suffer some hunger for it, so be it that they desire to be filled. For that woman of Samaria who had spoken with Christ at the well did some good unto her fellow-townspeople when, suddenly brought to admiring wonder at him [John iv., 7], she desired that her people also should have a share in the thing, and summoned them from the town for the purpose, that they might themselves hear Christ, who were yet men and eminent for knowledge while she was simple and hungry for the Word. But having received the food of the Word, she was perhaps herself superior, yet she grudged it not to others. How much of the Gospel food ye have in your store-houses is not clear, yet ye wish to seem so full that ye can belch it forth upon others. Indeed, as far as I can see, you have not up to now allowed unto others any knowledge of the Gospel teaching. But you seem to speak of everything rather vaguely, and if you deny this (as you will be right in doing) you cannot then deny that it is I alone you are aiming at.

XXXI. The traditions of the men of old deserve to be regarded with the more reverence, the more they are in conformity with the Gospel. But what do you call the traditions of the ancients? Those which the greed of certain individuals has recently devised? You will say, "No." Why do you not then present distinctly by name the traditions that you are trying so hard to have kept? Thus I, who am so in need of the heavenly food, and those like me, can see plainly which are to be retained and which let go. Please mention them all, whether of early or recent date, that the sore spot may be laid bare to the physician. For here seems to be the point in our ailment where it stings and is especially inflamed.

XXXII. Amen, if only you mean the Church of Christ and the bishops who are really bishops and not [John x., 8] thieves and robbers, but installed according to the rule of Paul to Timothy and Titus.

XXXIII. Here, unless it were now pretty well agreed by all that this whole thing was made at your instigation, you would expose our most kindly bishop to being laughed at in that you represent him as speaking with full confidence because prepared to render an account of his flock, though that I suspect is the lot of none besides him who said, "Father, of those that thou gavest me I have not lost one" [*cf.* John xvii., *12*]. Yet I could wish that, since you have taken so much time to get it up, you had done the whole thing a little more carefully, and did n't turn about so absurdly now to threats and now to entreaties, now weaving a veil of human tradition over the Gospel, now letting the Gospel go altogether and advocating only human tradition. You may be laughed at by the crowd as a certain bishop is laughed at all about to-day who ἐπισκοπεῖ [watches] over a flock within the diocese of our most Reverend Lord of Constance. For in his continued but vain struggles against a certain learned and truly pious preacher, he finally went so far in madness as to venture to say before the general crowd, even pouring out crocodile tears the while: "The difference between a real bishop to whom the sheep have been entrusted and him to whom the sheep have not been entrusted is that this fellow can even lead the sheep astray as he will and is not forced to give an account of his leading them astray, because he is not their shepherd, while on the contrary I, who am the lawfully appointed bishop, am compelled to give such an account of your sins, O my sheep, that though ye sin, not ye have to give an account yourselves, but I." And this view he supported by the words of Ezekiel [iii., 18], though he looked at them somewhat awry, for he left out this part— "The same wicked man shall die in his iniquity; but his blood will I require at thine hand." And when the crowd heard this mistake, they began to laugh and to say, "Bravo, good shepherd, who hast made us safe to-day!" But these things and things like them are not stumbling blocks of offence and error, and do not savour of heresy and impiety, oh no! Why? Because the servant who smote Christ in the face before Annas did no wrong [John xviii., 22], for he could not sin, being on the side of the high priest.

XXXIV. This that you quote from the seventeenth chapter of Deuteronomy, what has it to do here? There the question is about judgments, and in your view also the old law has been abolished as far as it has to do with ceremonials and judgments. What have ye to do with the Sacred Writings, which ye take into your hands so inappropriately, not to say clumsily? How much better it would have been not to touch these weapons of Achilles, which drag your untrained selves to destruction rather than help you in fighting, and to stay within the palisade! But if you maintain with all possible vigour that the thing concerns me, I will say, how do I not listen to the bishops? Nothing is easier, since they say nothing.

XXXV. Thank God that at last you grant even this to unhappy mortals, that the Gospel be preached to them. I should think you ought to have put this in at the beginning, and that you would have begun in this way: Since, then, the Gospel of Christ has been approved by Holy Mother Church, and our predecessors long ago directed in their sacred Canons and synodal Statutes that it be preached, it is our will and strict command and charge that every pastor or people's priest have a copy of the marginal notes of Guillerin of Paris,[1] and that from this every Sunday he expound to the people under our authority the Gospel according to the text, with a loud voice so that he can be heard. For once, if I remember rightly, I saw some bishop's synodal Statutes written in about this fashion, before I was anointed with the holy ointment. But you have kept this till towards the end, imitating certain rhetoricians, who bid one to keep the special points for the end of the speech that they may cling the faster. But if this had fallen out, would it not have been lawful to preach the Gospel? See into what a situation your affairs and words and notions have got! How neatly I could put my finger here upon your sore point; but I do not want to, lest some of its rottenness should touch the Most Reverend Lord of Constance.

XXXVI. I cannot understand in what sense you think the statement ought to be taken that without unity of the Church there can be no Gospel. For during the time[2] when the doctrine of Arius had infected almost the whole Christian world, so that those who were on his side not only were called ὀρθόδοξοι [orthodox], but were so powerful that they outlawed all the best people whose view of Christ was really sound, there was a Gospel, I take it, for both sides rested their case on it, and yet there was a tremendous split in the Church. Therefore there can be a Gospel along with a split in the Church. Here I know whither you would like to seek refuge, but you will be caught there, namely, that there is no Gospel for those whose views are unsound. Therefore Anastasius and Liberius,[3] though Roman Pontiffs, had no Gospel, because they agreed with Arius. Whose was the Gospel then? The Church's. Therefore there can be a Church with sound views, and this Church can have the

---

[1] Properly Guilielmus (Guillermus) of Paris (fl. c. 1485), a Dominican.

[2] The fourth century.

[3] Anastasius was pope 398 to 401; Liberius, 352 to 366. Their Arianism was very doubtful.

Gospel, even if it has no Roman Pontiff. But what can be more absurd than this according to the teachings and ordinances of men? But, not to run outside the subject, see how clearly I can divine that you had reference to that remark of Augustinus, to which all who exalt human traditions above the Gospel flee as to the protection of the shield of Telamon, "I should not believe the Gospel unless the Church had approved the Gospel."[1] Here I appeal to your sense of justice: tell me frankly whether you do not think that this remark of Augustine's was a trifle reckless or escaped him unawares. For suppose Augustine had never lived: there would still have been a Gospel, as the glad tidings of God's grace, there would still have been the covenant which God in his grace had entered into with the miserable race of man, and the same would have been true if, after he was born, Augustine had never believed it. Did any one before Augustine hold this view? Certainly not, for there is no record of it. Since the approval of the Church has not yet been spoken of distinctly enough, hear this further: Historians tell us that Matthew first committed the Gospel to writing eight years after Christ's ascent into heaven, because the necessities of the situation demanded it. Up to that time they had preached it from memory with only the aid of the inspiration of the Holy Ghost. Tell me, pray, what Church stamped the Gospel with approval then, and whose Gospel? Was it that which they all had in their memories? Country bumpkins! The Gospel could waver, therefore, and go wrong, after the manner of human things. Or was it the Gospel inspired by the Holy Ghost that had been sent by the Father and Christ? But it were impious if we said that that which God himself directs has need of human sanction. It remains, therefore, that Augustine uttered those words with more force than discretion, or else

---

[1] In his *Contra epistolam Manichæus quam vocant Fundamenti*, chap. v., ed. Vienne, 1891. *Corpus eccle. Latin.*, xxv., 191 *ff.*, p. 197, l. 22. English trans. in *Nicene and Post-Nicene Fathers*, iv., 131: "For my part I should not believe the Gospel except as moved by the authority of the Catholic Church."

that he would never have believed if he had heard that the Gospel was preached before it had been written down. For no man had then stamped it with approval, much less any general council. Here you concoct as answer, that it appears from the beginning of Luke that some approval had been given by the Church, for he tells us that many had tried to write down the Gospel [Luke i., 1, etc.]. This last I readily admit, for otherwise he would have said, "Matthew and Mark tried to write down Ἐυαγγέλιον [the Gospel] before me." But of those many since no Gospels exist it appears that they were rejected as not having been written with perfect faithfulness. Therefore four Gospels have been approved by the Church. I say to all this that I am very much surprised that while it is clear that "approve" should be understood here as "accept," some people are still so blind as to think that the Gospel would have had no existence, if it had not obtained the sanction of the fathers. The fathers did nothing but cut off from the original and genuine accounts the ἀπόκρυφα and νόθα, that is, those which came from an unknown or a false source. And something not so very different from this we see going on even now. When some Hercules strives to clear away the filth that has been dragged into the abode of the Gospel by certain vicious idlers, he is said not to approve the Gospel, but to rescue it and, like faithful Abraham, to bring it back from captivity in the enemy's country, to dig out the wells that had been loaded with rubbish by the Philistines [*cf.* Gen. xxvi., 15]. For how could it be that the divine should get its sanction from the human? Or how were it not the height of impiety to think that which (in the language of proverbs) sprang from the mouth not of man but of God, not valid unless it had received the approval of human ignorance? So we see it in the heathen poets; they make all the promises of all the gods invalid to which Jupiter had not nodded approval with that terrible brow of his. But Christ himself says [John v., 34], "But I receive not testimony from man," and a little later, "But I have greater witness than that of

John" [John v., 36], and again, "I receive not honour from men" [John v., 41]. Add to this what your own Canons teach [1, q. marcion.¹], that the Gospel consists not in the words of the Scriptures, but in their sense; not in the outside, but in the pith; not in the leaves of the language but in the root of its spirit. Again, imagine some one θεοδίδακτον [taught of God], as Paul was, who did not learn the Gospel from man; imagine some one enlightened in his heart from above and feeling comfort that no one can deny that his is a Gospel, will it wait to be a Gospel until the fathers have stamped it with approval? So learn at last that it is a Gospel when God deigns to illuminate a man freely with His grace, to draw him to Himself, and comfort him and make him at peace and free from all taint of sin. And when the poor man perceives it, no wonder he leaps with joy and exultation at the new and inspired message, and Paul gives his approval to this idea [Rom. i., 16]—The Gospel of Christ "is the power of God unto salvation to every one that believeth." Go now and say that the Gospel borrows its sanction from an assemblage of men, and if you say it, I know not how you will escape the brand of blasphemy. See meanwhile, also, how hard it is to put out from the hearts of men such long accepted opinions, even when false or erroneous. See, too, how crude a performance it is to patch together words however they have come into your head, as those words of yours are patched without any sort of learning—"only let it not remove any man from the fold and unity of the Church, without which there can be no Gospel."

XXXVII. That Christ is one, that, again, the Church founded upon a rock by the voice of the Lord is one, who will deny? Yet there are those who differ about the rock, some holding that it was a fisherman, others that it was the Creator of fishes and of all creatures. And which side judges the matter more soundly and correctly, even a slave will

¹ Corpus iur. can., canon 64, causa 1, questio 1.

easily decide, to say nothing of Œdipus,[1] because the words of Christ seem to point to his saying that he is himself the rock on which he is going to build the Church. For when he had called Peter by this name from "petra," a rock [Matt. xvi., 18], saying "Thou art Peter," if he had meant that Peter was the foundation stone of the Church he would not have gone back to the primitive word and said, "And upon this rock I will build my Church," but would have stopped with the name Peter in this way: "Thou art Peter, upon whom I will build my Church." As it is, in going back to the πρωτότυπον [primitive word], he makes it apparent that he meant himself by the rock upon which he would build his Church, as if he had said: "I, O Simon, for this full confession of my godhead will give to thee a name conformable to this confession, and from me, who am the rock (for Christ was the rock [I. Corinth. x., 4]), thou shalt henceforth be called Peter. And let not that name seem hard or rough to thee. This rock from which thou receivest thy name is the foundation stone of the Church." Besides, the agreement of the men of old to this interpretation is unanimous. Now the "seat" which you bring in here, I am inclined to think is nowhere spoken of in connection with this matter in the sacred writings, though I know well enough that mention is made of seats once or twice in the Gospel, as when Christ overthrew "the seats of them that sold doves" [Matt. xxi., 12], and when he upbraided the scribes and Pharisees for sitting unworthily in Moses' seats [Matt. xxiii., 2], but these passages are very unfavourable to your proposition. But if you mean that seat before which we shall all stand to give an accounting, I easily grant that as God is one, so is the throne one, where Christ is sitting on the right hand of God [Col. iii., 1], to which the same Apostle urges us to hasten with confidence, saying [Hebr. iv., 16], "Let us therefore come boldly unto the throne of grace, that we may obtain mercy, and find grace to help in time of need." If,

---

[1] Allusion to Terence, *Andria*, i., 2, 23, v. 194. "Davus sum, non Oedipus," meaning "I am no riddle solver."

again, you wish to be understood as speaking of the seats of men, nothing seems farther from the truth, for there are as many seats and chairs as there are banquet halls and courts and market-places. Even if I wished to deny that there are one altar and one priesthood, Paul would refute me [Hebr. xiii., 10], "We have an altar, whereof they have no right to eat which serve the tabernacle," and [I. Corinth. ix., 13], where he constantly speaks of only one altar. In the matter of the priesthood he would also confute me [Hebr. vii., 11], where he clearly proves that the old priesthood had been handed on to Christ, whom above [ch. iv.] he called the great ἀρχιερέα, that is, the highest priest (for the name "pontifex," pontiff, certain idolaters also used, whence I should like it better if we had taken the Greek name in its place), nay, by many arguments he established that Christ would be forever the ἀρχιερέα or High Priest according to the order of Melchisedec.

XXXVIII. Believe me, no prophecy of Orpheus himself is truer than that he that gathereth not unto Christ, spreadeth abroad, scattereth, wasteth [Matt. xii., 30].

XXXIX. That you should here again have spouted with incautious excess, I put up with only so far as to enable you to see how many absurdities will rise up against the Canonical Law of which you are, I believe, the champions, if what you propound in these words shall be accepted as valid. "False and impious and sacrilegious is whatever is set up by the favour of man to the injury of the order of the Church." Therefore, impious, false, and sacrilegious are those who maintain that the Roman Pontiff is the great high priest, the universal bishop, because the Church forbade any attempt at that in the African Council Di. 99 primae sedis.[1] It is false, impious, and sacrilegious that the suburban bishops whom we call suffragans and some call imitation bishops, do not distribute the bread of the heavenly word to the churches entrusted to them, because that is the especial, nay, the only function of a bishop, and one

[1] Corpus iur. can., c. 3, Dist. xcix.

who neglects to fulfil it is called a shameless dog 2. q. 7. He who neither—.¹ I pass by the directions of Christ who, in sending his disciples into the harvest, gave them no other command than to preach the Gospel to every creature [Mark xvi., 15]. I pass by Paul who says that he was sent, not to baptise, but to spread the Gospel [I. Cor. i., 17]. It will be false and impious and sacrilegious for priests to engage in warfare, because they should not mingle in mundane matters, according to the warning to which the whole subject of the third book of Decretals is devoted.² Yet you see even bishops in our days steeping themselves in their cups as much as the Leontines did, following after pleasures as much as the Crotonians, and in their tables surpassing even the Jews. That bishop will be false and impious and sacrilegious, who has rich and ostentatious furniture, such as we see them with in our days, even surpassing kings. For this was forbidden in the Council of Carthage Di. 41. A Bishop—.³ It is false and impious and sacrilegious if a bishop acts as umpire in mundane matters, because he does differently from what the order of the Church prescribes II. q. I. You, now—.⁴ Yet the money lenders to-day get their interest through no judges so successfully as through the bishops. It is false and impious and sacrilegious that the imitation bishops charge for the blessing of vestments and altars and shrines almost bushels of money, because that is forbidden in many places in the Canonical Law. Any bishops who forbid the priests to marry are false and impious and sacrilegious according to that formula of yours, because the Church once ordered that a bishop should be husband of one wife, according to the deliverance of Paul to Timothy and Titus dist. 26, passim,⁵ and the Council of Gangra forbids one to scorn a wife under pretence of religious scruples 28. dist. c. If any one,—and If any one decree—.⁶ What-

---

¹ Corpus iur. can., c. 32, c. ii., qu. 7.
² Ibid., Decretal. Gregori. IX., Lib. iii., Tit. 50.
³ Ibid., c. 7, Dist. xli.
⁴ Ibid., 29, Causa XI., qu. I.
⁵ Ibid., 1–5, Dist. XXVI.
⁶ Ibid., c. 14–15, Dist. XXVIII.

ever bishop exacts more than the two soldi which they call "cathedral" money is, by this definition of yours, impious and false and sacrilegious, because a decree was passed 10. q. 3, "This you—",[1] and there it was forbidden that more than has been mentioned be exacted from the parish priests. Time would fail me if I tried to gather together all the absurdities that would spring from this doughty principle of yours if it be not invalidated. Yet I beg you meanwhile to reflect how illusory and feeble those things are which are devised by a man however wise, if they be not according to the rule of the divine will and Scriptures. And this, if you will excuse me for saying so, has come upon you often, here and in other parts of this admonitory document. For when a little while before you had brought forward the words of Christ [Matt. xii., 30], "He that gathereth not with me, scattereth abroad," I began to look with eager attention to see whether you were getting ready to try to urge me, as you ought, to direct all my efforts more vigorously and strongly towards Christ. But it proved to be far otherwise. For, as I think, you brought the words in simply to support this $\dot{a}\xi\iota\omega\mu a$ [principle] of yours, and how well you did it, I fancy is sufficiently clear from what I have said. Yea verily, I beg of you by the gods, what do you think is blasphemy, pray, if it does not seem to you blasphemy to attribute to a created being that which belongs to God, to argue, or rather to trifle, in this way?— Christ said, "He that gathereth not with me, scattereth abroad," and then, not so much for the sake of satisfying one's desires as of showing them forth, to append "False and impious and sacrilegious is whatever is set up by the favour of man to the injury of the Church." Who does not see your sore point now? For while in your earlier remarks you always coupled the Gospel or the Gospel teaching or Christ or the Lord or the mastery of the Gospel with your traditions, here at last pain forces you to leave off any such covering. Who does not see whence these groans and sighs emanate?

[1] Corpus iur. can., c. 4, c. X., qu. 3.

XL. In saying "non deiicere et impugnare dictat ratio, etc." for "deiciiendas et impugnandas esse, nature does not dictate this sudden casting off with hostile violence, etc.," you indulge in a Greek construction, and with such you have about as much to do, as a jackdaw with a harp. I come back to the subject. The traditions of our predecessors, as I said a little while ago, we all look upon with the more reverence the more they savour of the teaching of the Gospel and the Apostles, and the farther they are removed therefrom, the less we accept them. But as to myself, I have done and shall continue to do unmoved the exact opposite of what you accuse me of. For, to speak for the sake of illustration, when the sheep entrusted to me heard of the ordinance of excommunication established by Christ [Matt. xviii., 17], "If thy brother shall trespass against thee, etc.," they began presently to argue with me, saying, "Then if one does not sin he cannot be excommunicated. For a law is not to be understood in any other sense than what accords with the intent of the lawgiver." And if I had not wrestled with them with the most urgent entreaty not to make any ill-considered disturbance, they would have cast off the bonds of excommunication on the spot. I am speaking of that excommunication by which we are excommunicated for a debt acquired by a loan or contract or in any other way. By this illustration you can see how fairly or unfairly I am considered a peacemaker or a sower of discord, when by pious prayers only I drive into line those who know that they are not bound by divine law to stay there, who might without harm to their consciences resist, partly because they confidently trust the divine promises, partly because they rely upon the freedom of their country and fear not every wind that blows. Hundreds of times I have said openly: "I beseech you by Jesus Christ, by our common faith, not to make any change rashly, but to show to all men by your endurance, if in no other way, that you are Christians, in that, on account of the weak brethren, you bear things that by Christ's law you do not need to bear."

XLI. Here you are caught by your own tracks, O Shrewmouse,[1] when, changing that number which alone is becoming to our Most Reverend Lord and which alone he has been in the habit of using, you come down to the singular and say, "For I do not admit that those people should here be listened to." For you never would have done this, unless you had meant to show by this mark that you were the author of this hasty[2] effusion, just as the reported maker of the shield of Pallas worked in an image of himself so cleverly at the top of the shield, that if it were erased or removed the shield itself would fall apart. But to draw your portrait more distinctly, so that you cannot think yourself unknown, I will say, you are he who once talked over many things with me privately,[3] and on another occasion you so far forgot yourself as to say that speech was a bodily exercise. For I remember the words still. And when all who were there laughed at you, ye gods, with what a labyrinth of words you tried to uphold the statement! How you contracted your brow and with what an angry look you tried to dispel the laughter! Yet to this extent I congratulate you that you are so great (in your own estimation at least) that even the good respect your anger, albeit influenced more by politeness than by your frown. I bid you, therefore, whoever you are, to refrain from the false charges with which you have been soothing your soul, and cease struggling so senselessly and obstinately against the revival of Christianity, or τὴν λεοντῆν [the lion's skin] will be stripped off you rather roughly, and you will repent when it is too late. Be it enough to have been pardoned three times. No one will be able to endure much longer your hiding yourself, like a cuttle-fish, in your own inky blackness. The good and also learned will at length seize their brushes and paint you in your true colours. But things will be all

[1] Reference to the Vicar-General Johannes Faber.
[2] Or is it a misprint for "delightful" (which he uses elsewhere)—festinæ for festivæ?—H. P.
[3] Zwingli writing to Beatus Rhenanus on October 12, 1520, alludes to this visit of Faber (*Werke*, n. e., vii., 354).

right, if you return to wisdom, or at least cease making up charges and stirring up our most pious bishop. Therefore, I urge you to come to yourself. For so far is it from my intending to yield to your attacks that I pray that, if I ever have to fight, I may have no other foe than you, though, on the other hand, I shall set no small value on your friendship, if you will take on again a spirit worthy of you. Now I will return to the question.

XLII. Who is so dull as to hold the same opinion in regard to the Apostles and to false apostles? From whom has this been heard among those who at this time are treating the teaching of Christ simply and sincerely? From no one surely except those who have set up their own abomination in the place of God. These are they who venture to spout things like these—"Who, pray, were the Evangelists? Who the Apostles? Were they not men? They could slip then, and go wrong and be mistaken. The Spirit of God is ever the same and can inspire some Thomas[1] in the latter days as well as the Sauls and Simons in the beginning." As if the Evangelists had handed down their own notions to us, after the fashion of your crowd, and did not assign to Christ alone all that they did, and write only what he did and what he taught. As if the Apostles had loaded the people with burdens like those of the false apostles. The Apostles preached the teachings of Christ in all their purity, for they raised the consciences cast down with terror at their sins up to good hope through the word of Christ which cannot deceive. To-day certain persons preach human ravings most wantonly, and try to frighten minds truly free, teaching that there is sin where there is no sin, and most cruelly murdering the soul. The Apostles taught that the Son of God out of pure generosity did not so much pardon the sins of all as give himself up as an expiatory offering for all. The false apostles preach to-day that no sin is so slight that it does not need to be washed out by human reparation. Peter suffered not that Cornelius should think him anything

[1] Aquinas.

Archeteles : Reply to Bishop's Admonition

more than man, saying "Stand up; I myself also am a man." [Acts x., 26.] The false apostles demand almost divine honours, and like Domitian suffer themselves to be called Lord God. The Apostles taught men only to recognise the grace of God, and its fulness brought to them through Christ. The false apostles cease not to shove upon the shoulders of men heavy and unbearable burdens, and compel them to buy off their wrongdoings for money as if they were merchandise, or, if there is no money, with clothing and food and drink or even their hearthstones. They spare not the orphan nor the widow. They must have money in any case, for they say God cannot be appeased without it. Go now and declare that the teaching of the Apostles can fall into such suspicion as that of the false apostles. As if any one were so stupid as not to see plainly what has been freely transmitted to us from the divine goodness by the Apostles, and what on the other hand has proceeded from human greed through hypocrisy.

XLIII. By general councils I do not know whether you wish the four to be understood which certain persons teach should be taken on the same footing as the Gospel, or all such councils. If the former, I should not want to detract at all from their value, though I cannot see how it is right to wish them regarded as of equal authority with the Gospel. Let those see to this who proclaim the doctrine. If you mean all general councils, I will ask you whether you hold that all should be held authoritative and kept with scrupulous care. If you say "Yes," I beg you to explain this difficulty, whether we must side with those who, according to di. 25, 26, 28, and 29,[1] have decided that a bishop should be husband of one wife, or with those who at the suggestion of evil spirits forbid his marriage. Shall we not have to go back to Scripture here? For John bids us not to believe every spirit, but to try the spirits, whether they are of God [I. John iv., 1]. But by what touchstone shall we try them other than that which has become the head of the corner

[1] Corpus iur. can., Dist. xxv., xxvi., xxviii., xxix.

[Ps. cxviii., 22; Matt. xxi., 42; Mark xii., 10], which was rejected of men, but chosen of God? He says that chastity cannot be required of a man unless it be given him from above. Therefore the Scriptures will be above the councils. For where the councils are at variance with each other there is no other way than by the Holy Scriptures of deciding which council comes nearer to the Scripture standard. And this method was always adopted by the men of old. And those Canons which are in harmony with the Scripture (for this alone is free from the possibility of deceit, as your own decrees hold di. 9. c. "I—")[1] will, of course, have to be accepted, and those not in such harmony will have to be rejected. I ask, I say, whether we ought now to obey the council which permits marriage to bishops or that which refuses it. You will say, no doubt, "That which refuses it." But I oppose to this the Synod of Gangra which pronounces anathema against him who holds that it is not lawful for a bishop to marry, and if you try it by the touchstone of the Gospel, the Gospel confirms this and Paul assents to it. If therefore this is to be done away by violent human ordinance, is not the divine forced to yield to the human? And what more dreadful abomination than this can be found? As if we wanted to patch up the divine with the human and so make complete what was imperfect before. For this is what you maintain, O $\mu\varepsilon\lambda\alpha\nu o\tilde{\upsilon}\rho\varepsilon$ [black fish]. I am going to direct my remarks solely to you now. You once said (you know where yourself) that Christ [John xvi., 12] said, " I have yet many things to say unto you, but ye cannot bear them now," for the purpose of reserving some parts of his testament to be afterwards spread abroad by Thomases and Scotuses. Hear what an impious thing it was to say: The Apostles were sad because they had heard that one of their own company should betray Christ, and because, though they had listened to his divine sayings, many of them had not sunk into the depths of their minds, for their sorrow prevented, when they heard the list of the evils to

---

[1] Corpus iur. can., C. 5, Dist. ix.

come upon them. Therefore, they heard many things to no purpose, and when Christ observed this, he preferred to put off the explanation of some things till the coming of the Holy Ghost, that he should make more intimately known to them the things they had not understood, and should refresh their memory of what he had said. For he had said [John xiv., 26] "he shall bring all things to your remembrance, whatsoever I have said unto you." So, here you have the word "you," that is, the Apostles, of course, not Thomases, Scotuses, Bartholuses, Balduses.[1] He added afterwards those words which you quote from chapter xvi., and distort to the detriment of the truth. For having said, "I have yet many things to say to you," to you Apostles, I say, he added: "Howbeit when he, the spirit of truth, is come, he will guide you into all truth" [John xvi., 13]. "You" he said, not "some," disciples of Aristotle rather than of Christ. But if the truth cannot lie, as it cannot, then the Holy Ghost guided you into all truth, O Apostles, so that you should understand more clearly the things that you had not thoroughly taken in before, and should boldly enter upon things which otherwise you would never have dared to begin, and should foretell under his inspiration things which no man knew were to happen. He made clear, then, to the Apostles by the guide of the Spirit, as he had promised, those things which they had not been able before to bear or understand. You see again how unfortunate you are when you turn over the Scriptures. I advise you to do nothing for some time but study carefully the way the learned treat them, and not take them into your hands on any point without a guide. Otherwise it may easily come about that you fall into some great and fatal blunder.

[1] Bartolus, born at Sassoferrato, in the Mark Ancona, Central Italy, 1313; died in Perugia, 1359, where he has a magnificent tomb in the church of San Francesco. He was the most famous of the dialectical school of jurists, and taught in Perugia University.

Baldus de Ubaldis, born 1319, 1324, or 1327, at Perugia; died at Pavia, 1400 or 1406. He was the most famous pupil of Bartolus, and taught in Bologna, Perugia, Pisa, Padua, and Pavia.

But that you may see how thoroughly worthless those things are that we fashion with a notion of offering something better than the divine, I will put things to you thus: That the New Testament is the most excellent that God is ever likely to bestow upon the race of man, you do not, I think, deny. If you deny it, read chapter viii. of Paul to the Hebrews, or rather the whole Epistle, and you will soon be ashamed of your denial. Now if Christ gave us that in incomplete form, he was evidently far inferior to Moses, who so thoroughly completed the Old that he forbade that anything be added or taken away [Deut. iv., and xii.]. Furthermore, if what was lacking was not added until the boggy utterances of Durandus[1] and the dicta of Scotus, the earlier generations had it in incomplete form until about the last three hundred years. The Apostles transmitted it unfinished, Christ, the Son of God, equal and like unto the Father in all respects, transmitted it unfinished. And what more blasphemous than that can be said? Yet they say nothing else who, under this pretext, as I have said, make human traditions equal or superior to the divine law, or maintain that they are necessary for salvation. Therefore they are blasphemous towards God, towards the Apostles, and towards the Fathers whom they champion with such zeal. But that you may understand me still better, listen. If without certain decretals of the councils, or the opinions of certain Sophists, one cannot be saved, then the Apostles were not saved, and the first fruits of the Christians were certainly not saved. For they did not have these decretals, they did not have these opinions, which are hardly yet clearly set forth. See whither you are taking yourself or rather whither truth is pushing you. Hence, in fact, our whole battle to-day is nothing but what Christ mentions in Luke [xvi., 14 *ff*.], "And the Pharisees also, who were covetous, heard all these things; and they derided him. And he said

---

[1] Bishop of Meaux, twenty-eight miles east of Paris. He was the chief representative of the Nominalists. He was born at St. Pourçain, eighty-five miles north-west of Lyons, about 1275; died at Meaux, 1334.

unto them, Ye are they which justify yourselves before men: but God knoweth your hearts: for that which is highly esteemed among men is abomination in the sight of God." Expound this passage to me, good Brother. You will doubtless find that we worship God in vain with the teachings and commandments of men. For a Christian ought to be "dead from these rudiments" and ought not to set up ordinances, since they are of no value [Colos. ii., 20]. Who, therefore, will not look with reverence upon any councils, pray, if they are in conformity with the divine law? Yet it seems to me that those have the better opinion who say, "If the councils are in conformity with the divine law, what need is there of crediting them with what they have simply worked over, instead of crediting the Holy Scripture itself, which, according to Christ's words, has the greater testimony? For the testimony of God is greater than the testimony of man, so that even the testimony of John the Baptist yields to it [John v., 36]. But if the councils contradict the divine law, who will not presently bring forward that saying of the Apostle, "we ought to obey God rather than men"? [Acts v., 29.] Therefore, we ought to be constantly on our guard lest something be set up some time that does not exactly square with the heavenly truth, which presents itself so simply that it can be easily grasped, and is so transparent and clear that it needs not to "receive honour from men" [John v., 41]. Therefore this is the one guide and master necessary to settle anything that may have come into dispute. Let them have done, therefore, who think that in these days any disagreement which arises among Christians as to the authority of Scripture can be settled by the councils of certain blind bishops, without doing all things under the lead of Scripture alone, which proceedeth from God and not from human desires. And by Scripture I mean not the letter which kills but the spirit that giveth life. I greatly fear, however, that what follows shortly after the words of Christ quoted above can be said of some of these people, namely, "But I know you, that ye have not the love of

God in yourselves."[1] You all, for I now come back to the whole group of you advisers, have the greatest reason to fear that those words may be justly applied by somebody to the Most Reverend Hugo, namely, that under your instigation he seems to love his coffers better than Christ, and to be looking out for wealth rather than salvation. But he will undoubtedly do the latter if you urge him to favour before all things the making the divine will and purpose as clear as possible to all men by the preaching of the Gospel. For in this way you will make his name worthy of heaven and immortality. But, wretched me! Why do I waste my labour and materials?[2] As if what pinches you through the whole course of your remarks were not clearer than light even to the purblind, though you imagine that you conceal it so nicely! The Most High God grant that the clouds may be scattered at last and that you may see the clear light! Amen. And may you not continue to force our excellent bishop to limp with both feet! Amen. But may you suffer him to run up rightly and without offence in the way and the law of God, untrammelled by the burden of human traditions! Amen and Amen.

XLIV. With regard to those who are commended to us as much by their lives as by their teaching, read your sacred Canons di. 9. c. "I—."[3] Thus you will find that in Augustinus's opinion you ought to have unhesitating confidence in those only who are the authors of those Scriptures which are called Canonical (and these are those which are contained in the Bible); other writers you should read with the feeling that, however pre-eminent they are for learning and holiness, what they write is not true because they in their holiness and learning believed it, but because by the power of the Canonical Scriptures they were able to convince their hearers of the truth of what not they themselves but the Spirit of God breathing in their words approved. Lo, here you have the Scripture as master and teacher and

---

[1] John v., 42.   [2] Plautus, *Pœnulus*, 332.
[3] Corpus iur. can., C. 5, Dist. ix.

Archeteles : Reply to Bishop's Admonition   265

guide, not the Fathers, not this misunderstood Church of certain people; and this you can read still more plainly a little farther on in the same di.[1] c. "He who does not know"—And meantime I want you to bear this in mind, that I make use of your Canons simply on your own account; for you seem to have as much confidence in them as in the Gospel or the teachings of the Apostles or the entire Scriptures bestowed upon mankind together by the divine goodness. It is not because I or any one who trusts in the divine utterances can accept those Canons as weapons of attack, except so far as they are not at variance with the divine utterances. But what need will there then be of yielding to the Canons and not rather to the Holy Scriptures?

XLV. Why, pray, do ye cling so tenaciously to ceremonials? You yourselves say they are to be kept only for a time. To what time do you postpone their abolition? Do you think we ought to pay no attention to the divine goodness now calling us away from these ceremonials? Do you suppose that anybody will have the courage ever to take up war against them again, if the present splendid intellects fail? Or that those are going to get off unscathed who display not so much indifference as hostility to the now budding Christianity? Have ye no fear of Him who said [Matt. xi., 23]: "And thou, Capernaum, which art exalted unto heaven, shalt be brought down to hell: for if the mighty works, which have been done in thee, had been done in Sodom, it would have remained until this day. But I say unto you, That it shall be more tolerable for the land of Sodom in the day of judgment, than for thee"? Have ye no fear, I say, that he will sometime threaten the peoples of Germany also, if they let the present opportunity pass?—And thou, Germany, whose stout and valiant heart I have drawn away from the uproars of war unto true piety, and have enriched with all manner of learning because thou hadst strength great enough for every sort of study, that thou mightest with learning and skill cleanse religion of the

[1] Corpus iur. can., C. 8, Dist. ix.

foul stains that some have cast upon it, and mightest trumpet it forth in all its purity, shall thy glory be exalted unto the heavens for this that thou didst, to be sure, make a beginning, but failed to carry the work through? Nay, verily. Thou shalt be brought down to hell, because thou hast disregarded the light coming into the world. For there is no nation so barbarous that it would have sunk down in such inactivity, if such opportunities had been offered it to establish true religion upon a sound basis. But the judgment that shall fall upon the unbelieving citizens of Sodom shall be milder than that which falls upon thee, etc. Here again you see how your whole discourse is an attempt to draw away to some shadowy good those who have already learned to worship the Father in spirit and in truth. If ceremonials are to be kept for a time, they are to be done away with sometime. What hinders their being abolished now, especially as the world is looking for this and all the good and learned are moving in this direction? But you will say, Wait till the time when no doubt certain τυφλεπίσκοποι, [blind bishops] will suffer them to be done away with. Do ye think that those whose life is a drunken spree, whose god is their belly [Phil. iii., 19], whose mules and drinking cups, as well as their ceilings, are loaded with gold, are ever going to return to right feeling so far as to allow a thing to be done away with when that will lighten their plates and coffers? In that case we shall abolish without any trouble many things that contribute nothing to salvation, and though retained can never satisfy the insatiable desires of certain persons, unless they be lowered. Therefore, do cease crying out, "Ceremonials, ceremonials," for ye will talk to deaf ears.

XLVI. Now for the first time we poor mortals learn that the Republic of Christ cannot exist without ceremonials, though it was never better off than at the time when there were the fewest possible ceremonials. We learn finally that the state cannot be carried on unless ψευδεπίσκοποι, [counterfeit bishops] purify the walls of the church with water and salt and ashes, grease the altars with holy oil, and dip the bronze of the bells in holy water. For if these things were neglected, all political order would fall to the ground, as if before these things were accepted cities had not been admirably governed. I do not deny, nay, I assert, that the teachings of Christ contribute very greatly to the peace of the state, if indeed they are set forth in their purity. But now that certain hypocrites have begun to care for their chests and not for Christ, I do not know whether anything could have happened more fatal to the cities. For how can it be that such things as these shall make for peace and quiet?—"We are the priests, you are the laymen: we are the learned, you are the ignorant: the keys are ours, the empty purses yours: it is for us to pass our days in leisure, for you to earn your bread by the sweat of your brow: you must be kept from adultery, we shall revel freely in every sort of lust: you shall pay tribute and taxes, we will soothe our leisure with your offerings: you shall keep watch and guard at night, we will snore on careless and free to high day: you shall keep off the foe from the town, our religion forbids us to free our countrymen from danger." I know what you are going to say to this, but pray be silent. Do not all these things belong to the ceremonials without which you say cities totter? But that Christianity which I advocate is adapted to all cities, obeys the laws and the magistrates of the nation, pays taxes to whom taxes are due, tribute to whom tribute is due, rates to whom rates are due. Under it no one calls any possession his own, all things are held to be in common; every one is eager to outdo his neighbour in kindnesses, to exercise all gentleness, to share his neighbour's burden, and relieve his need. For he regards all men as brothers, abhors blasphemy, embraces piety and helps it to grow among all. But why continue? It was an empty rather than a true statement, nay it was one of jealousy, that without the ceremonials cities and states would totter and fall, and it was made only for the purpose of rousing among the people hatred and resistance to the preaching of the Gospel. See how far from your style of speech the words of the false witnesses against Stephen were [Acts vi., 13]. "This man ceaseth not to speak blasphemous words against this holy place, and the law: For we have heard him say, that this Jesus of Nazareth shall destroy this place, and shall change the customs which Moses delivered us." Now I will add your words, "For thus all political order would fall to the ground." What would follow, I leave you to consider.

XLVII. I do not deny that the things which have been decreed by the general consent of all should be observed, but by those who decreed them, and only when they have received really the consent of all, and how far this seems to yourselves true in the present case is made quite clear by what follows.

XLVIII. "Or at least acceded to." From this term "acceded to" it appears that you mean things which certain people by the persistent use of their power have forced upon the simple body of Christians against their will and their remonstrances even. For after things came to such a pass that the Pontiffs declared themselves to be lords of all things, including the right to make laws at their own sweet will, and even claimed infallibility for themselves, what did they not venture to command? And, on the other hand, who was likely to court misfortune so far as to offer resistance, especially when the simple-minded crowd whom they vigorously oppressed, though not without the desire to rebel, yet did not dare to utter a murmur? Yet what is the use of refuting these things at length when it is clearer than light in these days of ours how that general consent came about or how the ceremonials were acceded to (to use your word)? For we see the things that you wish to make appear decreed by general consent cried out against by the crowd, and what you call accepted rejected. There you have your "general consent" and your "acceded to." Almost the whole business was done by command, and that with a wanton persistency not dictated by the spirit of Christ. For to bring forward one example out of thousands, no one objects to pious prayers in the consecration of churches,

Archeteles: Reply to Bishop's Admonition 269

but no one approves of superstitious punctiliousness. Every one naturally abhors extortion, abhors your Canons, abhors the oaths taken. And now, when such vast sums of money are extorted for ceremonials of this kind, you say that general consent or acceptance has been accorded, when nothing is less true. I will tell you here a thing that happened a few days ago, that you may see how truly assent is given in the exaction of money for consecrating churches. A certain suffragan[1] dedicated a certain church[2] and several altars in it—I do not wish to mention any names—and demanded as the price of the dedication twelve Rhenish gold pieces for the church, ten for the churchyard, and five for each of the altars. Then a priest[3] of more than usual spirit came forward and opposed to the performance Christ's words, "Freely ye have received, freely give" [Matt. x., 8], and said that the man was guilty of Simon's curse who ventured to sell the gifts of the Holy Spirit or thought they could be sold [Acts viii., 20]. Then that suffragan frowned, and said, "For this reason I will not treat with you in many words, because I fear running the risk of simony; therefore I will not make any bargain with you at all." For thus the sacrilege would be incurred, to which they have given the name of simony from Simon the sorcerer. "But," he continued, "I demand this amount of money of you, I do not bargain for it." So these poor people were forced to borrow twenty-six gold pieces to pay that counterfeit bishop, in order, forsooth, not to fall into the sin of simony with him.[4] Here you see clearly whether these burdens are acceded to or ordered. That counterfeit bishop preferred to command the money rather than to bargain for it. Go now, and say that things are acceded to which certain people have ventured to command with so much pride and arrogance. I

---

[1] Melchior Fattlin.   [2] That at Hettlingen in the canton of Zurich.

[3] Jacob Aeberli, also called Wagner, pastor of Neftenbach, of which church that of Hettlingen was a branch. These names are given by Finsler, *in loco*, p. 310.

[4] The complaint of Faber about a similar matter of non-payment is given in Egli, *Actensammlung*, Nos. 459 (Dec. 15, 1523) and 541 (June 11, 1524).

could tell hundreds of other things worthy of a smile about that suffragan—things that he has done or said, puffing himself up before the simple farmers, but my practice forbids. Everything will sometime be brought out into the clear light, if those swindling lovers of darkness do not stop darkening the light.

XLIX. Those who model their teachings upon the pattern of the Scriptures cannot be said to teach according to the whims of their own feelings, but those who go to work without resting on the authority of the sacred writings, contrary to Paul's directions to Timothy. For he gives him [II. Timothy iii., 14] the following admonition: "But continue thou in the things which thou hast learned and hast been assured of, knowing of whom thou hast learned them; And that from a child thou hast known the holy scriptures, which are able to make thee wise unto salvation through faith which is in Christ Jesus." Timothy had learned from Paul, and Paul from Christ, but both had been led by the same spirit into the knowledge of holy things. In these Paul bids Timothy continue, but they continue not in these, who according to what you say carry on this business as suits their own sweet will. They continue therein who εὐπροσέδρως καὶ ἀδιασπάστως, that is, constantly and undividedly cling to them, in the same Paul's words, knowing that all sacred Scripture was inspired by God, and is valuable for teaching, arguing, guiding, and for the discipline which is founded on righteousness, so that a man of God is perfectly finished and prepared unto every good work [II. Tim. iii., 15, etc.]. Those who give assent unto flesh and blood, regulate their teachings according to their own sweet will; those who give assent unto the spirit of God sweetly breathing from the Holy Scriptures and ever freshly blooming, regulate their teaching according to the thought and purpose of God. And He is by no means of recent origin, for the prophet called him the Ancient of days [Dan. vii., 22]. They, therefore, who refer all things to His purpose, and examine all things by the standard of His thought, do not set up a new standard, but go back to the old, old one, as Jeremiah also urges [vi., 16], "Stand ye in the ways, and see, and ask for the old paths, where is the good way, and walk therein, and ye shall find rest for your souls." You see that rest will be found in the old standard, not in the new one, to which you cling so obstinately, meanwhile accusing of innovations those who for this one thing alone urge war upon you and your likes, that they want to abrogate innovations too freely introduced and to restore the old by right of recovery, as it were. And this is lawful according to your own Canons [Dist. 9 "He who does not know—"].[1] There, to touch but briefly upon each point, you have put into the canon that γραφὴ θεόπνευστος, that is, a Scripture inspired of God, is to stand forever unshaken, but things written by the bishops can be torn out not only by councils but by anybody of any learning, provided such writings contain anything at variance with the divinely inspired. I have determined, however, if God will and if He shall duly inspire me, to write a special book upon this subject, to wit, upon the force and the use of the Holy Scriptures.[2] For we often use the sacred words very perversely.

L. If every word from the beginning of the Gospel had rested upon the voice of the crowd, where, pray, would Christianity be now? The Apostles were very few. And the Popes, how many nations and kingdoms have they converted to Christ, and Christ comforts them and encourages them to do it boldly without any hesitation because of their small number [Luke xii., 32]. "Fear not, little flock; for it is your Father's good pleasure to give you the kingdom." I might uncover here the marked foolishness which lies hidden under your words. For who of the heathen philosophers was ever so dull as to prefer the opinion of the crowd to the opinion of the few, of the wise few, of course? And

[1] Corpus iur. can., C. 8, Dist. ix.
[2] Reference to his sermon on "Clearness and Certainty of the Word of God," as his sermon which appeared on September 6, 1522, was called in the German. Gualther, in his Latin translation given in his edition of Zwingli's works, calls it *De certitudine et claritate verbi dei liber*.

what should we come to, if we rested to-day on the opinion of the crowd? Would it not be all up with you and with your teachings? Of so little moment ye think it whether ye spit out whatever comes into your head! I might treat you, I say, vastly less considerately and I have a right to, but I prefer to spare you, for I have a great hope that you will come back to yourselves and sing a palinode.

LI. "At least," you add "when they are not inconsistent with the divine law." Here I confess I do not understand you. If you are speaking of those midway things which in the view of the philosophers are neither good nor bad, why do you drag in such trifles here, where Christ's work is the matter in hand? Again, what have you, who call yourselves the champions of Christianity, to do with those people? He who gathereth not unto this, scattereth abroad. But how can you seem to gather unto Christ, when you gather unto that "which is at least not inconsistent with the divine law"? He that is not with Christ is against him. Therefore, if you are with these midway things, you are not with Christ. For Christ has nothing to do with the world. But if you wish to be understood as referring to laws which you admit are not of divine origin nor good, and which you yet say are not bad, what have you to do with such laws? Has any jurisdiction been entrusted to you over boundaries and aqueducts and rain water and neighbourhood rights? But even such ordinances I maintain have a sacred character when they correspond to the gauge of the divine will. Through their means justice can be administered and the peace secured which is Christ. Do ye think your real thought can still be hidden? Take away the treasure chambers and you will have done away with these enigmatical utterances. And I do not grant you that the treasure chamber is not inconsistent with the divine law, for it is contrary to love of one's neighbour. For he is deceived by certain counterfeit rites, is plundered and stripped, while the hypocrites devour widows' houses, and for a pretence make long prayer. Read Matthew xxiii.,

14, and you will find what the nature of those things is which you declare to be not inconsistent with the divine law. But, thank God, you have got so far that the things you were a little while ago venturing to palm off as of God, you are now satisfied to call by this made up and unintelligible middle name—"things which are at least not inconsistent with the divine law." Furthermore, not to discuss too long with you here, know that the whole law which you have undertaken to defend is holy. For, according to Paul's authority, it proceeded from God [Rom. vii., 12], "wherefore the law is holy, and the commandment holy, and just, and good." Thus this fiction of yours about the things which are not inconsistent with the divine law amounts to nothing, for whatever is good proceedeth from God [James i., 17], "Every good gift and every perfect gift is from above, and cometh down from the Father of lights." Hence, if these things of yours proceeded from God, they are good. If they did not proceed from God, as, according to your own testimony, they did not, then they are bad. If ye are priests of Christ, proclaim the law of Christ, that is good, holy, and everlasting. If ye are preachers of vanities, why sit ye in the holy place? The things that have not proceeded from God, but from man, are bad. For the good is good only through one characteristic and source, to wit, that it is from God, the fountain of all good. Otherwise we should be obliged to admit several fountains of good. For, if anything good could come out of man or out of any created thing, then the created thing would be a fountain and source of good, and it would not be true that every good and excellent gift is from God or that all things have been given unto the Son of God by the Father.

LII. When I came upon this beautiful comparison with the sailors, I wondered greatly where in the world you could have got it. And as I was thinking about it a certain learned gentleman who was there said that he had read much the same words in a collection of letters. Therefore, I beg of you, if this is the state of the case, return the thing immediately, before you are branded with the mark of theft. But as to the matter itself, I readily agree that a difference is unpleasing to you which you see is likely to fall out to your loss, and that you very greatly desire that all your opponents should yield to you, and reasonably. For you are held in high esteem by the untutored rabble both for your titles of honour and the reputation for that learning which you have drunk from the swamps of the Scotuses and Thomases. But, ah me, lend me your ear a moment. If you see a quarrel going on among the shipmasters, in whose number I take it ye are to be reckoned, why do you not yourselves yield? Is it because you think, as I have said, that all must yield to you and you to none? Or is it because you think you alone sail by the Pole-star, while everybody else is wandering all about the sky? But this would be pretty presumptuous and arrogant. For you also are men who can slip and go astray and be mistaken. But if you grant this, it were surely unfair to want everybody to yield to you unless you shall have first learned to yield to the Scriptures, and so the thing comes back to the Scriptures for decision, and if any one handles them properly he does not have to yield, as I have shown over and over again already. Therefore if I have anywhere handled the Scriptures improperly, you ought to have pointed that out. That you have never done, but all your remarks savour of that thing from the satire writer, "Such is my will and bidding. Be my pleasure reason enough."[1] On the other hand, if I have handled the Scriptures according to Christ's intentions, it will be your business to yield, and to cease from wranglings and strife, as you say, and to lend both ear and mind to the advancement of reviving Christianity, and to suffer the iron sinews of your neck to be softened by receiving the yoke of the Lord. For if with brazen brow ye try to charge upon and throw down the brazen wall of which Jeremiah speaks [i., 18, and xv., 20],

[1] Juvenal, *Satires* VI., line 223, where the text has *hoc* instead of the first *sic*.

ye shall come upon a stone of offence, and if the stone shall fall upon you, it shall grind you to powder. Mark these things carefully, I beg. On most of them enough has been said above.

LIII. When you desire to reach "some sort of" a harbour, what, pray, do you mean by this expression "some sort of" except that there are many harbours, not one harbour only? Look to it yourselves whether this is a pious remark. I will not suggest that by this term of yours you are representing certain commonplace and despicable harbours. If you are people who may not be contradicted, come, show us a sure harbour and goal. But I know what your difficulty is. There is a discussion as to whether we ought to obey the divine or the human. Here you are between the devil and the deep sea, for if you say that the human ought to yield to the divine, the treasure chamber falls and vain titles fall; if you say the divine ought to yield to the human, you fall yourselves into the depths of impiety. Why prolong the discussion? Did Christ come into this world to show us some sort of a harbour, and not a sure and safe one? Does he not say that man lives by the word of God and that he is worshipped in vain by the teachings and commandments of men? And when the Apostles said, "How can we know the way?" did he not reply, "I am the way, the truth, and the life"? [John xiv., 6.] If he is the way, why do ye not walk in him? If the truth, why do ye not trust in him? If the life, why do ye not seek life in him, instead of getting up "some sort of" a harbour? I might quote hundreds of passages from the Gospel writings, to show the impiety of that expression, but I will sound the recall. The Gospel, those good and glad tidings of the grace of God, confers upon poor mortals this blessing above all others, that it leads them to a sure harbour of salvation, which otherwise is absolutely unknown. So much for that fine and modest "some sort of."

LIV. Who is this one person? Is it Christ? But in him "are hid all the treasures of wisdom and knowledge"

[Col. ii., 3]. But he "of God is made unto us wisdom and righteousness and sanctification and redemption." [I. Cor. i., 30.] Is it another such? I know no other God but this one only, though many, at the cost of salvation, receive Him not. Is it some man? Have no fear. As a little while ago, in regard to strife, I argued with you at length, to prevent your falling into the mistake of thinking that everything must be yielded to yourselves, so now I am minded to regard it as very unsafe to swear allegiance to any human master, however learned.[1] For "cursed be the man that trusteth in man, and maketh flesh his arm!" [Jer. xvii., 5.]

LV. If counsels are sounder they ought undoubtedly to be followed. But I rest not upon the counsels of men, but upon the purpose and will of God. For if we neglect His will knowingly we shall be beaten with many stripes [Luke xii., 47].

LVI. You said "councils" here for "counsels," but I would not have you put down this criticism to a carping spirit. Your whole discourse is so incorrect and so hopelessly misspelled, that unless I had designedly covered over certain things, you would have become a laughing stock to every one of any sort of education. I am not sure, therefore, whether it was a slip or real ignorance that caused you to write "councils" for "counsels." If you will examine this whole section carefully, you will find it bristling with solecisms.

LVII. Without loss of his soul no man disregards Christ. For "he that is not with [Christ] is against [him]: and he that gathereth not with [him], scattereth" [Luke xi., 23], as I think you have heard by this time to the point of nausea. Now, no obstinate attempt is made to drag elsewhere but rather to Christ. For they drag elsewhere who call away from Christ to created beings. And further, those to whom a talent has been entrusted may not snore in idleness, but must labour with unremitting activity, that when the Lord

---

[1] Horace, *Epist.*, i., 1, 14.

Archeteles: Reply to Bishop's Admonition 277

cometh and demandeth an accounting they may deserve to hear "Well done, good and faithful servants," etc. In season and out of season must they be compelled to come in to the feast [Luke xiv., 23]. But since we have come to speak of this passage, to which certain persons [so Augustine] do violence, saying, "Lo, here we have Christ saying 'compel them to come in'; therefore the unyielding must be overcome by force and authority," I wish to rescue the passage from the continuance of this abuse. First, therefore, we see that a single servant was sent to compel them to the feas.. Now how could it have been that one man should compel a vast number, if he was to attempt it by force and authority, as these people wish? Secondly, no one tries to drive a person to a banquet or supper by violence. That would be exceedingly rude. Some people do, however, go so unduly far in urging as unwittingly to tear one's cloak by pulling, so that one of the commonest proverbial expressions among the Germans is "to rend one's cloak." Still all this is done in the name of friendship and not of authority, at least such as that with which this crowd hold up their heads. Friendship, to be sure has an authority of its own. Hence, I think, it is clear that in the above mentioned parable from Luke xiv., 23, "compel to come in" means nothing more than if you say, "Press them very urgently to come to the feast." For it is not likely that he who said that his kingdom was not of this world, forgot himself here and commanded that unbelievers be forced to come to him by the use of authority and violence on the part of his servants, to the unending hatred of the bidders. It were rather as, in the last chapter of Luke, those two disciples whom he joined as they were going to Emmaus constrained him, urging him after the fashion of friends, and not with the violence with which the Jews had dragged him before the judgment seat. Now I come back to the path. Those who wander in the darkness must be persistently dragged to the light, and compelled to come to the feast by words, not blows. For this even the divine Paul holds [II. Timothy iv., 2]:

"Preach the word; be instant in season, out of season; reprove, rebuke, exhort with all long-suffering and doctrine. For the time will come when they will not endure sound doctrine; but after their own lusts shall they heap to themselves teachers, having itching ears; and they shall turn away their ears from the truth, and shall be turned unto fables." Do you hear with whom one must labour in season and out of season? Nor can you make the objection that there is no need of urging out of season in our day, for you see all wickedness standing on the brink, and everything ready to fall into the depths of impiety. For I call it the depth of impiety, when we are turned from God to created things, when we accept the human for the divine, disregarding or even scorning the divine, and yet I have so far seen no one who cried out against this wickedness as it deserves. Though ears be so tender that they fear to hear a stinging truth, nay, resist and cry out, yet are they not on this acount to be forever humoured. And the gainsayers are to be vigorously convinced by the sound doctrine of the Gospel truth [Tit. i., 9].

LVIII. You think some allowance ought to be made for those who err with good intentions, and I think so too, if only the intention is good. It is an error with the best of intentions to think it unlawful to eat meat during Lent; it is an error with the worst of intentions not to point out to a Christian people the blessings that have been given unto them by God. For it is for this that we have received the spirit which is of God, not the spirit of the world [I Corinth. ii., 12]. For thus were the grace of God cast away or weakened [Galat. ii., 21]. Again, it is an error with the worst of intentions to say that if the chief Pontiff should bring down all souls to hell, yet could he not be deposed or punished; no man can even wink at errors like these and at the same time have good intentions. But as to the kind of errors you are talking about, to wit, the errors of ceremonials, hear what Paul says [Rom. xiv., 1]: "Him that is weak in the faith receive ye," that is, take him in a pious spirit, deal with him gently, teach him, do not deceive him with enigmatical doctrines. You have it here clearly stated that those who are weak ought not to be left in their weakness by those who are stronger, but ought to be received with pious teaching of the faith. Now whose duty do ye think this is? That of the more vigorous and more learned, no doubt, such as you are certainly thought to be by people in general. Therefore understand that it was your duty to fashion your discourse in this way: "O happy beings, to whom this great blessing is freely offered! For a time we were darkness, but now it is given us by the goodness of God to become light [*cf.* Eph. v., 8]. Ye have thought us learned, but if we had any learning it was imperfect and feeble, and that which was not wholly pure we did not venture to put forth for fear of evil results. Now that the truth is disclosing itself on all sides, take care not to miss it wherever it appears, and embrace it without dissenting voice, lest while some delay, and some obstruct, and some throw it away, it may be lost altogether, and your last state be worse than the first. For a neglected warning from God has ever caused great disaster," or something of this sort. As it is, when you cling so tenaciously to ceremonials and exert yourselves so in their defence, what do ye but hinder the truth? Be it said without malice. For by your own words ye weaken the power of ceremonials, and yet you champion preserving them till some indefinite time, though they might without any risk whatever be abolished simply by sound teaching. And they will be abolished all the same, though you struggle against it. Therefore, I advise you to do as they say Julius Cæsar did, when he saw that he could not escape death. He took care to gather the edge of his garments about him that he might fall in a suitable manner. So should you now that you see ceremonials tottering and almost ready to fall, strive to cause them to fall as fitly as possible—that is, not let them hold on so obstinately. You should immediately see to it how light can most speedily be let into the place of shadows. So will poor mortals not only feel no grief at the loss of ceremonials, but greatly rejoice that they have found the light so long denied them. In short, if ye put new wine into old bottles, the bottles will break, nor can the garment of Christ, which hath no seam, receive a patch of fresh cloth [Matt. ix., 17].

LIX. That a universal error has the force of right I am not inclined to allow even to unbelievers, much less to Christians. For Christ could not bear that men should wander in error [Matt. ix., 36], and Peter congratulates us because a little while ago we "were as sheep going astray, but are now returned unto the Shepherd and Bishop of [our] souls" [I. Pet. ii., 25]. And do you venture to take up again the defence of error, when even your own Canons cry out against it [di. 83[1]]?—"The error which is not objected to is approved, and the truth when not vigorously championed is crushed." See whither your blind malice leads you, namely, to forgetting yourselves and your own teachings, and to embracing certain empty trifles that nobody of any intelligence can stand. But I do not want to brandish my pen at you here, however much you deserve it. For I think it is clear enough and to spare to everybody how feebly, not so say treacherously, you are defending your side and your doctrines.

LX. But what are these new doctrines? The Gospel? Why, that is 1522 years old. The teachings of the Apostles? Why, they are almost as old as the Gospel. Those of the patriarchs and the prophets? Why, these are even older than the Sibyl's. Therefore, I beg of you to call things by their right names, so that we can be on our guard against these things that are so dangerous. But we shall do that in any case by this procedure. We shall try everything by the touchstone of the Gospel and by the fire of Paul. And when we find things in harmony with the Gospel, we shall keep them, when we find things not thus in harmony, we shall throw them out. Those who are thus deprived of

[1] Corpus iur. can., C. 3, Dist. lxxxiii.

some of their ill-gotten gains may shriek as much as they like. We shall not listen to these Stentors, and shall pass with deaf ear by the Sirens. For "we ought to obey God rather than men" [Acts v., 29]. But what am I doing, as if it were not clear what doctrines you hold to be new?

LXI. How this word "to rule" the Church of God pleases you! In Acts xx., whence you quoted it, some commentators put it in for "to feed," with damage to the sense. For Paul speaks thus to the bishops of the Ephesians, "Take heed, therefore, unto yourselves and to all the flock, over the which the Holy Ghost hath made you overseers, to feed the Church of God, which he hath purchased with his own blood" [Acts xx., 28]. Here you have the flock, the overseers, the congregation to be fed, not ruled, the congregation, not of man, but of God, because he won it by his blood. Why do ye use such an arrogant word? Shepherds, or feeders, feed, not rule.

LXII. Now since the Church was won for God by the blood of Christ ("For we were bought with the precious blood of the lamb without blemish," that is, Christ [I. Pet. i., 19]), what reason is there why certain persons should scorn us who are of the flock of Christ, and not only not regard us as Christians but not even as men? They are not satisfied, if through our kindness they are allowed to devote themselves to the care of their bodies at their leisure, unless they reduce us to slavery. But this is in violent opposition to the words of Paul when he says [I. Corinth. vii., 23], "Ye are bought with a price; be not ye the servants of men." What is the reason, I say, why this favour is never proclaimed, namely, that we are bought with the precious blood of Christ? Why are all things filled with false promises to squeeze out money? That were the way in which we could best be kindled to the love of God and a state of grace. We boast, indeed, of the blood of Christ that has been shed for us, but if any one, relying upon that, confidently believes that God will forgive his sins forever for Christ's sake, we straightway proclaim him a heretic! Stick closely to this expression which has fallen from you by design or accident, gentlemen, that Christ won the Church by his own blood. For it is the formula of salvation. Whoever, therefore, confidently believes it, belongs to that Church of Christ which he won by his blood. For faith alone is the ground of salvation. He who believes shall not see death forevermore [John viii., 51]. Strive to be reckoned in that Church which is sprinkled with the blood of Christ, that ye may hold in hatred the Church of the wicked. What have ye to do with the Church that rests on flesh and blood?

LXIII. If nothing is to be altered or changed, why has the communion been altered that used to be given under both forms, according to the institution of Christ and the usage of the Apostles? Or rather why has it been mutilated? Why has the function of bishop been changed into that of prince? Why is marriage forbidden [to the clergy]? Why are hundreds of other things altered? Christ and the Apostles and the general opinion are all opposed thereto. Are ye mightier than God, that ye have ventured to forbid what Christ left free? Or wiser than God, that ye complete what God inadvertently left unfinished? Or so stupid, that you think you are going to persuade consciences free in Christ not to regard as lawful what they know is lawful by the divine law, even though you shout till you are hoarse?

LXIV. Yet you modify your remarks a little later after this fashion, "until those whom it concerns come together for the business of the Church," etc. This I fancy, is likely to come about when "the Parthian drinks the Saône and Germany the Tigris."[1] For I want you to be convinced that in these days of ours there are going to be men who will rage against the champions of a purer Christianity as violently as in the days of old the Jews raged against Christ himself. For how can it be that those whose ceilings gleam with gold and their mules with gems and their attendants with silk, should voluntarily accept any limitation or reform in all these things? They would easily come to an

---

[1] Vergil, *Eclogues*, i., 62.

agreement if they might order everything according to their own purposes and not according to the intent of Scripture, but this will certainly not be accepted by the world which is already well instructed in the Gospel everywhere (I had almost said better instructed than those same high priests), and cannot in any way be torn away from it. When they see something proclaimed that does not square with the Gospel, they simply make a laughing stock of them that sit in Moses' seat, and lay heavy burdens upon men's shoulders but will not themselves touch them with so much as the tips of their fingers [Matt. xxiii., 4]. This is the reason, I say, why I have no hope that the councils will ever be compelled to obey the Scriptures, unless the unanimous agreement of princes brings that about. But it is wonderful how well certain sly dogs[1] know how to prevent this by dazzling the eye with the delusions of functions and honours and priesthoods and deceiving with empty hopes. In vain therefore shall we expect any modification of view from them.

LXV. The Scriptures can be compared together not only by those whose concern you say it is but also by those who trust in God and in His word and who are pining with longing for Him. For it can happen that if the bishops betake themselves to the study of the Scriptures in their usual manner, without regarding the general and common consent, they may prove to be all or in great part unversed in the sacred writings. How, then, shall they make any sound decision in regard to the less transparent parts of Scripture? But even if they be ever so learned, may it not happen that all of them have some illusion, while some layman may show a clear vision in the matter? (I do not want you to snap at me with that silly statement, "The councils cannot be wrong." For even your own people have not maintained that unreservedly, but have modified it thus: "The council cannot be wrong in matters which are of the faith.") Would not violence be done the Scrip-

---

[1] This looks like a pun upon *catulus*, "puppy," and a *catulus* as diminutive of *catus*, "shrewd, crafty," though I do not find such a word.—H. P.

tures, and the man whose view was sound be not left free to hold sound views, and those who were eager for the light of truth be forced to dwell in darkness? And this the divine Paul also warned us against [I. Corin. xiv., 29], saying, "Let the prophets speak by two or three, and let the others discern. If anything be revealed to another that sitteth by, let the first hold his peace. For ye may all," he says, "prophesy one by one, that all may learn, and all may be comforted" [I. Corin. xiv., 29–31]. The passage, I think, is clear enough to you. You see, therefore, that any one may prophesy, though in a certain order, that all may learn the truth of the Scriptures, and all may be comforted by the Word of God, which alone can give repose unto human longing. I want to leave you here for reflection from time to time the shameless statement of a certain smatterer, who ventured to proclaim in a public assembly that it was not lawful for laymen to know or to read the Gospel, but only for those to whom that function had been entrusted, namely for our little priests and masters. Would that some Apollo would give him ass's ears because he does not remember or does not know that Christ said [Matt. x., 27], "What I tell you in darkness, that speak ye in light: and what ye hear in the ear, that preach ye upon the housetops." And again, "Preach the Gospel to every creature" [Mark xvi., 15]. But they confront me presently with the Gordian knot: If it is not lawful for any persons to make some definite proclamation in regard to the truth of Scripture, there will arise countless errors. For every one will maltreat the Sacred Writings at his own sweet will. Country bumpkins! Do ye not see that the spirit of God is everywhere like unto itself and ever the same? The more unskilled a man is in human devices and at the same time devoted to the divine, the more clearly that spirit informs him, as is shown by the Apostles and by the foolish things of this world which God hath chosen. And as it is a spirit of unity and harmony and peace, not of strife and dissension, it will inspire even the most ignorant, sobeit that they are pious, in such manner that they will understand the Scriptures in the plainest way according to God's purpose. This the prophet Joel foretold [ch. ii., 28]: "I will pour out my spirit upon all flesh" (he does not say, upon courtiers and bishops only); "and your sons and your daughters shall prophesy," etc. And the same thing is plainly set forth in Acts [ch. x.], because while Peter yet spake, the Holy Ghost fell on the untaught household of Cornelius and upon Cornelius himself, and Peter, seeing this, perceived that the Holy Ghost had not limited himself to the Jews only or to the Apostles [Acts x., 44–48] (for he is no respecter of persons), and he bade that they be baptised. And when other Apostles, still having something of the Jewish arrogance left and thinking that that which had been wrought upon them should not be distributed among the crowd, demanded an explanation of Peter's action, he answered at length and finally said, "For as much then as God gave them the like gift as he did unto us, who believed on the Lord Jesus Christ; what was I, that I could withstand God?" [Acts xi., 17.] And the same sort of thing certain persons are doing to-day. As soon as some pious and learned man has set forth something from Scripture rather more simply and clearly than usual, they break out with, "Who gave thee authority to teach thus? It belongs to the Fathers only." You would think they expected with their authority to frighten God from daring to inspire any one to teach sound doctrine. In short, the disagreement which is rife to-day seems to me to come from nothing else than that you do not concede that we have a full share in the spirit of him who has numbered all the hairs of our heads, and [*cf.* Matt. x., 30, etc.] in whose sight we are of more value than the fowls of the air. We turn to our own decrees and imagine that not we receive honour from the Scripture, but it from us, and that the source of the wisdom of God is so hemmed in by our authority that it cannot inform any one except through us, though he bids his own to be of good cheer in regard to knowledge and the adornment of speech; for that at the critical moment the Spirit will be at hand and will remind us of all that Christ has said unto us. And certain Brothers and Fathers, living in ill-employed leisure, were not satisfied with his teaching and believed it not. So they ventured to try to give a better one, and that has resulted most disastrously. For in place of the teachings of Christ, the worship of Aristotle has sprung up, and instead of men of Apostolic character, apostates have arisen; instead of men of thrift, men greedy of gain; instead of piety, superstition; and instead of simplicity, madness and hypocrisy. Finally it has come to such a pass that nor law nor right nor heaven nor God's words can bring these goats over from the left to the right side. For they have drunk in other teachings than those of the Spirit, though if they had ever been properly imbued with the teachings of the Spirit, things never could have come to such a pass that none should be more densely ignorant of the heavenly teachings than those who venture to subordinate them to their own opinions, and to claim for themselves alone the right of expounding them. Therefore, to come to an end at last, it is not the function of one or two to expound passages of Scripture, but of all who believe in Christ. "For he whom God hath sent speaketh the words of God: for God giveth not the Spirit by measure unto him" [John iii., 34].

LXVI. You bid us pour forth prayers by which God may be appeased by the restitution that is due him, as if prayers were a sort of money by which the punishments due our sins could be bought off, and not a means of beseeching the mercy of God, that he may not enter into judgment with us, but may take pity upon us according to his great mercy. For as to a price for the doing away with punishment, you know, I think, that Christ was made a sacrifice for us to take away the sins of the people [Hebr. ix., 12], and that "he hath made him to be sin for us, who knew no sin; that we might be made the righteousness of God in him" [II. Cor. v., 21]. But the testimony of Paul would not be so strong, if Christ had not very clearly said the same thing in Luke, xxii., 19, "This is my body which is given for you," and a little later, "This cup is the new testament in my blood, which is shed for you" [Luke xxii., 20]. Hence I do not see how those can be acquitted of blasphemy who attribute to their own prayers and the works that they sell that which belongs to Christ alone. The Heavenly Father willed that he should make restitution for us, and by this free sacrifice draw to him those that could not yield to the works of laws and ceremonials. And this Paul again shows more clearly than daylight [Eph. i., 7], saying of Christ, "In whom we have redemption through his blood, the forgiveness of sins, according to the riches of his grace; wherein he hath abounded toward us in all wisdom and prudence; having made known unto us the mystery of his will, according to his good pleasure," etc. But this market of prayers makes them πρὸς τὰ ἄλφιτα [very like barley groats], and we set out merchandise for sale, as it were, we who have filled our coffers with this sort of hypocrisy and Persian trifles, so that all the granaries are full, the sheep fat, the walls solid, and all would go well, if only he were dumb who is going to say some day, "Fools, this night shall your souls be required of you, and then whose will these things be that ye have laid up?" [Cf. Luke xii., 20.] Κεφάλαιον [the sum of the matter is], it is βαττολογία [silly talk], if any one expects after the fashion of the heathen to propitiate God by his much speaking [Matt. vi., 7]. We ought, nevertheless, to pray without ceasing, and to imitate the importunate widow [cf. Luke xviii., 3], but not to advertise our prayers, that is, offer them for sale with a price attached, in this fashion, "These are worth so much or so much," as that word "restitution" which you add seems to hint. We ought rather to trust ourselves wholly to the divine goodness.

LXVII. Would that ye had the same feelings towards us that he has whom you have made the sponsor of your designs. You know, I think, how the proceedings recently in the Council of Zurich came out, namely that your charge was met in a Christian spirit, and that this pained one of the delegates so much that he could not assuage his grief in any other way than by sending this delicious admonitory document to the Chapter, so as to make me blush again, as he hoped would be the case when the larger part of the assembly turned their gaze upon me as the person at whom this little tale was pointed. It was this fatherly affection, I fear, that influenced you to draw our most pious bishop into that scheme. For there is no other explanation of the proceeding, since the gist of the whole admonition seems to be all of a piece with the earlier course of action. Fatherly affection admonishes in a fatherly spirit, calls home, warns privately, listens with gentleness to the son who makes reparation, does not get together a meeting secretly by night, nor drag the offender before the body of priests and counsellors, but urges him once and again to turn from his sin according to the teaching of Christ [Matt. xviii., 15 foll.], and finally, if he still persists, turns him away in sorrow. And that you may do, when, by the instrumentality of Holy Writ, you have shown me guilty of any error in regard to Christ's doctrine. For you cannot win in any other way, unless, perhaps, you choose to have recourse to force. Then I shall be as defenceless before you as sheep before a wolf; for Christ sent out his disciples like sheep into the midst of wolves. [Matt. x., 16.] You can kill, I admit, so can a highwayman; you can hold one a prisoner, so can a fever, but in bed; you can torture with various punishments, so can the plague, the cholera, and other diseases. Therefore I say and proclaim unto you, that if you wish to maintain that I have not taught the Gospel doctrine truly, try it not by threats nor flattery, not by snares and secret devices, but by the open warfare of Holy Writ and by public meeting, following the Scripture as your guide and master, and not human inventions. For otherwise ye will not accomplish anything more than Xerxes accomplished when he forced the sea, as he fancied, to endure blows and shackles.

LXVIII. That we may abide in the unity of Holy Mother Church, we beseech thee to hear us. That we may abide in obedience to those set over us, that is, to our good magistrates, we beseech thee to hear us. That thou wilt teach the counterfeit bishops so much humility that they will regard themselves not as rulers and men set over us, but, according to Peter's words [I. Pet. v., 1], as $συμπρεσβυτέρους$ [fellow elders], we beseech thee. That thou wilt illumine them with thy light that they may know the true Church which is thy bride, we beseech thee to hear us. That thou wilt open to them the fountain of living water, we beseech thee to hear us [cf. Jer. ii., 13]. From the worn-out wells that they have dug and that have not the living water, save us, O Lord. From the unbearable burdens that they lay upon men's shoulders, save us, O Lord [Luke xi., 46, and Matt. xxiii., 4]. Bid them bear them and practise what they preach. If they cannot in any other way be persuaded to suffer thy yoke to be easy and thy burden light, force them to do it, O Lord [Matt. xi., 30].

LXIX. For thus it will come to pass that thy Church shall enjoy the deepest peace and tranquillity. For thou seest, Most Holy Jesus, that their ears have been shut up by worthless whisperers and sycophants and gain-seekers, in consequence of whose noise, even though they hear thy voice, they cannot recognise it nor obey it, for these men block their way and impose upon their singleness of heart. For where in all the diocese of Constance have thy teachings been received with such universal acceptance as at Zurich? Is deeper peace to be seen (alas, for these times of ours!) in any canton of Switzerland? Yet have they dared, under pretence of bringing about peace where there was no dissension, to strain every nerve in order to sow tares among the good seed. Thou knowest there was no need of that splendid delegation of three scholars recently, which yet they ventured to suborn, having dragged in Hugo, whose natural sentiments in regard to thy teachings are not unsound. But they could not make out that my teachings were one whit against thy law. And now thou knowest also in what spirit they have written to me. As for myself, there is no need to call thee to witness in what spirit I do all that I do. Thou knowest how far aloof from all strife and uproar I have kept myself from early youth, yet thou hast not ceased to call me to this duty of battle in spite of my unwilling protests. Therefore I may now rightly appeal to thee to finish unto the day of the Lord the good work which thou hast begun, and if I ever build anything less worthily than I ought, cast it down; if I lay any other foundation than thee, destroy it, that thy flock, led and inspired by thy spirit, may come to the knowledge that it shall lack nothing, if it be led and fed by thee as bishop and shepherd. For thou, O Son of God, art the defender and advocate of all who put their hope in thee. If then thou failest them, thy name will be a weariness and mark of scorn to all mankind. They will mock thee as the Jews mocked thee as thou wast hanging from the cross, for they will say: "Lo, this fellow began to build and could not finish." O then, sweet vine, whose vintner is the Father, and of whom we are the branches, abandon not thy planting and thy building. Thou hast promised to be near us to the fulness of the ages, and hast bidden us to be of good cheer when brought before kings and potentates, for that the spirit would protect us at the critical moment, and inspire us with words whereby they should be compelled even against their will to hear testimony of thee. Put, therefore, fit words into the mouths of all who seek thy glory and sanctify thy name, that they may speak before the princes of this world things acceptable unto thee and profitable for unhappy mankind. For so it shall come to pass that we, who are members one of another and one body in thee our one and everlasting head, shall form thy one and only bride whom Paul betrothed to thee without spot or blemish [Eph. v., 27], and that Church shall be abandoned which is naught but stains and defilement, since the name of God is through it made of ill repute. Thou livest and reignest as God with the Father and the Holy Ghost world without end. Amen. I foresee that I shall seem to you unduly to have made all things worse, for the minds of most theologians nowadays have this in common with courtiers, that they think nothing pious or holy or right except what they have themselves done. If they make proclamation, it must be held as law; if they condemn, the condemnation must be accepted; if they make untrue accusation, they must not be answered. And we see, too, that nature has somehow ordained that those who are most prone to attack others are most averse to seeming to have done it. And if ye are so minded, I have no ground for good hope of you, for ye will continue to wail that an unworthy thing is done in that a pastor has ventured to resist his bishop, and ye will not take in good part this little admonition with which I have tried to dissuade you from stirring up our bishop. But that will not frighten me a bit. Nor will the fact that you turn to abuse and call me promiscuously a quarrelsome bird and villain and sycophant have any more effect than rain has upon the donkey, for I have so toughened my skin that I simply scorn these weapons. And as to the matter itself, so far am I from yielding to you that unless you leave me and mine—that is, the sheep of Christ—in peace and quiet, I shall proceed to deal with you far more roughly, without fear of your words or your frowns. You must deal with me by means of the Holy Scriptures bestowed upon us by God (and do not forget that point), and they must not be twisted. You must not use things devised by the vanity of man, and you must come to close quarters and not fight by laying mines. As soon as I perceive any tricks, I shall expose them. Be it enough to have been pardoned this time for having ventured to disturb the peace under pretence of restoring peace. If you persist, as I hope you will not, in the plan you have begun, of not speaking the name of Zwingli, while yet attempting to make it known by all sorts of side thrusts and to hold it up to disapproval, I shall certainly not spare your names but shall challenge you by name to single combat as Menelaus challenged Paris, and if you scorn me so far as to refuse to come forth, I will proclaim your reluctance to the whole world. But heaven forbid! I hope, now that you have learned that your darts have been fittingly blunted, you will not renew the battle, but will surrender yourselves soul and body to God. For you see how unsuccessfully so far those who champion human traditions and visions and οὐδὲν ὑγιές [what is wholly unsound], have engaged with the pious defenders of the Gospel. But if it shall be given to you from above to return to reason, know that I shall be so wholly yours that none shall more strenuously canvass for your friendship, none more boldly come forward to champion your cause. The Most High God cause all the hearts of all nations to be so illuminated by the divine ray that they may become one in one faith and forever possess him who is one, Amen. Farewell.

ZURICH, Aug. 23, 1522.

> Wrath and jealousy burst in bits all bishops
> Who in spite of their name are wolves voracious!
> Now once more, as in days of old, refulgent
> Shines the light of the Gospel's truth upon us,
> Notwithstanding the doughty three-tongued Satan
> Sent to quench it; for God remaineth master
> Yea (and verily speak I truth as prophet),
> Their authority, all their sway of tyrants,
> Sins of simony, keys and canons human,
> Cruel murderers of the people's conscience,
> Rows on rows of the wares those men call sacred,
> Bulls, anathemas, and dark superstition—
> These, all conquered, the message of the Gospel
> Leads, and ever shall lead, in hard-won triumph.
> Who in spite of their name are wolves voracious,
> Wrath and jealousy burst in bits all bishops!
>   CONRAD GREBEL[1]
>   In gratitude for the restoration of the Gospel.

---

[1] Grebel was born in Zurich, 1489, and died of the plague in Maienfeld, Canton Graubünden, 1526. He became a leader of the Anabaptists in Zurich and so was opposed by Zwingli, who earlier had admired and aided him; indeed was the means of his conversion from a licentious life.

Index

Abstinence. *See* Fasting
Adrian VI, Pope, 12-13
Aeberli, Jacob, 269
Agapetus I, Pope, 186, 187
Agathius of Bern, 1
Anastasius, Pope, 248
Aristotle, 79-80, 261, 286
Arius, 235, 248
Augsburg, 17
Augustine, Bp of Hippo, 64, 172, 187-188, 249-250, 264, 277

Baden convention (1512), 45-46
Baden disputation (1526), 16-17
Baldus de Ubaldis, 261
Baptism, 108
Bartolus, 261
Basel, 2
Basil the Great, 234
Bern, 3, 17, 18, 20
Bible. *See* Scripture
Bishops, 99-100, 189, 226, 231, 246-247, 253-255, 266, 281, 282
Blansch, Martin, 12
Blarer, Thomas, 58
Bologna, 37
Boniface I, Pope, 186
Boschenstein, Andrew, 10
Brendlin, Nicholas, 113, 117, 198-202
Brunner, George, 206n
Buenzli, Gregory, 2-3

Cappel Wars, 21-22
Catabaptism, 11, 14-16, 292n
Celibacy, 150n, 166, 254. *See also* Chastity
Cepronius, James, 10
Ceremonies, 116-118, 121-123, 127, 208, 213-214, 216, 219, 265-269, 279-280
Charles V. Emperor, 63, 64, 215
Chastity, 156-164, 166, 177-194, 235, 260. *See also* Celibacy
Chrysostom, John, 79, 191
Church, the, 117, 126, 213, 248-249, 251-252

Cologne, 60
Constance, 16
Councils, 64, 186, 214, 259-260, 263, 271, 282-283
Custom, 105-109, 125, 128, 205, 214-215, 223, 230, 245-246, 262

Death, 56, 57, 234
Deusdedit, Pope, 186
Dingnauer, Johannes, 48
Duns Scotus, Johannes, 238, 260, 261, 262, 274
Durandus de Sancto Porciano, Bp of Meaux, 262

Eck, Johann, 16, 17, 60
Einsiedeln, 7, 55
Engelhard, Henry, 116, 125, 126
Ennius, Bp of Verulam, 13
Episcopacy. *See* Bishops
Erasmus, Desiderius, 48, 55, 58, 130, 197-198
Eucharist, 12, 14, 17, 282
Euripides, 139

Faber, Johannes, Vicar Gen. of Constance, 12, 16, 257, 264, 269n
Faber, John, canon of Zurich Minster, 165
Fabricius, Erasmus, 113, 165
Faith, 78, 108, 171, 190, 282
Fasting and abstinence, 70-112, 113, 117, 121-122, 123-125, 235
Fattlin, Melchior, 113, 114, 116, 118-119, 198-202, 269-270
Felix III, Pope, 186
Ferdinand the Catholic, 37
Foix, Gaston de, Duke of Nemours, 38-39
Food, 73-112, 121, 122, 124-125
Freedom. *See* Liberty
Froschauer, Christopher, 70-71, 130

Gangra, Council of, 184-186, 260
Gelasius I, Pope, 186-187
Geroldseck, Theobold, 7

Index

Glarus, 5
Grace, 79
Gospel, the, 248-251, 262
Grebel, Conrad, 292
Greek language, 5, 7-8, 10, 36
Gregory I, Pope, 88
Guilielmus of Paris, 248

Haller, Berthold, 19
Hebrew language, 10
Hedio, Kaspar, 48, 49, 197
Henry VIII, King of England, 63
Hilary, Bp of Poitiers, 186, 191
Hofmann, Konrad, 197
Hofmeister, Sebastian, 15, 206n
Hohenlandenberg, Hugo von, Bp of Constance, 12, 113, 151, 197, 198, 208, 288, 289
Holy Ghost, 261, 285
Hormisdas I, Pope, 186
Hosius, Bp of Cordova, 186
Hübmaier, Balthasar, 15-16
Hummelberg, Michael, 197

Idleness, 9-10
Images, 14
Indulgences, 59, 64
Intercession of saints, 11, 12

Jerome (Eusebius Hieronymus), 182
Jesus Christ, 169-172, 238-240, 275-276, 281-282, 286-287, 290
Joner, Wolfgang, 130
Jud, Leo, 11, 15, 116n, 130, 165
Julius II, Pope, 36, 46, 65-66

Kilchmeyer, Jodoc, 165

Lambert, Francis, 11
Law, 80-81, 84-85, 86, 111, 159
Leo X, Pope, 59, 60, 215
Liberius, Pope, 248
Liberty, Christian, 102, 103-104, 106, 111-112, 208, 220
Lord's Supper. *See* Eucharist
Loreti, Henry, 36
Louis XII, King of France, 37
Louis II, King of Hungary, 63
Louvain, 60
Love, 220
Lüti, Henry, 114
Lupulus, Heinrich, 3
Luther, Martin, 9, 17, 58-65, 176, 216n

Macrinus, Melchior, 197
Manichaeus, 235
Manx, Felix, 11
Marburg, Colloquy of (1529), 17
Marcion, 235
Marriage, 158-164, 177-194, 282
Mass. *See* Eucharist
Maximilian I, Emperor, 46
Megander, Caspar, 19, 165
Melanchthon, Philipp, 17
Mercenary service, 68-69, 137-138, 142-144, 146
Meyer, Sebastian, 197
Murner, Thomas, 17
Myconius, Oswald, 8, 15, 48, 196; Life of Zwingli, 1-24

Nepos, James, 49
Nicholas I, Pope, 187

Oechsli, Hans, 129
Oecolampadius, Johannes, 22
Offence, 89-104, 118, 127-128, 155, 162, 163, 191

Papacy, 58-59, 60, 62, 63, 64, 65-67, 144, 253, 268
Paris, 60
Paul, The Apostle, 65, 219, 238, 251
Pavia, 41-45
Peace, 132-133
Pensions, 6, 19
Peter, the Apostle, 65, 74, 102-103, 121, 159, 252
Picus of Mirandola, John, 6
Pistoris, Huldreich, 165
Preaching, 172-177
Prierias, Sylvester, 58n, 60
Prophets, false, 242-244

Ravenna, 37-39
Reason, 61
Repentance, 211, 258-259
Rhenanus, Beatus, 257n
Righteousness, 169, 172
Roesch, Ludwig, 36
Röschlin, Rudolph, 116
Röust, Mark, 119

Sabbath, 81-82, 107
Sabellius, 235
Salvation, 117, 126, 262, 281-282
Sam, Konrad, 197

Index

Sardanapalus, 229
Sax, Huldreich von, 42, 45
Scandal. *See* Offence
Schinner, Matthias Cardinal, 39-40, 45
Scotus. *See* Duns Scotus, Johannes
Scripture, 6, 61, 72-73, 110-111, 128, 201, 207, 224, 236, 259-260, 262, 263, 264-265, 270-271, 283-286, 288, 291
Sforza, Maximilian, Duke of Milan, 46
Silverius, Pope, 186
Sin, 135
Stähelin, Georg, 165
Steiner, Werner, 165
Stumpf, Simon, 165

Tetzel, Johann, 58n
Theodore I, Pope, 186
Thomas Aquinas, 88, 238, 258, 260, 261, 274
Tithes, 113
Toledo, Council of, 188
Trachsel, Balthasar, 165

Tradition. *See* Custom
Tschudi, Valentine, 36

Utinger, Heinrich, 156n

Venice, 37-41, 44-45
Vergil, 27
Verona, 40
Vienna, 3

Wanner, John, 113, 118, 198-202
War, 130-131, 139-142, 145-146
Watt, Joachim, 35
Wildhaus, 2
Will, 83
Wimpina, Konrad, 58n
Works, 85

Zinck, Francis, 13
Zug, 18
Zurich, 8, 10, 14-16, 21, 56, 68, 113, 287-288
Zwick, Johannes, 197
Zwingli, Huldreich (father), 2
Zwingli, James (brother), 35, 36

Scriptural Citations

Genesis
1:27 132
2:7 132
3:5 137
3:10 157
11:1-9 137
14:13ff 201
26:15 250
34:1-2 145

Exodus
2:11 218
15:1-2 135

Leviticus
26:3ff 148
26:14ff 148

Deuteronomy
4:2 .... 110-111, 262
12:32 .... 111, 262
16:19 142
17:12 .... 213, 247
32:15 136
32:30 137

I Samuel
8:10-27 135

II Samuel
24 136

I Kings
11:9 227
12:11 163

Nehemiah
9:30 100

Psalms
24:1 96
34:9 228
51:18 216
52:7 136
55:9 .... 210, 234
69:9 210
77:3-4 176
81:8-12 86
118:22 260
119:90 203
137:1 146

145:18	103
147:10-11	141

Proverbs

1:26	226
3:11-12	141
9:9	131
11:9	137-138
21:30	141

Isaiah ... 11

1:23	227
3:4	100-101
5:8-9	66, 139
5:11-12	66
5:20	143, 152, 233
6:9	224
8:9-10	141
28:15	137, 229
30:9-13	174
45:23	93
48:18	229
48:22	229
55:10	104
56:10	182, 231
56:10-12	100
58:6	88
61:8	227

Jeremiah ... 11

1:18	274
2:13	105, 289
6:14	200
6:16	271
7:4	206
9:1	146
15:19	228
15:20	274
17:5	276
23:15-16	243
23:16-17	212, 242
51:1-5	140

Ezekiel

3:18	247
5:11	233
13:3-7	206
22:18	219
24:10	219
29:17-21	140
34:13-14	220

Daniel

7:22	270

Hosea

1:7	148

Joel

2:28	285

Amos

5:5	233
5:13	210, 234

Micah

2:2-3; 8-9	138-139

Wisdom

5:3	226

Baruch

3:16-18	66

Matthew ... 8, 238, 249

4:4	177
5:10	103
5:18	170
5:22	84
5:29-30	99, 221
5:37	170
5:39, 44, 45	142
6:7	287
6:16	88
6:26-29	170
6:30	78
7:5	221
7:16	138, 227
9:17	280
9:36	280
9:36-38	218
10:8	269
10:16	231, 288
10:27	284
10:30	285, 289
10:32-37	90
10:34-36	121, 229
11:23	265
11:25	123
11:28	84, 239
11:29	170
12:25	240
12:30	240, 253, 255
13:37-39	221
13:41	99
15:3	221
15:9	109, 102, 204, 219
15:11	79n
15:11-14	103

Index

15:13	125, 184
15:14	104
15:17	73
16:8	78
16:17	126
16:18	252
16:19	105-106
17:24-27	98
18:6	100, 191
18:7	98, 118, 140, 191
18:8	99
18:9	221
18:10	191, 234-235
18:15ff	288
18:17	256
18:18	105-106
18:20	242
19:4-6	179-180
19:10-12	156, 157, 159, 178, 179
19:17	105
19:21	240
21:12	252
21:25ff	203
21:42	260
22:21	122
23:2	252
23:4	283, 289
23:10	236
23:13	101
23:14	272-273
23:16	206
23:18	206
24:23	81, 242
24:24	242
24:35	170, 203
24:48-51	91
25:13	107
25:23	277
26:69ff	134

Mark

2:23-28	80-81
2:24	104
7:15	73, 77, 124
9:42	99
12:10	260
13:13	232
13:21-22	242
16:15ff	154, 220, 254, 284

Luke

1:1	250
5:31	171, 218
5:32	172
6:11	174
6:22	205
6:26	205
6:38	240
9:62	228
10:3	231
10:20	205
10:31	232
11:23	213, 240, 276
11:46	289
11:52	101
12:20	287
12:32	271
12:45	91
12:47	276
13:1-3	147-148
14:23	277
14:26	90
16:14-15	262-263
16:15-16	77
17:1	98
17:20	83
18:1ff	240
18:3	287
18:11	172
18:11-13	85
21:17	232
22:19-20	287
22:20	111
22:26	236
22:35	83
23:34	169
24:29	277

John

1:16	170
2:17	210
3:3	169
3:33	223
3:34	286
4:6	153n
4:7	245
4:23	170
5:34	250
5:36	250-251, 263
5:39	221
5:41	251, 263
5:42	263-264
5:44	239
6:40	170
6:63	159
7:37	153
8:12	204, 223, 241
8:32	220

8:51	282
10:1	231
10:4	231
10:8	241, 246
10:9	170
10:10	241
10:11-12	210, 224, 232, 239, 241
10:30	241
14:1	241
14:6	159, 223, 275
14:26	261
14:27	228
15:7	134
15:9	134
16:2	219
16:6	170
16:12	260
12:12-13	261
16:33	229
17:3	93
17:11	132-133
17:12	246
17:20	153
18:22	247
21:25	172

Acts

	238
4:12	171
5:29	174, 176, 205, 263, 281
5:34-42	117, 125, 152, 175
5:41	230
6:13	268
7:51	223-224
8:20	269
9:5	207
10:9-15	74
10:15	112, 159
10:26	258-259
10:34	81
10:44-48	285
11:17	285
14:19	175
15:10	121
16:3	97, 101, 104, 118, 128
17:17	167
18:9	175
19:23ff	175
20:17	189
20:28	99-100, 281
20:29	225
28:17-29	224

Romans

1:16	167, 251
1:28-31	133-134
3:4	223
5:7	169
7:12	273
8:28	135
8:31	148
9:3	218
12:18	92
13:7	122
13:8	111
14-15	92-94
14:1	101, 278
14:23	78
15:1	104
15:6	200

I Corinthians

1:12	208
1:17	254
1:27	123
1:30	276
2:2	103
2:12	93, 278
2:15	230
3:3	222
3:19	225
3:21	82
6:12	74, 104
7:1-2	160, 180
7:8-9	180-181
7:9	160
7:21	135
7:23	281
7:25	160, 181
7:28	162
7:32	150n
7:35	82, 161
8	94-96
8:8	75
9:13	253
10:4	252
10:11	141
10:23-33	96-97
10:25	75-76
11:16	222
11:31	99
12:12ff	152
14:29-31	284
15:10	241
15:32	229

Index

II Corinthians
3:6 84
5:21 286
11:5 241
12:6 241
12:11 241
13:8 103

Galatians 238
1:9 111
2:1 .... 118, 128
2:3-5 .... 102, 104, 128
2:5 223
2:12-14 102-103
2:21 278
3:15 111
4:9-10 .... 84, 85
5:1 .... 111, 162
5:15 237
5:19 163
6:10 169

Ephesians
1:7 287
2:3 171
2:10 171
4:1-6 133
4:16 152
4:28 169
5:8 279
5:27 290

Philippians
1:18 227
2:6 169
3:19 266

Colossians
1:18 .... 152n
2:3 275-276
2:16 76
2:16-23 106-109
2:20 .... 84, 263
3:1 252

I Timothy 238
1:4 126
3:1ff 161, 182, 254
3:12 182-183
4:1-5 .... 76, 161, 183
5:20 231

II Timothy 238
3:2 234
3:6 228
3:14-17 270
4:2-4 277-278
4:10 229

Titus
1:5-6 161
1:5-7 188-189
1:9 .... 221, 278
1:13-15 77-78
1:15 73

Hebrews 238, 262
1:1 169
4:14 239
4:16 252
7:11 253
8 262
9:12 286
10 171
13:4 .... 162, 190
13:9 78-79
13:10 253
13:17 122

James
1:17 .... 105, 273
3:2 221

I Peter 238
1:11 245
1:19 281
2:7 204
2:16 162
2:25 .... 225, 280
5:1 289
5:8 236

II Peter 238
1:10 134
2 244-245
2:3 223
2:4ff 137
2:19 212
2:20 .... 174, 228

I John
3:6 134
4:1 .... 185, 204, 221-222, 259

www.ingramcontent.com/pod-product-compliance
Lightning Source LLC
Chambersburg PA
CBHW050336230426
43663CB00010B/1877